MARCH TO THE FINALS

The History of College Basketball's Illustrious Finale

Alan Minsky

MetroBooks

MetroBooks

An Imprint of Friedman Fairfax Publishers

©1997 by Michael Friedman Publishing Group, Inc.

Library of Congress Cataloging-in Publication Data available upon request.

ISBN 1-56799-387-7

Editor: Nathaniel Marunas
Art Director: Jeff Batzli
Designer: Diego Vainesman
Photo Editor: Wendy Missan
Production Manager: Jeanne Hutter

JH HH

Color separations by Ocean Graphics International Company Ltd.
Printed in China by Leefung-Asco Printers Ltd.

10 9 8 7 6 5 4 3 2 1
For bulk purchases and special sales, please contact:
Friedman/Fairfax Publishers
Attention: Sales Department
15 West 26th Street
New York, NY 10010
212/685-6610/685-1307

Visit our website:
www. metrobooks. com

Photography Credits

©Allsport USA: 2, 87, 94, 95, 96, 104, 106

AP/Wide World Photos: 10, 11, 28, 32 bottom, 35, 36, 41, 50 top, 55, 67 both, 99, 103

©Rich Clarkson/NCAA Photos: 9, 22, 24, 26-27, 43, 46 bottom, 62 left, 63, 66, 68, 69, 71, 73, 74, 75, 81, 83, 92, 108, 109

©Focus on Sports: 6, 85, 88, 89, 91, 93, 97, 98, 101, 102

©Michael C. Hebert/Spurlock Photography: 5

©Long Photography: 50 bottom, 76

©Brian Spurlock: 7, 72, 100, 105

UPI/Corbis-Bettmann: 12, 13, 14, 15, 17, 18, 19, 20, 21, 29, 31, 32 top, 33, 37, 38, 39, 40, 42, 45, 46 top, 47, 48, 51, 52, 54, 57, 58, 61, 62 right, 64, 65, 70, 79, 80, 84, 90

12.98

C O N T E N T S

Introduction

The National Collegiate Athletic Association (NCAA) men's basketball championship tournament has evolved into one of the most, if not the most, exciting sports events in the world. Every year America's top college teams compete in the sixty-four-team, single-elimination tournament for the undisputed national championship. One by-product of the dramatic rise in basketball's popularity throughout the nation over the past few decades is the tremendous increase in the number of exceptional college-age players. These talented youngsters fill the ranks of the major college teams, the best of which make it to the NCAA tournament. Thus, all sixty-four squads that reach the tournament are rife with talent and most are capable of beating even the highest-ranked teams on any given night. None of the sixty-four teams is there to lose, to see the end of their dream, but sixty-three teams do lose, and only one emerges victorious.

Whereas older, professional athletes meet defeat with adult, stoic composure, eighteen- to twenty-two-year-old youngsters, who are on teams that rarely lose during the regular season, sometimes unravel in the face of a defeat that destroys their lifelong dream. Likewise, the student-body faithful, who have traveled to the neutral-site game, support their peers with a fervency unmatched in American sports. Thus, any NCAA tournament game can become an emotional spectacle of the first order; even the most detached viewer of a game on television is liable to get swept up in the excitement. Both teams do everything in their power to try to win. With every basket,

the jam-packed, bipartisan crowd erupts. As the game draws to a close, the drama grows—and if it's a close contest down the stretch (as it usually is), the tension builds to a riveting crescendo.

The NCAA tournament was born in 1939 and instantly became one of the two most prestigious tournaments of the college basketball season, alongside the then-one-year-old National Invitational Tournament (NIT). The two rival postseason tournaments competed for supremacy until the gambling scandal of 1951, in which many prominent players admitted to accepting bribes in exchange for influencing the outcome of games. The NIT suffered more damage than the NCAA in the fallout from the scandal. Consequently, since 1952, the winner of the NCAA tournament has been recognized as the undisputed national champion in men's basketball.

While the tournament has expanded from the original eight-team format to the present-day field of sixty-four (and the popularity of both the sport of basketball and the tournament itself has grown in spectacular leaps and bounds), one thing has always remained constant in the NCAA tourney: the thrill of the games themselves. As unbelievable as it may seem to a contemporary fan weaned on the high-flyin', gravity-defyin' game of the 1980s and 1990s, college basketball in the 1940s and 1950s was just as dramatic, just as exciting to the fans, as it is today.

From 1939 to the present, countless tournament games have gone down to the wire, resolving in often unbelievable scenarios. Seemingly invincible Goliaths

have been slain by improbable Davids. Virtual unknowns have stepped to center stage and, in one fleeting moment, made their indelible impression on history. Witness, for example, Lorenzo Charles, who in 1983 rose out of obscurity and in the space of less than one second sealed a national championship for North Carolina State and gained immortality. The tournament has also been the proving ground for many a great titan, where the likes of Bill Russell, Lew Alcindor, and Bill Walton led their teams to resounding victories over the best competition the nation had to offer.

Whatever the end result, each and every year the tournament has seen the unfolding of a unique and (usually) thrilling tale. While it is true that in some years the championship game has been little more than the coronation ceremony for the hands-down favorite, most NCAA tournament games, from the first round to the title game, deliver edge-of-your-seat excitement. There is no annual sporting event anywhere else in the world that has generated as much drama over the past fifty-eight years than the NCAA men's championship basketball tournament.

Opposite: Tip-off! At center stage, North Carolina's Eric Montross and Michigan's Chris Webber jump for the ball to begin the 1993 NCAA finals inside cavernous New Orleans Superdome in front of the largest television audience ever to watch a college basketball game. This championship showdown between legendary coach Dean Smith's Tarheels and Michigan's precocious and hyper-talented "Fab Five" (who as sophomores were in the finals for the second straight year) lived up to the pregame hype. Above: In a rite of passage for the young American scholar, the Syracuse student body shows their true colors at tournament time.

Chapter

Beginnings, Controversy, and Growth: **1939–1954**

Seen through the prism of today's basketball—a high-flyin', rapid-pace spectacle featuring feats of awe-inspiring athleticism—the game at midcentury may seem like a slow-motion joke: a bunch of white guys, slaves to gravity, taking set shots and underhand runners. But at the time of the first National Collegiate Athletic Association (NCAA) tournament, in 1939, people already thought of basketball as an exciting, high-scoring game. Since its invention by Dr. James Naismith in Springfield, Massachusetts, in the winter of 1891, basketball had only gained in popularity. Colleges began fielding teams shortly after the turn of the century and the sport became increasingly exciting to watch as the rules and the framework of the game were improved; by the thirties fans began to flock to gymnasiums in every region of the country to watch college hoops. As more people played basketball in more places, the rate of innovation increased; every year, it seemed, captivating new approaches to the sport arose. And as the first sixteen years of the NCAA tournament testify, the young sport was able to generate tremendous drama, year in, year out.

While today the NCAA is firmly established as the premier collegiate sports organization, overseeing virtually all intercollegiate competition among major schools in all sports, this was not always the case; the NCAA evolved into its position of preeminence (though to this day it does not encompass every major sports program; some schools, particularly all-black universities, participate instead in the NAIA [National

Association of Intercollegiate Athletics.]). The NCAA began around 1905 and had its roots in standardizing rules for competition for the nation's premier schools, most notably the Ivy League universities (the Ivy League was not yet an official conference) and the Big Ten. Following the success of the National Invitational Tournament (NIT) in its initial year, 1938, the NCAA decided to inaugurate a national championship tournament in men's basketball to be played each spring following the conclusion of the regular season.

By 1939, the NCAA had grown to where it could sponsor a national basketball tournament and be confident that the champions of the nation's leading conferences would accept invitations. This didn't mean, however, that the NCAA owned postseason rights to the best teams in the nation. Many of the country's top teams were not members of major conferences, and thus were not bound to the NCAA. For instance, several independent Catholic schools—such as Notre Dame, Holy Cross, and De Paul—had developed strong basketball traditions.

The NIT also had a distinct advantage over the NCAA because the entire NIT tournament was played at Madison Square Garden in New York, basketball's high temple. The New York area had become a hotbed of basketball—with strong independents such as New York University (NYU), Long Island University (LIU), and City College of New York (CCNY)—and the NCAA regional selection process allowed only one team from this powerful region to participate. Therefore, teams often

bypassed the NCAA for the NIT and the bright lights of New York City. To counter the prestige of the NIT, the NCAA tourney was frequently played after the NIT event in the years from 1939 to 1951 so that teams could compete in both. And, from 1943 to 1950, the NCAA final was played in Madison Square Garden seven out of eight years. Still, the relationship between the two tournaments was such that it was frequently unclear which team truly deserved the appellation "national champion." Perhaps because of this confusion, the Associated Press (AP) began its college basketball wire service poll in 1948–1949. So, despite the competition from the NIT, the NCAA tournament established itself between 1939 and 1954 as a championship event that teams strove to participate in.

The primary force that elevated the more inclusive NCAA tourney's status was the growing popularity of basketball nationwide. On playgrounds across America kids were increasingly drawn to the exciting game, and during winter, in youth centers and school gymnasiums, coaches taught these same kids the fundamentals of team basketball. The game itself evolved rapidly during these years. Numerous different styles of play competed for prominence throughout the land; some teams used a fast-paced running game, while others relied on disciplined half-court offenses that worked for a good shot. The jump shot was a recent innovation, although most coaches

The 1940 NCAA champion Indiana Hoosiers: the player holding the ball is Marv Huffman, the tournament MVP.

still discouraged it in favor of the set shot from long range. Toward the end of World War II, during which basketball was tremendously popular among American GIs, big men Bob "Foothills" Kurland of Oklahoma A&M and George Mikan of De Paul revolutionized the sport with their powerful inside presence. Still, the dominant style of play through the forties was the "New York Game"—in which teams employed a motion offense that featured passing, picks, players cutting to the basket, and long-range, open, two-handed set shots—which emphasized endurance and agility. Some teams, most notably Adolph Rupp's Kentucky Wildcats, competed against the New York style with more of an open running game, and teams with a quality big man used a slow, low-post offense.

The 1939–1954 era had a number of great stars who competed in the NCAA tournament, but the biggest names were the coaches who were forging revolutionary theories and building consistent winners. Indiana head coach Branch McCracken perfected a weaving fast break that carried the Hoosiers to the 1940 title. The 1940 runner-up, Kansas, was coached by the legendary Forrest "Phog" Allen, who was a disciple of Dr. Naismith himself, and was instrumental in formalizing the game's rules through the years. Henry Iba structured an offensive strategy that suited the needs of his superstar Bob Kurland and led to consecutive NCAA titles at Oklahoma A&M. CCNY coach Nat "Mr. Basketball" Holman was a New York basketball legend who managed to incorporate the freewheeling, improvisational moves associated with New York street ball into a disciplined offensive scheme, and in the process led his team to both the NIT and NCAA crowns in 1950, an unequaled feat. But by the end of this era basketball's most respected and influential strategist was none other than the "Baron of the Bluegrass," Kentucky coach Adolph Rupp, who led the Wildcats to three NCAA titles in four years (from 1948 to 1951). Rupp's teams emphasized discipline, athleticism, and fast-paced basketball.

However, both Rupp's and Holman's respective programs were rocked by the infamous point-shaving scandal of 1951. The scandal involved contests held at Madison Square Garden where bookies

Dr. James Naismith, the man who started it all, invented basketball in 1891 at the Springfield, Massachusetts, YMCA.

would collect bets on the outcomes of the games. In the spring of 1951 an investigation revealed that over the past few years gamblers had successfully bribed players on favored teams to keep those teams from covering the point-spread. In other words, if a team was favored by 8 points, gamblers would pay players on the favored team to prevent their team from winning by 8 or more points. The scandal devastated many programs, especially those in New York City. The debacle severely tarnished the public's perception of big-time basketball, but it hurt the New York–based NIT more than the NCAA tournament. The NCAA immediately disassociated itself from Madison Square Garden, where all college games were banned except for those of the NIT. But the truly devastating blow to the NIT was the collapse of New York City powerhouses like CCNY, LIU, and NYU. Before the scandal, talented players from the New York area remained close to

home, at colleges that competed for a spot in the NIT. Following the scandal, New York's unparalleled pool of basketball talent spread throughout the provinces, among colleges that traditionally competed for NCAA bids.

Only eight teams, one from each of the designated regions, made the NCAA tournament in its early years. The eight regions were organized geographically and loosely constructed around the major conferences. Thus George Mikan's great De Paul teams were excluded twice because Chicago is in the heart of Big Ten country (and the Big Ten was the conference with the strongest ties to the NCAA), and numerous New York powers inevitably missed the tournament each year, all of which added to the prestige of the NIT. After the NCAA tourney expanded to sixteen teams in 1951, there were more at-large entries for independents and a greater number of conferences included. However, a significant legacy of the original tournament structure, that each major conference could only send its champion to the NCAAs, remained intact until 1976, even after the tournament expanded to twenty-two and twenty-four teams. Consequently, many great teams, often ranked as high as the top five, had to settle for a spot in the NIT, long after the NCAA was established (in the 1950s) as the premier postseason competition. Of course, a positive side of this structure was the added intensity it lent to conference regular-season races and postseason league championship tournaments, like the one the Atlantic Coast Conference (ACC) traditionally used to determine its representative in the tournament.

The eight teams selected for the 1939 NCAA tournament were divided into two regionals. The four Eastern teams grouped in Philadelphia were Brown from region one (roughly the Ivy League), Villanova from the Mid-Atlantic, Wake Forest from the Southeast, and Ohio State from the Big Ten. The New York schools were grouped in the Mid-Atlantic region, but when the powerhouse teams of 1939, LIU and St. John's, both declared their intent to play in the NIT, the NCAA selected Villanova, perhaps because of its drawing power in Philadelphia. The four Western teams were all from major conferences: Oklahoma from the Big Six (for the next eleven years the region five representative was determined by a playoff between the Big Six and Missouri Valley Conference champions, which meant that Oklahoma reached the tournament by knocking off Oklahoma A&M in 1939); Texas from the Southwest conference; Utah State from the Skyline; and Pacific Coast champion Oregon, who won the conference's northern division and then triumphed over the southern champion, California, in a best-of-three playoff.

The first NCAA tournament game was played at the Palestra in Philadelphia between Brown and hometown Villanova. The Wildcats did not disappoint their faithful fans, turning back the Ivy League champs 42–30. In a high-scoring affair (for the time), Ohio State trounced Wake Forest 64–52 in the second half of the doubleheader. The next day the Buckeyes' Jimmy Hull poured in a tournament-high 28 points to lead Ohio State University (OSU) past Villanova in a romp, 53–36, and win them a spot in the NCAA final game.

The Western regional was played before meager crowds at San Francisco's Coliseum. In the first round, Oklahoma and Oregon moved easily past Utah State (50–39) and Texas (56–41), respectively. The Oregon Ducks were not only a strong and talented team led by two All-Americans (the only two in the tournament)—six-foot-eight-inch (203cm) low-post player Urgel "Slim" Wintermute and five-foot-eight-inch (173cm) guard Robert Anet—but had also gained experience throughout the season by playing the grueling regular-season schedule (31 games, 8 more than any other tournament team) that coach Howard Hobson organized for the Ducks. Oregon played not only the 20-game Pacific Coast Conference schedule, but also exhibition games against noncollegiate amateur opponents as well as tough road games against Eastern and Midwestern powerhouses like CCNY, St. John's, and Bradley. Thus, by the postseason the Ducks were familiar with the varied

styles of ball played around the country. This experience paid off at tournament time, as Coach Hobson and the Ducks knew how to adjust to their opponents. In the West final, Oregon led 21–14 at the half, altered its strategy in the locker room, and routed the Sooners in the second half, winning 55–37.

The final was played at Patton Gym on the campus of Northwestern University in Evanston, Illinois. Playing against a Big Ten school, the Ducks recognized the need for a fast start and responded by scoring the first 6 points of the game. However, the Buckeyes recovered and stayed close; the score at the half was 21–16, advantage Oregon. Ohio State had succeeded in the East with an

completed and the champion, Colorado, and the runner-up, Duquesne, were both in the NCAA field. The tournament promised to be memorable. Joining Duquesne in the East regional were Western Kentucky, Indiana, and Springfield College. Indiana joined the fray when Big Ten champion Purdue declined the invitation. Tiny Springfield College was an outgrowth of the very YMCA where Dr. Naismith invented the game, and many felt the team's selection was a tribute to Naismith, who had recently died. Colorado, Big Six co-champion Kansas, Southwest Conference king Rice, and the University of South Carolina (USC) prepared to do battle in the West.

Seven-foot (213cm) -tall Bob Kurland, perhaps the greatest star of the NCAA tournament's first decade, towers over his fans and a radio announcer after the Aggies trounced Baylor in the 1946 Western regional final.

impressive display of firepower, but they were unable to overcome Oregon's tight defense. The Ducks won pulling away, 46–33, to become the first ever NCAA champions.

Eight new teams qualified for the tournament in 1940. The overall winning percentage of the 1940 NCAA field was .871 (compared to .776 in 1939) and the teams had a plethora of All-American candidates. The NIT had already been

The West opened with an intriguing matchup as the NIT champ, Colorado, faced off against the team many felt was the best in the country, USC. The two All-Americans on the court—USC's Ralph Vaughn and the Buffaloes' Jack Harvey—cancelled each other out. The difference came from the Trojans' six-foot-five-inch (196cm) center, Joe Riesing, who showed the NIT champs the exit door, 38–32. Kansas topped Rice 50–44 behind Howard Engleman's 21 points. The next night, nine thousand partisan fans packed the arena in Kansas City to cheer on Kansas against the favored Trojans. The contest was the first classic in tournament history. USC led 21–20 at intermission and it remained close throughout. The Trojans clung to a 1-point lead with seventeen seconds left, when, to the delight of the crowd, Engleman scored a basket to lift the Jayhawks into the finals with a 43–42 victory.

The East regional was played in Indianapolis, thus the Indiana Hoosiers had the same home advantage that Kansas had enjoyed in the West. However, Springfield couldn't have beaten the Hoosiers if the game were on Mars; Indiana crushed the small school 48–24. Duquesne squeaked by Western Kentucky in the other first-round contest, but the Dukes couldn't get past the Hoosiers. Indiana won 39–30 to advance to the finals.

The final matched up two coaching geniuses, Indiana's Branch McCracken and Kansas' Dr. Forrest "Phog" Allen. The Hoosiers' success in 1940 was a direct result of McCracken's ingenuity. Indiana ran a weaving fast break offense that boggled opponents and became the prototype for generations to come. Phog Allen's contributions to the sport were

Wyoming's Kenny Sailors, the 1943 NCAA tournament MVP, pursues a player from St. Francis College. Sailors' sensational backcourt play perfectly complemented the powerful low-post game of Wyoming's two big men, Milo Komenich and Jim Weir.

already too numerous to list. Allen had played college ball for Kansas from 1905 to 1907, and his coach had been none other than Dr. Naismith himself. By Allen's senior season, Naismith thought so highly of him that he selected Allen as his successor. Allen left Kansas for a while, but returned in 1919 and established an unparalleled winning tradition. Revered by all who followed college roundball, Allen was the cofounder and first president of the National Association of Basketball Coaches. From

this position, Allen was instrumental in formalizing the game's rules and, in the late thirties, initiating the NCAA tournament. Allen was not only a brilliant coach, with a tremendous winning percentage, but also a great teacher. Many of Allen's varsity players went on to coach the game themselves, foremost among them: Ralph Miller, who won more than 500 games during his career at Wichita, Iowa, and Oregon State; future North Carolina coaching great Dean Smith; and the greatest coach of the generation that followed Allen, Adolph Rupp.

The 1940 championship game was played at Kansas City's Municipal Auditorium, so the Jayhawks enjoyed the same home-court advantage as in the Western regional. The partisan crowd roared its approval as Indiana started slow, failing to score a field goal in the first eight minutes of the game. But Indiana then executed its fast break to perfection, storming to a 32–19 halftime lead. The crowd had little to cheer about in the second half, as the Jayhawks failed to mount a substantial rally. The Hoosiers won 60–42. Indiana's Marv Huffman, who played well throughout the tourney, was named Most Valuable Player (MVP). However, the key to the victory was teamwork; McCracken's troops functioned like a well-oiled machine, and they raced back to basketball-crazed Indiana with the NCAA title.

In 1941 the NIT was played simultaneously with the NCAA tournament because the NIT's organizers, recognizing the success of the 1940 NCAA tourney, feared that the newer event would usurp the NIT's status as the premier postseason tournament. Indeed, the lure of playing in front of a packed Madison Square Garden, and in a field full of independent Eastern powerhouses, allowed the NIT to remain top dog for a while. However, only Duquesne turned down an NCAA invitation for the NIT in 1941, and the NCAA field came from across the country, while the NIT's was concentrated in the East.

Once again all eight participants in the NCAAs were new to the tournament. Pittsburgh replaced Duquesne as the representative from section two. Joining the Panthers in the East were Dartmouth, North Carolina, and surprise Big Ten champ Wisconsin, who had finished ninth in the conference a year earlier. The four Western teams were Arkansas, Wyoming, Washington State (who beat Stanford for the PCC title), and Creighton, who topped Big Six champ Iowa State to become the first team to qualify for the tourney from the Missouri Valley Tournament.

The East regional was played in the home state of the Big Ten champ for the second straight year, which reflected the organizers' concern that the event would not yet attract sizable audiences on a neutral court. The Badgers thrilled their fans with a 51–50 first-round victory, which was decided when sophomore John Kotz buried 2 free throws in the final minute to lift Wisconsin past Dartmouth and its All-American, Gus Broberg. The other first-round game in the East, between Pittsburgh and University of North Carolina (UNC), produced the lowest-scoring affair in tournament history as the Panthers held UNC's high-scoring All-American George Glamack to 9 points and triumphed 26–20. In front of fourteen thousand fans the next night, the Badgers trailed by 6 at halftime, but rallied behind Kotz and All-American center Gene Englund to catapult past the Panthers in the second half for a 36–30 victory. For the third straight year the

Big Ten representative would play for the title. At the Western regional in Kansas City, favored Arkansas squeaked by Wyoming behind the play of guard Johnny Adams while Washington State, led by six-foot-seven-inch (201 cm) center Paul Lindeman (who scored 26 points) pasted Creighton 48–39. In the regional final a small crowd showed up for a contest without a local favorite and Washington State pulled an upset over the Hogs, 64–53.

On the basis of its two solid victories, Washington State was favored in the championship game. Experts predicted that the Badgers could not contain the Cougars' running game. However, from the opening tip, Wisconsin (looking like relics from an even earlier era with their striped red and white socks and knee pads) controlled the game's tempo with its deliberate offense. In the battle of centers, Englund got the better of Washington State's Lindeman. Wisconsin held the Cougars scoreless for one nine-minute stretch in the first half and held a 21–17 halftime lead. The Badgers worked their patient offense to create openings behind Washington State's defense for high-percentage inside shots. After suffocating the Cougar offense for another five-minute stretch in the second half, Wisconsin had things under control. They held on for a 39–34 victory. Kotz was named MVP.

Wisconsin's victory seemed to confirm the Big Ten's reputation as the top basketball conference in the nation. The Big Ten had won

Wisconsin's John Kotz led the Badgers to the 1941 NCAA title and was named tournament MVP in his sophomore year. Two seasons later, the sharpshooting forward would become the all-time leading scorer in Big Ten history.

two consecutive NCAA titles and played in all 3 championship games. However, the Badgers' improbable run to the title would be the Big Ten's last hurrah for some time; it would be twelve years before another Big Ten school would reach the NCAA finals.

World War II would eventually affect every sphere of civilian life, but the Japanese attack on Pearl Harbor on December 7, 1941, and the United States' subsequent entry into the war had little effect on the 1941–1942 college basketball season. Almost all teams honored their commitments to the tournaments and few varsity players enlisted before the season ended.

Colorado and Stanford were the two powerhouses in the West in 1942. In the first round Colorado downed Kansas, and Stanford snuck by Rice after blowing a big lead. The regional final was a much-anticipated clash between titans, but it turned out lopsided as the Cardinals, behind sophomore sensation Jim Pollard (17 points), pulled ahead of Colorado early and cruised to a 46–35 victory. In the East, things didn't hold to form as Big Ten champ and tournament favorite Illinois, dubbed the "Whiz Kids," fell to Adolph Rupp's Kentucky Wildcats, 46–44. Dartmouth downed Penn State and then, in front of a disappointing crowd of three thousand in New Orleans, walloped Kentucky 47–28.

Stanford figured to be the heavy favorite in the final, but young Pollard, who had led the Cardinals through the West regional with 43 points in 2 games, fell ill with the flu. Pollard was the most talented player on a team that featured a rotation of seven Bay Area natives, all of whom were medium-sized for college ball. Coach Everett Dean, who coached Indiana for fourteen years before moving West in 1938, exploited his players' low-post skills by posting one of his "guards" close to the basket where he could overwhelm the smaller man trying to defend him. Although this meant that all the Stanford players could score, with Pollard out, Stanford's title run seemed in jeopardy. Coach Dean knew that Jack Dana and Fred Linari would fill in for Pollard, but he wondered who could make up Pollard's point production.

The first half of the final, played in Kansas City for the third straight year, was tight. Dartmouth held a slight lead until Stanford sophomore Howard Dallmar tied the score at 22 and Dana added a bucket at the buzzer to give the Cardinals a 2-point lead at intermission. In spite of Pollard's absence Stanford looked composed, Dana and Linari were playing soundly, and Dallmar had stepped up to assume a larger role on offense. Still, the game was close and Dartmouth had an All-American, George Munroe, whom they could go to at crunch time. But it never came to that, as the Cardinals took control of the game after intermission. Dartmouth never mounted a comeback and the unflappable Cardinals pulled away from the Ivy Leaguers for an inspirational 53–38 victory. Dallmar was named MVP. Ironically, the Cardinals were unable to repeat as the PCC champ in 1943 after losing Pollard (who would eventually go on to a long and illustrious career in the NBA) to the armed services. Many have speculated that Dean's team would have become the first dynasty of college basketball's tournament era if not for the war. As it was, 1942 turned out to be the Cardinals' only appearance in the NCAA tournament until 1992.

Utah's Arnie Ferrin controls the ball against Dartmouth in the 1944 championship game. The three Dartmouth players are Harry Leggat (17), Bobby Gale (4), and Audley Brindley; the Utah player at the far left is Wat Misaka, one of the few Asian-American players of note in American basketball history.

World War II had a major impact on the 1942–1943 college basketball season as many players were drafted or enlisted. Thus, some schools resorted to playing freshmen on the varsity in order to field a team. De Paul's freshman center George Mikan, too tall for the armed services at six feet nine inches (206cm) (and still growing), was a second-team All-American. The dearth of available players did cause many schools, though none of the traditional powers, to cancel their entire varsity schedule. Travel restrictions forced more cancellations. Many college teams made up for cancelled games by playing squads from regional military bases, where basketball was tremendously popular. Still, competition remained strong enough that both the NCAA and NIT decided to stage their tournaments.

As in the previous year, Illinois was deemed the top team during the regular season. They went undefeated through the Big Ten regular season and lost only

1 game, to Camp Grant. However, the Whiz Kids declined the NCAA's invitation, which allowed Mikan's De Paul team to accept its first invitation to the NCAA tourney. Dartmouth's Stan Skaug had emerged as an All-American and had led the Indians to another Ivy League title. New York University became the first of the perennial New York powerhouses to play in the NCAA tourney, though most felt St. John's, Fordham, and Manhattan, all of whom went to the NIT, were Gotham's strongest teams. The NCAA's decision to invite NYU was, no doubt, motivated by the decision to play the East regionals and the finals at Madison Square Garden. Georgetown rounded out the East. The West regional in Kansas City included a tall, powerful Wyoming team, PCC champ Washington, Texas, and Oklahoma, who represented the Big Six after league champ Kansas declined an invitation.

A crowd of 16,491 flocked to the Garden for the opening round in the East. De Paul downed Dartmouth 46–35 behind Mikan's 20 points and a defense that held the Indians without a field goal for the game's first eleven minutes. To the dismay of the New York crowd, Georgetown cruised to victory over NYU in the other regional semifinal behind the Hoyas' own dominating center, six-foot-eight-inch (203cm) John Mahnken. Thus, the Eastern final offered one of the first great matchups between big men in basketball history. Not only did Mikan and Mahnken have similar sounding names, but they were also the focus of their teams' respective strategies, which was uncommon for centers up to that time. Of course, Mikan would go on to become the first dominant superstar of the NBA after the war, forever changing the role of the big man in the sport. But Mikan had not yet matured fully by 1943, and in the Eastern final game he was outgunned 17 points to 11 by Mahnken before the Georgetown center got in foul trouble. However, with Mahnken forced to the bench, Mikan began to dominate the game with his defense, batting away numerous Georgetown shots as they approached the basket (the goaltending rule would be adopted before the 1944–1945 season, largely due to Mikan's use of the ploy). Late in the game, with Mahnken still on the bench and De Paul holding on to a slight lead, the Hoyas discovered that banking their shots limited Mikan's effectiveness. Sparked by the playmaking of floor general Danny Kraus, Georgetown mounted a comeback and pulled off a thrilling 53–49 victory, thus ending Mikan's only NCAA tournament appearance.

The West regional also featured some thrilling basketball. Texas' John Hargis scored a tournament record 30 points, as the Longhorns came from behind to beat Washington, 59–55. Wyoming's two high-scoring big men, Milo Komenich and Jim Weir, led the Cowboys past Oklahoma, 53–50, in a game that was tight throughout. In the regional final, the Longhorns' fast-paced offense staked them to an early 12-point lead, but Wyoming was too strong and consistent beneath the basket, and the Cowboys came back for a 4-point victory despite Hargis' 29 points.

The final attracted a sizable but noncapacity crowd to the Garden for a game billed as another battle between big men: Georgetown's Mahnken versus Wyoming's Komenich and Weir. As it turned out, the low-post game took a backseat to an exciting floor show featuring two guards, the Hoyas' Kraus and the Cowboys' Kenny Sailors. Wyoming led 18–16 after a dismal offensive performance by both teams in the first half. After intermission, Georgetown snuck out to a small lead when Kraus was forced to the bench with 3 fouls (4 was the limit until the 1943–1944 season).

After thirty-four minutes of play, Wyoming still had only scored 26 points and trailed the Hoyas by 5. Then, keyed by Sailors, the Cowboys exploded for 11 straight points in three minutes. The Hoyas regrouped, pulling back to within 3 with two minutes remaining, but Wyoming then slammed the door in their face, rallying for 9 unanswered points to close out the game. In a year in which large, powerful centers were more prominent than ever before, Cowboys guard Kenny Sailors led all scorers with 16 points, woke his team from its slumber down the stretch, and was appropriately named the tournament MVP. A few days after their victory in the finals, Wyoming squared off against NIT champion St. John's in the Red Cross Classic, a game organized to raise money for the war effort. Wyoming won 52–47, earning the NCAA bragging rights over the NIT.

The climax of the next college basketball season was perhaps the most improbable in history. By the spring of 1944, WWII had transformed the college basketball landscape significantly. While many schools had trouble even fielding teams, those universities with military training facilities were allowed to recruit on their campus any of the military personnel who had not exhausted their eligibility. Dartmouth had a military training facility where many East Coast draftees landed; consequently the Indians were able to add former Cornell star Bob Gale and Harry Leggat, previously of NYU, to an already sound team led by All-American and actual Dartmouth freshman Audley Brindley. The coup de grace was Dick McGuire, widely considered to be the top player in New York, who played almost the entire season for St. John's before he joined the army. Right before tournament time McGuire became a member of the Dartmouth five. It was appropriate that a school with a military training facility should become such a roundball juggernaut, since the only teams that could possibly beat Dartmouth were those playing on U.S.

Following the 1944 title game, tournament MVP Arnie Ferrin shakes hands with NCAA president Philip O. Badger in front of the championship trophy. Badger is handing Ferrin a watch, awarded to all the players on both teams.

military bases throughout the country and across the globe—or so it seemed.

Joining the Indians in the East regional were Temple, Big Ten champ Ohio State, and tiny Catholic University from Washington, D.C., who got a bid because most southern schools cancelled their seasons (and Kentucky had opted for the NIT). Dartmouth overwhelmed Catholic and the Buckeyes handled Temple in the first round; Dartmouth then dismissed Ohio State, who put up a valiant fight behind Arnie Risen's 21 points, 60–53.

The West regional was something out of the twilight zone. The four teams that accepted bids to the tournament were Pepperdine (because the PCC called off its playoff); two Big Six schools, Iowa State and Missouri (because the Skyline conference suspended its competition); and Arkansas, which won the SWC title in a playoff with Rice. However, an automobile accident involving a few members of the Arkansas team on their way to the regional in Kansas City left the Razorbacks unable to compete. As chance would have it, the Utah team was on its way back home from New York City, where they had just lost to Kentucky in the first round of the NIT. Utah, due to its impressive 18–4 record, had been offered a place in the NCAA tournament and freed from any obligation because the Skyline conference was in suspension; Utah coach Vadal Peterson chose to compete in the NIT. However, the NCAA committee realized that the Utes would be passing near Kansas City on their way home and extended them an opportunity to replace Arkansas in the draw. Disappointed from their showing in the NIT, the Utah players voted to accept the unorthodox invitation. The Utes, whose average age was below nineteen and whose star was freshman Arnie Ferrin, took full advantage of the opportunity by jumping all over Missouri in the first round and posting a solid victory over Iowa State in the regional final. So in one of the most bizarre turns of events in the history of American sports (but strangely suited to the 1943–1944 college basketball season), the Utes were headed back to New York City, where

they hoped to play the role of David against a Goliath called Dartmouth.

The 1944 final was one of the great games in the annals of the NCAA tournament. Utah was able to control the tempo of the contest with its patient offense and pressure defense, while Dartmouth played nervously, making many turnovers. Still, Dartmouth led 18–17 at the break. Utah moved in front early in the second half and held a slim lead. The two Utah stars in the game were Ferrin, who would lead all scorers with 22 points, and five-foot-seven-inch (170cm) guard Wat Misaka, a Japanese-American. Ahead 36–34 with a few minutes left to play, the super-quick Misaka and the Utes were able to maintain possession until the game's waning seconds. They played keep-away; the four times they were fouled they chose to take the ball out-of-bounds rather than shoot free throws (teams were given this option when a nonshooting foul occurred, until a rule change before the 1949–1950 season). However, Dartmouth regained possession with seconds left and McGuire hit a miraculous bank shot from half court at the buzzer to send the game to overtime. In the first extra period in tournament history, Utah grabbed a 40–38 lead on the strength of Arnie Ferrin's 4-for-4 shooting from the free throw line, while the Indians shot a collective 2-for-4 from the charity stripe. McGuire tied up the score again. So with time winding down, the Utes held for the last shot; with three seconds left Herb Wilkinson buried a one-hander from the top of the key, and the Utah Utes were the improbable NCAA champions.

And the Utes' storybook season wasn't quite over. Utah got to face the NIT champion, St. John's, in the second Red Cross benefit that matched up the NCAA and NIT champions. In the semifinals of the NIT, the McGuire-less St. John's team had defeated the same Kentucky team that had eliminated Utah from the NIT in the previous round. However, since leaving New York in defeat, the Utes had gained enough experience to last a lifetime. At Madison Square Garden, in front of a sellout crowd all pulling for St. John's, the Utes

downed the Redmen 43–36. Once again the NCAA won bragging rights over the NIT, and the Utes completed a Cinderella story/revenge fantasy for the ages.

The 1944–1945 season was the first year of the "Big Man" in college basketball. The sheer size of De Paul's George Mikan, Oklahoma A&M's Bob Kurland, and Bowling Green's Don Otten made them ineligible for active military duty, and while most of their basketball playing peers were training for combat, this triumvirate of giants was revolutionizing the sport. Mikan, Kurland, and Otten proved that an agile big man is the greatest weapon a team can possess, able to dominate both offensively and defensively and to control the boards. Basketball purists were so fearful that these giants would make a mockery of the game that they pushed through the goaltending rule for the 1944–1945 season, which did a little to lessen the big men's capacity to nullify the opposing team's offense. However, these three centers ruled the 1944–1945 season. Mikan and Otten would square off in the NIT final, while Kurland would led his team into NCAA battle. The rule change forced the big men to refine their skills: Mikan concentrated on developing the low-post offensive moves that served him so well throughout his storied NBA career, and Kurland remained foremost a defensive weapon in coach Henry Iba's conservative system (though Kurland could also score, just as Mikan could still stifle opponents).

While Iba's Oklahoma A&M Aggies were busy stifling opponents, a new trend toward wide-open, fast-paced basketball was sweeping the rest of the West. Oregon and Arkansas played in a record-setting first-round scoring bonanza in the NCAA, in which the Razorbacks triumphed. But Oklahoma A&M was able to hold the Hogs to just more than half their previous night's total in the next round, in a decisive 68–41 Aggie victory. In the East a talented NYU team coached by the great Howard Cann and featuring forward Sid Tannenbaum and center Dolph Schayes moved past Tufts and then faced off against Ohio State, who got revenge on Kentucky in the first round for a regular-season loss. The

Buckeyes led NYU by 10 points with only two minutes to play, when the Violets began to try to steal the ball at every opportunity and fouled if they failed. Ohio State fell into Cann's trap, stepping up to the free throw line and missing their shots (instead of adopting the winning strategy from the previous year's final, when Utah preserved its lead by taking the ball out-of-bounds, which remained an option). With each missed Ohio State foul shot and subsequent NYU basket, the capacity New York crowd grew louder and louder. With thirty seconds remaining, the game was tied. It went to overtime and the Violets beat the demoralized Buckeyes by 5.

The final presented an interesting matchup between a Western team and a traditional New York power. In each of the two previous seasons, the West had produced NCAA champions who had beaten a New York team in the Red Cross showdown. Both Wyoming and Utah were playing in a less disciplined, more open style than the traditional New York game. Now another Western team, playing yet another style (one that worked methodically for an open shot without employing the traditional motion offense), was coming to New York City to challenge NYU. As it turned out, the final was a virtual replay of a regular-season meeting between Oklahoma A&M and NYU, in which the Aggies won 44–41. Once again, the Aggies succeeded in controlling the tempo with a patient offense featuring Kurland and an airtight defense that never allowed the NYU scorers to develop a rhythm, holding Schayes and Tannenbaum to a combined 10 points. Iba, Kurland, and the Aggies had turned winning basketball into a science; they had such confidence in their skills that they seemed in absolute control whether they were maintaining a 3- or 30-point lead. The Aggies won the final, 49–45, and Kurland, who led all scorers with 22, was named tournament MVP.

De Paul's George Mikan and Oklahoma A&M's Bob Kurland reach high for the ball. Basketball's first two outstanding big men squared off twice during their college careers. Kurland's Aggies captured the first showdown and Mikan's Blue Demons won the rematch (pictured here) 46–42.

However, the main event was yet to come: the Red Cross benefit match between De Paul and Oklahoma A&M—that is, Mikan versus Kurland. Mikan's Blue Demons had blitzed through the NIT, winning their 3 games by an average of 28 points. At the benefit, the basketball world was riveted and Madison Square Garden was packed to the rafters. However, the event itself was a letdown. Both Mikan and Kurland fell into early foul trouble; the De Paul big man was disqualified with six minutes remaining in the first half. Mikan managed 9 points in his fourteen minutes, while Kurland contributed 14. Likewise, the Aggies got the better of the Blue Demons, 52–44. Alas, a postseason rematch was not in the cards since the NCAA continued to snub De Paul in favor of a Big Ten representative. The year 1945 also turned out to be the last year of the Red Cross benefit game; the NCAA champion had dominated all three of the grudge matches with the NIT winner, a harbinger of things to come.

The big story of the 1945–1946 season was the continued dominance of Mikan and Kurland. The defending NCAA champion Aggies suffered only 2 defeats all season, both on the road, one of which was against Mikan's De Paul team. Perhaps the most significant game of the Aggies' season was their final regular-season contest at St. Louis, Kurland's hometown. In a departure from his trademark offense, Iba pulled Kurland aside before the game and told him to play with abandon on offense, to try to score as much as possible. "Foothills" Kurland, who averaged 19 points a game, went wild, pouring in 58 points as the Aggies crushed St. Louis 86–33 (in a previous meeting, Oklahoma A&M had won 39–27). On that night in St. Louis, Kurland's offensive potential was finally unleashed.

The Aggies returned to their typical strategy in the NCAA tournament, where they handily disposed of Baylor, 44–29, and the Cal Bears, 52–35, a team that also employed an Iba-type, defense-first approach. Meanwhile, in the East, UNC stymied NYU and then got past Ohio State in overtime to reach the finals. The Tarheels featured All-American John Dillon and his accurate hook shot, but it was center Horace "Bones" McKinney, a six-foot-six-inch (198cm) twenty-seven-year-old ex-serviceman, who had the unenviable task of trying to contain Kurland in the middle. McKinney did an honorable job keeping Foothills away from the boards, but the Heels' center fouled out early in the second half, with his team trailing by 3. Kurland scored the game's next 7 points. But UNC still had a lot of fight in them and snuck back into the game with pressure defense and a series of hook shots by Dillon. With their lead down to a single point in the final seconds, the Aggies had to inbound the ball. UNC put three men around the man out-of-bounds, but Aggie A.L. Bennett was up to the challenge; in an ingenious move, Bennett rolled the ball, in a bowling motion, through the Tarheels' feet to a teammate (a relatively riskfree effort, since kicking the ball is a violation; in a few years a rule was established allowing no more than one player to pressure an inbounds pass). The play led to a final layup and the Oklahoma A&M Aggies became the first repeat NCAA champion.

In addition, Bob Kurland was named tournament MVP for the second straight year. Unlike rival big man George Mikan, who went on to become the NBA's first superstar (with the Minneapolis Lakers), Kurland bypassed a career in the pros despite numerous lucrative offers. He did continue to play basketball, however—for the Phillips Petroleum Company team in the Amateur Athletic Union (AAU) and as a member (and star) of the 1948 and 1952 U.S. Olympic basketball teams, which won gold medals both years.

The landscape of the college basketball world changed dramatically in 1946–1947, not only because of the graduation of Kurland and Mikan, but also because of the return of numerous stars from military duty. John Hargis returned to Texas, Arnie Ferrin to Utah, Kenny Sailors and Milo Komenich to Wyoming, Danny Kraus to Georgetown, and Gerald Tucker to All-American form at Oklahoma. All had further honed their skills while in the armed services. (Basketball's great popularity on U.S. bases during WWII not only led to the establishment of the sport's first "major" professional league, the NBA, in the late forties, but also contributed to the spread of the game internationally.)

The West region in the NCAA tournament was stacked with talent. With its racehorse style, led by Hargis and a speedy playmaker, five-foot-ten-inch (178cm) Slater Martin, Texas lost only 1 regular-season game. In contrast, Big Six champ Oklahoma structured its team around the low-post game of rock-solid Tucker, a Charles Barkley prototype at six feet four inches (193cm). Sailors and Komenich led Wyoming back to the postseason and Oregon State topped UCLA to claim the PCC crown. Tucker worked his magic down the stretch to lift the Sooners over an Oregon State team frustrated by Oklahoma's stifling interior defense. Slater Martin's one-handed basket in the final thirty seconds lifted the Longhorns to a hard-fought 42–40 victory over Wyoming, who played deliberately to slow down Texas. The regional semifinal turned into a classic between two natural rivals. Texas tried to run whenever possible, while the Sooners tried to control the pace. The Longhorns got the better of Oklahoma in the first half and led 29–22 at intermission. But Oklahoma successfully controlled the pace after the break and built a 7-point lead by holding Texas to 5 points during the first thirteen minutes of the second period. Texas fought back, forced turnovers, and, with fifty-three seconds remaining, tied the score at 53. After the Sooners failed to score, Texas took the

Kentucky guard Ralph Beard, one-fifth of the Fabulous Five, moves in for a layup on a fast break.

Kentucky's Jim Line (left) and Wally "Wah Wah" Jones battle Holy Cross' sophomore sensation Bob Cousy for a loose ball in the 1948 NCAA Eastern regional final. The Wildcats dismissed Cousy and the defending national champions 60–52.

lead on a free throw. The Longhorns then denied Tucker the ball down low, challenging the Sooners to try their hand from the perimeter as time wound down. Sooner Bob Pryor, who had yet to score a field goal all game, buried a long set shot. For the third straight year a team from Oklahoma would play for the NCAA title.

Holy Cross, led by its star George Kaftan, carried a 20-game winning streak in the tournament. Joining the Crusaders in the East were Wisconsin from the Big Ten; CCNY, making its first appearance in the NCAAs; and Navy, who got the Southern bid when both Kentucky and North Carolina State opted for the NIT. The Midshipmen were coached by Ben Carneval, who had led UNC to the previous year's final. However, Navy was unable to stay with

Holy Cross in the second half and lost 55–47. Likewise, Wisconsin led early against CCNY but, to the delight of the New York crowd, CCNY won going away. Holy Cross, which played all its games on the road because the team did not have its own gymnasium, did not figure to be unnerved by a huge partisan crowd rooting against them. However, Holy Cross began tight and CCNY took the lead early. Under coach Nat Holman, CCNY incorporated a potent fast break into a "New York" motion offense. But Holy Cross was equally adept at an up-tempo game; every Crusader could handle the ball well when they ran their weaving fast break, and burly Kaftan anchored a strong half-court offense with his ability to score in the paint and out-rebound taller men. The well-conditioned Crusaders also played tenacious

defense, which wore down their opponents. This was the pattern against CCNY; in the ten minutes before halftime, the Crusaders negated an 11-point CCNY lead to go up 2 at intermission, and after the score was still close with ten minutes remaining in the game, Holy Cross began to dominate on defense and pulled away for an easy victory.

The final matched the Crusaders against Oklahoma, which ran a slow, controlled offense. The game moved at the Sooners' pace in the first half and Oklahoma led 31–28 at intermission. But Holy Cross came out running in the second half and, employing their pressure defense, moved ahead. While the Sooners trailed by only 3 points with

CCNY's Floyd Lane controls a rebound from North Carolina State's Sam Ranzino while the Beavers' Ed Warner (4) and Irwin Dambrot (5) look on during the 1950 NCAA Eastern Regional Final, won by CCNY 78–73.

three minutes left, the Crusaders had worn them out. Holy Cross converted Sooner misses into easy baskets down the stretch and claimed the national title with a 58–47 victory. George Kaftan was named tournament MVP.

Throughout the 1991–1992 NCAA tournament, announcers and journalists often noted that the Michigan Wolverines' "Fab Five," a charismatic quintet of talented freshman, recalled the "Fabulous Five" of the 1948 NCAA champion Kentucky Wildcats. However, whereas the Fab Five were enthusiastic upstarts overflowing with confidence and raw, undisciplined talent, the Fabulous Five channelled their formidable athleticism and refined skills into

cohesive teamwork that annihilated opponents. Kentucky coach Adolph Rupp, who relentlessly sought improvement and innovation, molded the experienced and talented Wildcat players into a dominant team that set the standard for the era.

Sadly, the point-shaving scandal of 1951 would taint the reputation of Rupp's marvelous teams from the late forties; at the time, however, everyone was in awe. The Wildcats won the NIT in 1946 and then were runners-up to Arnie Ferrin and Utah in 1947. In 1948, Kentucky was

led by three players with All-American credentials: powerful six-foot-seven-inch (201cm) center Alex Groza, who led the team in rebounding and scoring; super-quick guard Ralph Beard, who was the team's floor general and also had a deadly shot; and six-foot-four-inch (193cm) forward Wallace "Wah Wah" Jones, who had a knack for coming up with crucial baskets. Talented swingmen Cliff Barker and Ken Rollins filled out the Fabulous Five starting unit, although defensive specialists Dale Barnsdale and Jim Line both played about as much as the starters; also, Rupp had faith in many of the players on his bench. Only Rollins was a senior among Kentucky's top players. The Wildcats preferred a brisk pace; they ran flawless fast breaks and moved the ball quickly in the half-court offense to generate opportunities. All the Wildcats were sticklers on defense, and Groza and Jones were demons on the boards. Still, Kentucky wasn't perfect; their 29 victories were balanced by 2 defeats, both by 1 point, to Notre Dame and Temple.

Rupp chose to accept the NCAA's invitation (instead of the NIT's) because he had never won the event before. The only school that was given much of a chance against the Wildcats in the NCAA field was defending champion Holy Cross. The Crusaders were loaded with firepower in the spring of 1948. Flashy sophomore guard Bob Cousy had emerged as a floor general extraordinaire and last year's NCAA MVP, George Kaftan, was back. Kentucky routed Columbia in the first round, while Holy Cross did the same to Michigan. The next night Madison Square Garden was packed for the showdown. Kentucky began by attacking the basket and never relented. The Wildcats had a 13-point lead late in the first half, but the Crusaders rallied both before and after halftime. So Rupp called on Wah Wah Jones, renowned for his clutch shooting, to stem the tide. Jones hit 2 consecutive baskets and the Wildcats were never threatened again. Throughout the game, a Wildcat tag team of Rollins and Barnstable was able to contain Cousy.

Baylor knocked off Wyoming and Kansas State to win the West, but few gave the Bears much of a chance against the Fabulous Five. Baylor tried to stay close by slowing the pace. They succeeded in holding the Wildcats to 13 points after seven and a half minutes, but they were only able to tally 1 point themselves. Kentucky built a 24–7 lead and coasted the rest of the way. The final score was 58–42. Groza led a balanced attack with 14 points and was named MVP. Adolph Rupp, known in Kentucky as the "Baron in the Brown Suit" and to out-of-staters as the "Baron of the Bluegrass," reigned atop the college basketball world.

As far as the University of Kentucky basketball program was concerned, the 1948–1949 season promised to be every bit as rewarding as the previous campaign. The AP poll was born at the beginning of the season, adding a new twist to the college hoops landscape. Kentucky sat comfortably atop the poll throughout its inaugural season, although the Wildcats' regular season was not without a blemish (St. Louis stunned them early on). After the loss Rupp decided to increase Groza's role in the offense. The strategy worked flawlessly. The Wildcats won the remainder of their games by an average margin of 25 points. Finishing the regular season 29–1, Rupp planned an ambitious final month for his team; since the NCAA East regional in New York wasn't set to commence until after the NIT, Rupp accepted invitations to both parties.

The postseason didn't go exactly as the Baron planned; in fact, the only people who could have anticipated all the upsets in the NIT were some high-stakes gamblers and low-integrity players. The NIT had expanded to twelve teams, with the four top seeds getting byes to the second round. Among the bottom eight seeds were all four of the traditional New York powers: NYU, St. John's, Manhattan, and CCNY. The organizers had a brainstorm that none of the New York teams would face each other in the opening round. Madison Square Garden was packed as the stunning events began to unfold. Bradley, Bowling Green, Loyola (Illinois), and unheralded San Francisco swept the four New York schools in what became known as the

Some of the Kentucky Wildcat players and coaches pose for a picture after narrowly defeating Illinois in the 1951 Eastern regional final. Front and center is head coach Adolph Rupp (holding the glasses); on Rupp's right side is star center Bill Spivey (77).

"Manhattan Massacre," which a few years later would become truly infamous. Even more stunning was the series of upsets in the second round. Number one–ranked Kentucky, number three St. Louis, number five Western Kentucky, and Utah all lost to the first round winners. Kentucky's 61–56 loss to Loyola (Illinois) seemed thoroughly shocking at the time, but two years later, as the scope of the point-shaving scandal was becoming evident (and just after Rupp had confidently, self-righteously, and naively pronounced that no gamblers could get near his players), Groza, Beard, and Barnstable confessed that they had shaved points versus Loyola. Anyhow, both underdogs won again in the finals, and then San Francisco completed its string of "upsets" to claim the NIT title.

The NCAA field in 1949 was not as weak as the previous year but paled in comparison to the NIT. The NCAA tournament consistently produced a

strong winner, but its selection process left out too many strong teams. Barring another upset, or more secret meetings with shady characters, Kentucky figured to repeat as champions. The Wildcats waited for a week in New York between tournaments, giving them ample time to ponder their defeat (and, for some, their uneasy consciences). Their first round opponent was Villanova, led by scoring machine Paul Arizin, who had once tallied a record 82 points in one game. Groza and Arizin got into a scoring duel in which each ended up with 30 points, but Kentucky won the game handily, 85–72. Rupp castigated his team for their porous defense after the game, and in the next round versus Illinois, the Wildcats played their first vintage game in almost two weeks, routing the Illini 76–47.

Oklahoma A&M emerged from the Western regional, where they came from 5 points down in the final two minutes to squeak by Wyoming in the first round, and then squashed Oregon State, 55–30, in the regional final. Their win gave the final, which was played in Seattle, some interesting subtexts. Favorite Kentucky was trying to become the second team to repeat as the NCAA titlist by defeating Oklahoma A&M, the only other college to do so previously; Kentucky was also trying to equal its opponent's record of two championships, while the Aggies were trying to move well ahead of the pack with an unprecedented third title (in five years). More intriguing still was the showdown between the coaching legends Adolph Rupp and Henry Iba. The contrast between their coaching styles could not be more pronounced: Rupp advocated an up-tempo style, aggressive-ly attacking the basket; Iba preached the antithesis, a patient offense that allowed the Aggies to control the pace of the action while they looked for high-percentage shots. The Aggies were no pushovers in 1949, although they lacked a dominant player, à la Bob Kurland. The issue at hand was whether the Aggies' slow tempo and tight defense could contain the multifaceted Wildcat attack. The answer was yes, almost. Iba succeeded at controlling the game's pace, and the score stayed low; but the Aggies couldn't stop Alex Groza, who (despite fouling out and missing thirteen minutes of the game) doubled all scorers with 25 points. Kentucky cruised to its second consecutive NCAA crown with a 46–36 victory. Groza also repeated as tournament MVP.

Groza, Jones, and Beard were all named consensus All-Americans, making the 1948–1949 Kentucky Wildcats the only team ever to have three All-Americans. Rupp lost this most accomplished group of players to graduation, leaving the Baron to rebuild (which he did in a jiffy). However, Groza, Jones, and Beard did not part ways after college; instead they stayed together to form the nucleus of an NBA team that they organized and partly owned, the Indianapolis Olympians. Also joining the star trio on the Olympians were former Wildcats Cliff Barker and Joseph Holland. The team was an instant success, winning the NBA's Western Division behind a brilliant season from Groza, who fin-

Legendary Kansas Coach Forest "Phog" Allen talks to his troops before the 1952 championship game. Note how pensive and attentive the Jayhawk players are; the venerable coach was more of an educator than a fiery leader, even before the biggest game of the year.

ished second in scoring to George Mikan and first in field goal percentage. The Olympians struggled in their second season, however, although Groza remained a topflight star. The team made the playoffs but were shut down immediately by Mikan's Lakers. Then, faced with being exposed for their actions, Groza and Beard confessed along with former Kentucky teammate Dale Barnsdale to shaving points in the loss to Loyola at the 1949 NIT and in a game at Tennessee. Consequently, Groza and Beard were both banned for life from the NBA. The Olympians survived for two more undistinguished seasons before folding, a sorry end to such a promising tale.

The 1950 postseason provided a brief glimpse into the potential of New York City college basketball, as a racially integrated team from CCNY managed to win both the NIT and the NCAA tournament, an accomplishment unrivaled in the annals of college hoops. Sadly, however, members of the same CCNY team were arrested in February 1951 for their role in the point-shaving scandal. The demise of the CCNY, LIU, and NYU basketball programs followed. Only one year after its greatest triumph, New York City basketball was moribund.

The CCNY Beavers got off to a slow start in the 1949–1950 season. Coach Nat Holman, a member of the legendary "Original Celtics" of the twenties and thirties, had decided to start four exceptional first-year players to complement one senior, but the group needed time to jell. Two of the four sophomores, forward Ed Warner and guard Floyd Layne, were African-Americans. Black players were commonplace on the major New York college teams, but never before were a team's two stars both black. Holman thought nothing of it; if they were good enough to lead the team, that's what they would do. CCNY was in Harlem, and the neighborhood embraced the team. To accommodate his new players, who learned to play basketball in the wide-open style of the New York streets, Holman moved away from the orthodox half-court motion offense, incorporating more fast breaks and even encouraging jump shots when a player proved he

could knock them down. As the CCNY players grew more familiar with each other, the team came together, and in the second half of a 17–5 regular season the Beavers defeated all the other major New York schools. Toward the end of the season the Beavers' offense was fluid, with each player seamlessly integrated into the team's attack on the basket.

CCNY began the NIT against last year's surprise champion, San Francisco. The Beavers disposed of the Dons handily, 65–46. Next up was third-ranked Kentucky. The Wildcats hoped for the third straight season to win the NCAA crown, even though they had lost four out of five starters from last year's legendary squad. Jim Line had picked up the slack and seven-foot (213cm) sophomore center Jim Spivey was improving rapidly. The Wildcats had won 14 straight. Holman figured six-foot-six-inch (198cm) Ed Roman, his regular low-post man, would get nowhere against Spivey, so the coach put swift six-foot-three-inch (191cm) forward Ed Warner in the middle. Warner had learned his game on the city's playgrounds and knew all the slickest moves. Warner took the slow, plodding Spivey to town and laid him to rest by going around him, over him, under him, and by him for 26 points. Considering that Rupp usually went out of his way to avoid scheduling games against racially integrated teams, Warner's abuse of his protégé had to be irksome. But nothing matched the final score, CCNY 89–Kentucky 50, the worst defeat ever in the history of Kentucky basketball. After the game, Rupp admitted he was impressed and predicted that CCNY would take the title. The semifinals brought a matchup against number six Duquesne, which stayed a little closer than Kentucky, but fell by 10. Only Bradley, the top-ranked team in the country, stood in the way of an NIT title. The Braves were led by All-American forward Paul Unruh and guards Gene Melchiorre and Bill Mann, but the Beavers won the NIT title with a 69–61 victory. Warner led the way with 16 points, for a tournament total of 87, and was named MVP.

The day after the NIT finished, CCNY was extended an invitation to the

NCAA tournament. Two-time defending champion Kentucky was snubbed in favor of North Carolina State. The Wolfpack responded to the opportunity by setting a record for team scoring with 87 points in a victory over Bob Cousy and Holy Cross. CCNY squared off against Big Ten champ Ohio State and its All-American Dick Schnittker in a peculiar opening-round game that the Beavers were lucky to survive. CCNY led 56–54, behind center Ed Roman's hot hand from the perimeter, when things took a turn for the strange. The Buckeyes refused to come out of their zone, so the Beavers simply held the ball near mid-court for five minutes. When Ohio State finally came out of the zone the Beavers were able to run the clock down past two minutes, which meant they could hold the ball for the rest of the game (in a rule change before the 1949–1950 season, a team could no longer refuse foul shots in favor of the ball, but in the final two minutes retained the ball after taking the shots). Things looked good for CCNY, but they bungled twice. Despite this, Buckeye Bob Burkholder missed a potential game winner at the buzzer and CCNY's glorious fortnight continued. The regional final was another nail-biter. The Beavers held a slight lead down the stretch, but the Wolfpack didn't cave in. Future coaching legend Vic Bubas had a chance to tie the game in the final seconds but missed, and CCNY won the hard-fought contest by a deuce. Meanwhile, Bradley ousted UCLA and Baylor in the Western regional to set up a rematch of the NIT final in the NCAA championship game.

The NCAA committee had decided some time earlier to bring the final back to New York, but they couldn't have envisioned the circumstances: a rematch of the NIT final, in the same building, with the same home-court advantage for CCNY. Furthermore, Bradley had logged countless hours in airports, planes, and hotels, while the CCNY players were living at home. The tired Braves trailed throughout and were down 11 with ten minutes remaining. The Braves were able to close the margin to 5, but then the clock moved past the supposedly magic two-minute mark, after which

CCNY had suffered so much grief against Ohio State. The final was no different. With CCNY ahead 69–63, just under a minute to play, and Braves stars Unruh and Mann fouled out, Bradley guard Gene "Squeaky" Melchiorre miraculously revived the moribund Midwesterners. Squeaky shifted into a higher gear, and in just twenty seconds made 2 steals and 2 layups to go along with a teammate's free throw. The Beavers were addled and Holman called time-out, but to no avail; soon the ball was back in the hands of the Braves, who trailed by 1. The five-foot-eight-inch (173cm) Melchiorre drove the lane, elevated as high as he could, and released the ball with a fully extended arm. The Beavers' only starting senior, Irv Dambrot, timed his jump perfectly and swatted the

as the number one-ranked team in both the NIT and NCAA finals. In contrast, by the middle of the 1950–1951 season, CCNY was struggling with 6 losses when the point-shaving scandal broke. A month later, all four of the Beavers who had turned the program around the previous year as sophomores were implicated. It turned out that 4 of their 6 losses had been intentionally "tanked" for payoffs. CCNY dropped the quartet, including the great Ed Warner, and like all those implicated in the scandal who did not firmly establish their innocence, they were banned for life from the fledgling NBA. CCNY suffered even more disgrace when it was revealed in the wake of the investigation that grades were altered for players, including Irv Dambrot, so that they could gain admission to

The year 1951 hangs like a toxic cloud over the history of college basketball, although the events of that year were necessary to bring back honest competition. No matter how sympathetic one may feel toward Alex Groza or Ed Warner because their brilliant careers were wiped out and they were never given a second chance, one must remember that they had had ample time and opportunity to come forward and save their sport from degenerating into a farce and a swindle. In contrast, Manhattan college star Junius Kellogg went to his coach when former teammate Hank Pope offered Kellogg one thousand dollars to influence the outcome of an upcoming game vis-à-vis the point-spread. Coach Norton and Kellogg then reached District Attorney Frank Hogan and the investigation was under way. The whole process went in phases as each wave of implications and confessions brought new leads. Some rough final figures for the investigations were that 86 games were fixed from 1946 through 1950 in twenty-three cities by thirty-seven players from twenty-two colleges, but these numbers almost certainly fail to reflect the true extent of the tampering.

While all this was surfacing, the NCAA was preparing to host an expanded tournament. The new setup would include sixteen teams, with eleven automatic bids for conference champions and five at-large bids (three in the East, two in the West). The eleven conferences were the Yankee, Ivy, Big Ten, Southern, Southeastern, Big Seven, Missouri Valley, Southwest, Skyline, Border, and the PCC.

Once again Kentucky entered the tournament ranked number one, on a 21-game winning streak, and were heavy favorites to win their third NCAA title in four years. The Wildcats were built around seven-foot (213cm) "Big Bill" Spivey, an immovable force in the middle who was developing offensively. Rupp also struck gold with freshmen Cliff Hagen and Frank Ramsey. Kentucky ousted interstate rival Louisville, 79–68, and managed the difficult task of defeating St. John's in front of a New York crowd. The East regional final between the Wildcats and Illinois was the game of

Coach Allen greets his star center, Clyde "Mountain Man" Lovellette, near the end of the 1952 title game. MVP Lovellette tallied 33 points, giving him a record 141 points for the tournament, in the Jayhawks' 80–63 romp over St. John's.

ball to a teammate, who drove the length of the court uncontested as the Garden exploded. Dambrot won the tournament, while CCNY won the year.

In 1950, CCNY had the greatest postseason ever in college basketball history and it seems that their accomplishment will never be equaled. They not only won both of the competing championship tournaments, but in the process defeated the twelfth-, sixth-, fifth-, third-, and second-ranked teams as well

CCNY (a 3.0 grade point average was mandatory). Consequently, CCNY dropped major college basketball. Nat Holman faded into obscurity. The Beavers' glorious ascendancy—which produced some truly memorable basketball—and infamous demise had occurred within the course of just one year.

the tournament. The Illini featured two star guards, Rod Fletcher and Don Sunderlage. The game was close all the way, but things looked bleak for Kentucky when Spivey, who had led the way with 28 points and 16 rebounds, fouled out with three minutes remaining and left Kentucky clinging to a 1-point lead. Kentucky's Shelby Linville took the reins in Big Bill's absence. Linville pushed the lead to 3, but Illinois rallied to tie the score at 72 with less than a minute to play. Linville moved Kentucky back ahead, but Sunderlage responded to tie the game up with twenty-nine seconds left. As the Wildcats moved the ball downcourt, Frank Ramsey saw Linville open near the basket and got him the ball, and Linville scored his third straight bucket. After a time-out Sunderlage attempted a hook shot from medium range, but it clanked off the rim and Rupp's Wildcats were headed to Minneapolis for the finals. In the Western regional, number two–ranked Kansas State slipped past a feisty Arizona team that fought back from a 21-point deficit to lose by only 2, and then breezed past Brigham Young. The Wildcats expected a tussle against third-ranked Oklahoma A&M, but the Aggies were playing their third game in as many days and had nothing left. Kansas State embarrassed Iba's Aggies. They built a 37–14 lead by halftime and coasted to an easy victory.

The final was an all-Wildcat affair. For Kansas State to have a chance, six-foot-seven-inch (201cm) center Lew Hitch would have to contain Spivey. All was well through the first half, as Kansas State led 29–27. Spivey was more productive in the second half (he finished with 21 points and 22 rebounds), but the big story after intermission was Kansas State's eight-minute scoring drought. By the time the Midwesterners regained their touch, Kentucky was out of reach. Rupp had won his third title in four years. Spivey deserved an MVP honor but none was awarded.

The year 1951 signaled the dark end to an era in which college basketball had grown tremendously. The response to the point-shaving scandal demonstrated how college basketball had become too large to be controlled by small-time crooks; the bloodletting that occurred was tantamount to growing pains. After the scandal, college basketball would regain its footing and continue to evolve into a larger, nationwide arena (New York would no longer be the focal point of the college basketball universe). The new era began in 1952, the first year of the Final Four.

At the start of the 1951–1952 season, Bill Spivey was expected to lead the defending champion Kentucky to another title. However, by midseason Spivey himself was implicated in the (still-expanding) betting scandal and suspended from the Wildcats. Spivey's trial ended in a hung jury, which despite Big Bill's protestations of innocence was sufficient to end his college career. Spivey was also banned from the NBA (in violation of his rights), but did play on some semipro teams. Even without Spivey, Kentucky was a force; led by All-Americans Cliff Hagen and Frank Ramsey, the Wildcats stormed into the tournament with a 28–2 record and were favored to repeat as champions.

For the first time in its history the NCAA tournament was organized into four regionals—East, Mideast, Midwest, and West—consisting of four teams each. The winner of each regional would advance to the Final Four to determine the national champion.

Kentucky breezed past Penn State in the first round of the East regional and then squared off against St. John's, the only New York power not to derail its program after the point-shaving scandal. Earlier in the season, the Wildcats had crushed the Redmen 81–40. Kentucky featured its legendary fast break, but the Redmen, having learned from their first encounter with the Wildcats, devised a strategy to upend Rupp's number one–ranked troops. The Redmen utilized a deliberate offense, but whenever Kentucky gained possession, the St. John's players raced back at breakneck speed to defend their basket. The Redmen's All-American Bob Zawoluk was on fire and staked the underdogs to a 6-point lead. The frustrated Wildcats tried to rattle St. John's with aggressive defense, but only fell into foul trouble.

Behind Zawoluk's 32 points, St. John's held on to produce the season's biggest upset, 64–57, and become a member of the inaugural Final Four. Second-ranked Illinois was able to get by fourth-ranked Duquesne, 74–68, in the Mideast regional final, despite 29 points by the Dukes' All-American Jim Tucker. In the West, Santa Clara was able to hold off a late comeback by Wyoming, sparked by Cowboys guard Larry Esau, and advanced to Seattle with a 56–53 victory.

The Kansas Jayhawks, coached by living legend Phog Allen, were the heavy favorites in the Midwest regional in Kansas City. At a time of crisis for the young sport, Allen's mere presence reminded fans of what intercollegiate athletics were supposed to be about. While Allen built a winning tradition at Kansas that continues to this day, he always emphasized the educational value of basketball. Like Dr. Naismith before him, Allen viewed competitive sports primarily as a way to build up a young man's character. By the late forties, Allen had sensed that the college game was veering into troubled waters and railed against the atmosphere in Madison Square Garden long before the point-shaving scandal broke. Ironically, he fielded his best team in years during the season following the scandal; the venerable coach was poised to take center stage just when his sport needed him most.

Allen's 1951–1952 Jayhawks compiled a 22–2 regular-season record and seemed capable of earning their legendary coach the one thing missing from his résumé: a national title. Kansas' main weapon was the massive six-foot-nine-inch (206cm), 245-pound (111kg) Clyde Lovellette, deemed the "Mountain Man" (though he hailed from Indiana), who led the nation in scoring with a 28.4 average. The Jayhawks easily dismissed Texas Christian to set up a showdown with St. Louis in the regional final. The night belonged to Lovellette. Showing that he possessed a silky touch to go along with his wide body, Clyde poured in 19 first-half points to keep the otherwise cold-shooting Jayhawks even with St. Louis, 27–all. But Lovellette was just warming up. He added 25 points in the second frame to establish a new tournament scoring record (44) and the Kansas Jayhawks won pulling away.

The inaugural Final Four was held in Seattle. Upstart St. John's squared off against Illinois in the first national semifinal and Kansas faced underdog Santa Clara in the nightcap. The Redmen's disciplined style once again paid early dividends against Illinois, as St. John's built a 10-point lead midway through the first half. But the Illini bounced back, converting a high percentage of their possessions and taking a slim lead early in the second half. However, as in its game against Kentucky, St. John's kept its composure and Zawoluk got a hot hand at the right time, scoring 10 of his 24 points in the final ten minutes. Up by 6 with a couple of minutes left, the Redmen went into a stall. The strategy backfired, as Illinois moved within 2 and stole the ball with seconds left, but a desperation shot at the buzzer failed to connect and St. John's survived. The Kansas–Santa Clara contest provided no such thrills, as the favored Jayhawks overwhelmed the Broncos, 74–55. Kansas held Ken Sears, Santa Clara's freshman star, to 1 point. Lovellette led all scorers with 33.

St. John's had already upset the two top-ranked teams in the nation to reach the final, so overcoming number three Kansas should have been a breeze. It wasn't to be. The disciplined offense and hustling defense of St. John's did not disorient the well-schooled Jayhawks, who, led by the Mountain Man, took the upper hand early and built up a 41–27 lead by intermission. The only glimmer of hope for the Redmen came early in the second half when Lovellette was called for his fourth foul of the rugged contest. Coach Allen elected to keep his star in the game, and unfortunately for St. John's, Lovellette displayed the necessary discipline to avoid collecting another foul. The huge center once again scored 33 points, establishing a new tournament record for points (141) as well as for rebounds (69). The final score was 80–63. Lovellette was named MVP and Phog Allen was finally a certified NCAA champion.

There are two footnotes to Kansas' first NCAA crown. First, it must have given Allen, who frequently equated

New York City with all that was wrong with college basketball, a special sense of satisfaction to capture the title over St. John's. Second, the 1952 Jayhawks were not only tied to basketball's storied past, through Allen's Naismith pedigree, but the team also had a connection to the college game's glorious future in the person of a backup guard by the name of Dean Smith.

The 1953 national championship game was a classic between two traditional powers, defending champion Kansas and Indiana. A rematch of the 1940 final, the game once again pitted the schools' two famed coaches, Kansas' Phog Allen and Indiana's Branch McCracken, against each other. Unlike Indiana's lopsided win thirteen years earlier, the 1953 showdown was nip and tuck from start to finish. At no point were the two teams separated by more than 6 points—it remains the most closely contested final in tournament history. With under a minute to play, the score tied 68–68, and the Kansas City crowd going crazy following a clutch layup by the Jayhawks, the Hoosiers slowed down the pace and prepared to take the final shot.

The 1953 championship game was a brilliant, but not really fitting, conclusion to a college basketball season best remembered for the tremendous increase in scoring brought about by three off-season rule changes, all of which led to more free throw shooting. First, a team could no longer waive off a foul; second, players got two opportunities to convert a 1-shot defensive foul; and third, in the final three minutes of the game, 2 shots were rewarded for all fouls. Free throw shooting became key to a team's success. Teams with good free throw shooters drove to the basket whenever possible to exploit the new rule. As point totals rose, more and more teams converted to fast-breaking offenses. Free throw shooting went up 30 percent and scoring increased a record 10 percent over the previous season. Teams began to top 100 points on a regular basis.

The NCAA tournament expanded again in 1953, this time to twenty-two teams; six teams would be rewarded first-round byes. Kentucky was conspicuously absent in the East regional. The

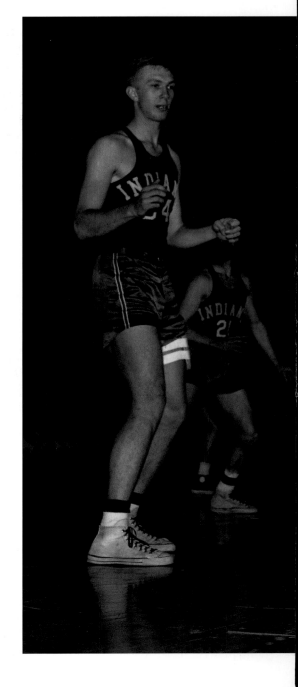

Wildcats were serving a one-year probation, stemming from the point-shaving scandal, from both the Southeastern Conference and the NCAA tournament. Louisiana State University (LSU) took advantage of the void. Led by six-foot-ten-inch (208cm) All-American Bob Pettit, a scrappy scoring machine who would go on to a brilliant NBA career, the Tigers advanced to the Final Four with solid victories over Lebanon Valley (who upset Fordham in the first round) and Wake Forest. In the West, Washington, led by Bob Houbregs, was the favorite. After a first-round bye, Washington dismantled crosstown rival Seattle behind a record-setting 45 points by Houbregs. The Huskies then faced Santa Clara and Ken Sears. The game went back and forth until the Huskies

Indiana's Charley Kraak dribbles around Kansas' Al Kelley during the 1953 NCAA title game while his Hoosier teammates Dick White (41), Bob Leonard (21), Don Schlundt (34), and Phil Byers (14) look on. Future coaching legend Dean Smith (22) lingers downcourt.

took the lead for good, 51–50, on a long set shot by Houbregs with about ten minutes to play. Houbregs outscored Sears 34–23 and Washington won handily 74–62.

The number one–ranked team in the nation, Big Ten champ Indiana, was placed in the Mideast regional. The Hoosiers featured six-foot-ten-inch (208cm) All-American Don Schlundt, deemed "Mr. Inside," and backcourt man Bob Leonard, "Mr. Outside," alongside a strong supporting cast. Nonetheless, De Paul, fresh off a thrilling 74–72 win over Miami of Ohio in the first round, almost derailed Indiana, but the Hoosiers escaped with a 82–80 win. Indiana's next foe, Notre Dame, had defeated them earlier in the season by a point. This time, Schlundt, who grew up literally next

door to Notre Dame in South Bend, Indiana, took things into his own hands, scoring an amazing 30 points in the first half and 42 overall, to pace the Hoosiers to a comfortable victory and a place in the Final Four.

The Kansas Jayhawks were not expected to contend for the NCAA title in 1953, having graduated all five of their starters from last year's championship squad. In preseason, Coach Allen said he'd be surprised if his team won 5 games. But overlooked center B.H. Born emerged as a star (though not on par with the likes of Clyde Lovellette) and the Jayhawks jelled into an exceptional team during the course of a season in which Kansas was cast in an unfamiliar role, the underdog. In the only four-team regional, the Kansas Jayhawks slipped by Oklahoma

City and Oklahoma A&M to return to the Final Four in 1953.

Neither of the semifinals in Kansas City was particularly dramatic. Indiana handled LSU, 80–67. Pettit got his customary points, but Schlundt matched his total. With the two stars negating each other, Leonard and the other Hoosiers easily outclassed the remaining Tigers. In something of a surprise, Kansas trounced Washington in the other semi. The Jayhawks jumped ahead early when their pressing defense thoroughly disoriented the Huskies, causing numerous turnovers. Any hope of a comeback was extinguished when Houbregs fouled out early in the second half. The final was 79–53 and the surprising Jayhawks were 1 victory away from repeating as national champions.

After ten minutes, Indiana led Kansas 21–19. At the half, it was tied at 41. With ten minutes remaining, the difference was 1 point, 59–58, advantage Indiana. Kansas' Born fouled out with 26 points, but his teammates did not cave in. Down the stretch, as the tension mounted, every shot, every pass gained in significance. Phog Allen and Branch McCracken drew on all their years of studying the game to devise their strategies. And it came down to the game knotted at 68, Indiana with the ball, and the clock ticking down to half a minute when the Jayhawks fouled Bob Leonard, an exceptional free throw shooter....But he misses! The partisan crowd in Kansas City erupts, but under the new rules he gets one more try. Leonard steps to the line, eyes the basket, and sinks the shot. The Jayhawks bring the ball upcourt, looking for the winning basket. But they're unable to get into a smooth rhythm; they, no doubt, miss Born, who was the focus of their half-court offense. The clock is ticking down, past ten, past five...the ball is in the hands of backup Jerry Alberts, who puts up a shot to win the title. It misses and Indiana is crowned the 1953 NCAA basketball champion.

The offensive explosion continued during the 1953–1954 season. Furman's six-foot-three-inch (191 cm) Frank Selvy, who averaged an unprecedented 41.2 points per game, led the assault on the record books. The 355 points he tallied from the charity stripe during the season remains on the books, just as his 100-

A group of jubilant Hoosiers carry their coach, Branch McCracken, off the floor after Indiana clinched the 1952–1953 Big Ten title at Illinois. It was Coach McCracken's first conference crown. Indiana won the NCAA title in 1940, but finished second in the Big Ten to Purdue, which declined the NCAA tournament's invitation.

point explosion against Newberry stands as the single-game record for a Division I player. However, Bevo Francis of tiny Rio Grande College actually set the scoring standard for the record-breaking season, totaling 113 points against Hillsdale.

As the 1954 NCAA tournament approached, Kentucky once again seemed head and shoulders above the rest of the pack. Following their suspension in 1952–1953, Rupp's Wildcats were back with a vengeance, routing most of their foes on the way to an unblemished 25–0 season. Then, with the team poised to sweep to a national title, the NCAA declared that three of the Wildcats' top stars—Frank Ramsey, Cliff Hagen, and Lou Tsioropoulas—were ineligible because they were in their fifth year of college. With his team in disarray, Rupp

chose to stay home for the postseason. Kansas, who was ranked seventh, also missed the tournament when it lost a coin flip with Colorado, who was unranked, to determine the Big Seven champion.

Thus, before it even started, the 1954 tournament was missing some of its luster; and then the upsets began. In the Midwest regional, fourth-ranked Oklahoma A&M was favored to advance but was derailed by a Bradley squad that had won just a few more games than it had lost. Bradley only got invited to the tournament because the NIT, in a desperate attempt to compete with the NCAAs, had lured the more highly touted teams into its tournament by extending invitations at midseason. The Bradley Braves played an all-out, run-and-gun offense; their strategy was to attack the basket at all times. Henry Iba's Oklahoma A&M Aggies, playing on their home court in Stillwater, probably figured they would crush the Braves in the regional final, but Bradley maintained a slight lead throughout and then won pulling away, 71–57, to earn a trip to Kansas City.

The results of the Mideast regional were even more astounding. Defending champion Indiana, with only 1 loss all season, was favored to win the region, although Notre Dame and LSU figured to be worthy foes. Penn State didn't seem to stand a chance in this powerful grouping and barely survived against Toledo in a first-round match. But Penn State more than held its own versus LSU. Close all the way, the Nittany Lions withstood a 34-point performance by

Bob Pettit and dominated the game's closing minutes to post a 78–70 upset. Then Notre Dame and Indiana staged a classic. When the dust settled, the number two–ranked defending champions were eliminated by the narrowest of margins, 65–64. The Fighting Irish, perhaps too high from their glorious win over their in-state rivals, didn't give enough thought to unheralded Penn State. Led by Jesse Arnelle's 5 first-half steals and Ed Haag's long-distance set shots, Penn State stunned the Irish, 71–63, in the regional finals.

No obvious favorite reigned in the West; once-defeated Seattle seemed strong, as did Santa Clara. Pacific Eight champ USC, with 12 defeats, was a long shot. Idaho State got the upsets started by snapping Seattle's 26-game winning streak with a 77–75 upset in the first round. Santa Clara moved through the first two rounds easily and squared off with USC, who had dismissed Idaho State. The Trojans led throughout most of the regional final, but Santa Clara moved ahead late. Down by 3 with only three seconds left, USC needed a miracle and got one when Roy Irvin scored on a tip-in and was fouled. He sank the free throw and the game went to overtime. After five more minutes, the score was tied again, thanks to a last-second Trojan free throw. In the second overtime, the first in tournament history, USC went ahead 66–65 on a free throw. Frustrated by the Trojans' persistent comebacks, Santa Clara decided to hold the ball for the next four minutes for a final shot. The strategy backfired when USC stole the ball with seventeen seconds left before Santa Clara ever took a shot.

The only pretournament favorite to win its region was La Salle, who was led by its All-American Tom Gola. However, in the very first round, La Salle trailed Fordham by 2 with four seconds left, following a tip-in basket by Fordham. La Salle called time-out to set up a play, and everyone in the arena expected Gola to take the shot. The Explorers inbounded the ball to Gola and the Fordham defense collapsed on him, so Gola drilled a pass to teammate Fran O'Malley under the basket for an easy bucket. La Salle pre-

vailed in overtime, 76–74. Gola averaged more than 20 points and 20 rebounds in the next two rounds as the Explorers romped through the rest of the regional.

In Kansas City, La Salle continued its hot streak and Penn State's unlikely run ended in the first national semifinal, the Explorers posting a convincing 69–54 victory. The Bradley-USC contest was

Two years before capturing the 1954 NCAA crown, La Salle shocked the college basketball world by taking the 1952 NIT. Coach Ken Loeffler's Explorers were led by co-MVPs Norm Grekin and freshman Tom Gola (17). Two years later Gola would earn the NCAA tourney's MVP.

more engaging. USC jumped ahead early and led by as much as 11, but the Braves narrowed the gap to 6 at halftime. The Trojans maintained their lead after intermission, but Bradley turned it on as the game wound down. With sixty-three seconds remaining, the Braves finally took a 1-point lead, 71–70, and never trailed again.

In the finals, 1 point separated Bradley and La Salle at intermission when La Salle coach Ken Loeffler, who always preached man-to-man defense, told his troops to switch to a zone defense. The move stymied the high-octane Bradley attack. Unable to penetrate the zone effectively, the flustered Braves took to launching outside shots. The Braves shot below 20 percent in the second half, while La Salle went on a tear and pulled away to win the national title. Gola was named tournament MVP. La Salle's 92–76 victory was the highest-scoring NCAA final yet.

By the end of the 1953–1954 season, college basketball had bounced back from

the shock of the 1951 point-shaving scandal and gained a new and truer stability. On the court, the game was characterized by an explosion in offensive production that thrilled fans across the country. Heading into the 1954–1955 season, La Salle, led by returning senior Tom Gola, was poised to defend its national championship against the likes of Kentucky and

other traditional powers. Everything seemed status quo. What no one envisioned was that the previously unheralded center of the University of San Francisco (USF) Dons, Bill Russell, was about to revolutionize the sport with his innovative defensive techniques and airborne style of play that would lift USF to consecutive national titles on the strength of the team's stifling defense. No other single player has ever made such an impact on the game's evolution. Simply put, basketball-before-Russell and basketball-after-Russell are two different games; the modern era began in 1955.

Chapter

Evolution of Offense and Defense: **1955–1963**

Basketball evolved into the modern era in the mid- to late fifties. Bill Russell took the game above the rim with his shot blocking and dunk shots, Wilt Chamberlain carried it even higher, and Elgin Baylor seemed suspended in midair on his drives to the basket. Meanwhile, Jerry West perfected the jump shot and Oscar Robertson excelled as the first large point guard/point forward, twenty years before Magic Johnson and Larry Bird came on the scene. These great players' groundbreaking techniques spread through the game like wildfire; soon every kid shooting baskets in his backyard and every high school coach across the land was playing a profoundly different game—more athletic, more airborne—than the basketball played a decade earlier.

The game during this period became something that would be recognizable to today's fans, who are apt to say that no players from previous generations could compete with today's top performers, given the evolution of the game and improvements in conditioning. But few could argue that the likes of Russell, Chamberlain, Baylor, West, and Robertson would ever be anything less than superstars, even today. These five men and many of the other top players of the late 1950s/early 1960s did things on a basketball court that are still in great demand today—and did them brilliantly.

A significant factor in the transformation of basketball from the late forties/early fifties to the late fifties/modern era was the increasingly visible role of African-American players in major college ball. Basketball had evolved dif-

ferently in "white" and "black" America. De facto segregation in the North and legislated segregation in the Jim Crow South contributed to these different trajectories. Thus, "black" basketball was not solely the product of the streets and playgrounds of ghettos in large Northern cities, but also of organized all-black teams. The two most famous of these teams were professional touring teams: the New York Rens in the twenties and thirties and the Harlem Globetrotters (from Chicago, oddly enough) in the thirties and forties. The Rens and the Globetrotters were serious, competitive teams; and they played a distinctly black style of ball, featuring more individual improvisation, in-air play, and fancy dribbling and passing. The 1950 CCNY team that won both the NIT and NCAA titles had two prominent black stars and successfully incorporated these players' contrasting approach to the game into a cohesive whole (as in the late forties did Holy Cross, whose star, Bob Cousy, though white, played in the style of New York schoolyard ball). Still, traditionalists claimed that "street ball" maneuvers could not be integrated successfully into an overall team concept. This claim was soundly discredited in the late 1950s as Russell, Chamberlain, Baylor, and Robertson all led their teams to the Final Four.

These innovations changed the way college ball was played on both the offensive and defensive ends of the court. The late 1950s/early 1960s was a peculiar era in college basketball in that the top teams in the nation were either offense-oriented or defense-oriented; that is,

they emphatically emphasized high-scoring offense or airtight defense. The early 1950s had seen a nationwide explosion in scoring. Then, the nation's top defensive team, Bill Russell's University of San Francisco Dons, won back-to-back titles, and basketball's top teams split into two camps. For five years, from 1959 through 1963, the nation's top defensive team squared off against the nation's top offensive team in a series of remarkable NCAA finals. It was an innovative era, an era of offense versus defense, new strategies, and new ways of playing.

The 1954–1955 campaign marks an important turning point in the history of college basketball. At a time when scoring records were being established across the country, Bill Russell came on the scene and reestablished the primacy of defense. Over the next two seasons the six-foot-nine-inch (206cm) shot-blocking center would lead the Dons to consecutive NCAA titles. In fact, the Dons' only loss during the two-year span came at the hands of John Wooden's UCLA Bruins led by a star named Willie Naulls, whose skills matched up fairly well with Russell's. UCLA defeated the Dons early in the 1954–1955 season. It was Russell's last defeat at USF; the Dons' center got his revenge on Naulls and the Bruins during the next season and again in the 1956 NCAA tournament. However, the

Kansas' seven-foot (213cm) sophomore sensation, Wilt Chamberlain, skys above the fray for an easy 2 points against San Francisco in the 1957 NCAA semifinals. Behind Chamberlain, the Jayhawks routed the two-time defending champion Dons 80–56. Of course, San Francisco was without Bill Russell, the player most instrumental in their back-to-back titles, who had graduated after the previous season.

loss to the Bruins kept the Dons from becoming one of only two teams in history to post back-to-back undefeated national championship seasons; ironically, Wooden's Bruins managed the feat, during the first two years of the "Walton Gang" (1971–1972 and 1972–1973). Nonetheless, the Dons closed out the Russell era with an unprecedented string of 55 straight victories (which the Dons expanded to 60 in their first season after Russell), a record that stood until the Walton Gang came along.

Bill Russell had an inauspicious beginning to his brilliant basketball career. Tall but lanky, Russell played on his high school varsity team in Oakland, California; while he had a strong physical presence, he was far from being a star. Russell figured that his basketball playing days were over after high school, but he was tapped for a traveling California All-Star team because they needed another player. This exhibition team played a wide-open style—similar to black schoolyard ball—that appealed to Russell. Frustrated by his lack of offensive skills, especially dribbling and shooting, Russell realized he could exploit his athleticism in another way, by stopping offense. Thus, Russell developed his own physical style of defense, featuring airborne shot blocking, unlike anything seen before in basketball. When Russell returned from the All-Star tour, he was surprised by an offer of a basketball scholarship from USF. There, Russell became a dedicated student of basketball and worked with his roommate, K.C. Jones, to develop his revolutionary defensive style. Russell and Jones had the blessing of coach Phil Woolpert, who emphasized defense anyway, but it was Russell himself who came up with the innovations that he unveiled on the basketball court.

In the winter of 1952–1953, the unheralded center from Oakland led the USF freshman team to a successful 19–4 season with his uniquely aggressive, shot-

Bill Russell rules the airwaves. Top: Russell skys to reject a hook shot by Iowa's Milt Scheuerman during the 1956 finale. Bottom: Surrounded by the opposition (including Tom Gola, 15), Russell controls the boards against La Salle in the 1955 NCAA finals.

blocking defense and tremendous rebounding. The next year, Jones, USF's costar, missed the season due to appendicitis, but Russell graduated to a varsity team that finished 14–7. However, he was not readily accepted by some of the veteran Dons, who resented the center's different and dominating style of play. So no one was really prepared for what transpired during the 1954–1955 season, when Jones returned and Russell truly came of age. Teams would show up to play the Dons, move into their standard offenses—working the ball around, trying to create a good shot, finding an apparent opening—and then, seemingly from out of nowhere, Russell would appear to block the shot. Russell would single-handedly take teams out of their offenses. Likewise, Russell dominated both the offensive and defensive boards like no one before him. He was literally playing head and shoulders over everyone else, and he integrated his revolutionary style of play into a fluid team concept. The Dons won their first 2 games, lost to UCLA, and then closed out their schedule with 21 straight wins.

USF ascended to the top of the wire service polls heading into the NCAA tournament. Kentucky suffered the most stunning upset of the season when Georgia Tech's Joe Helms hit a one-handed twelve-footer (3.5m) with eleven seconds left to lift the Yellow Jackets over the Wildcats, 59–58. In the process they snapped Kentucky's sixteen-year in-conference unbeaten streak, 129-game at-home winning streak, and 54-game regular-season unbeaten streak all at once. Nonetheless, the Wildcats entered the tournament ranked number two. Defending champion La Salle was number three.

While Kentucky was upset in the regional semifinal by Marquette, La Salle stormed through the East regional, winning by an average margin of 32 points. USF breezed through the first two rounds, but then faced a serious challenge in the West regional finals in the form of Oregon State and its seven-foot-three-inch (221cm) center Swede Halbrook. The game was nip and tuck all the way. The Dons' second-leading scorer, Jerry Mullins, twisted his ankle early

San Francisco Mayor George Christopher (crouched down, wearing the ribbon pinned to his lapel) celebrates the USF Dons' second consecutive national title on March 23, 1956. Bill Russell is on the far right, while K.C. Jones is in the dark suit crouched down next to Russell.

on and contributed only 2 free throws. However, Russell dominated Halbrook and the Dons escaped with their narrowest victory of the season, 57–56, when the Beavers missed a last-second shot.

The Dons defeated Colorado in one of the national semifinals, while La Salle handled Iowa (who had eliminated Marquette). Thus, the 1955 final was a much-anticipated showdown between the nation's top offensive team, defending national champion La Salle, and the nation's stingiest defensive team, from the City by the Bay. From the opening tip-off it was all Dons. K.C. Jones held Gola to only 1 basket for one twenty-minute stretch and outscored the La Salle All-American 24–16. Russell added 23 points, grabbed 25 rebounds, and was named tournament MVP. The Dons led 35–24 at halftime and cruised to a 77–63 victory.

Cruise is exactly what USF did the next season as well. Ranked number one from start to finish, the Dons swept all their games, winning by fewer than 10 points only twice during the regular season. The only adversity the Dons faced all season came at the beginning of the NCAA tournament, when they learned that K.C. Jones was ineligible for the tournament as a fifth-year senior. But this setback hardly affected the Dons as they crushed all four of their opponents to become the first-ever undefeated NCAA champions.

The dramatic highlight of the tournament came in the first round of the East regional when little Canisus overcame second-ranked North Carolina State, 79–78, in four overtimes. Canisus then advanced past Dartmouth before falling 60–58 to Temple, which was led by its dynamic backcourt of Hal Lear and Guy Rodgers. USF spanked UCLA in the first round, 72–61, pounded seventh-ranked SMU in the national semifinals, and then breezed past Big Ten champion Iowa (who had knocked off Temple in the semifinals). Russell closed out his magnificent college career with a 26-point, 27-rebound performance in the 83–71 victory and was named MVP for the second straight year. The USF Dons of 1954–1956 were clearly one of the greatest teams in the history of college basketball, and Russell was one of the game's all-time great players.

No sooner had Russell graduated from USF than another dominant big man came on the scene—Wilt Chamberlain. However, Wilt's basketball career would contrast sharply with Russell's, especially when it came to winning championships. Seven feet one inch (216cm) tall, with the agility of a point guard combined with the strength of an ox, Chamberlain was a force of nature, virtually unstoppable. Most opponents hoped merely to contain the giant: whole teams ganged up on Wilt just to slow him down. The college basketball world seemed ready to concede the next three national titles to Kansas, but it didn't turn out that way.

Chamberlain was already a legend before his first college game. Wilt averaged 45 points per game at Philadelphia's Overbrook High School, which he led to back-to-back public high and citywide championships. Every major college in the country, from all-white Southern schools to Harvard, recruited Chamberlain. The young giant chose to attend Kansas in part because he was impressed with Phog Allen, who visited Philadelphia twice to seek him out. Allen was as much an educator as a coach intent on winning. Unfortunately for Chamberlain, Allen turned sixty-five, the mandatory retirement age, the year before Wilt began his varsity career. Despite the loss of its coach, Kansas was ranked number one at the start of the 1956–1957 season on the strength of Chamberlain's reputation.

When the Jayhawks lost by 2 to Iowa State (their only other regular-season loss came to Henry Iba's Oklahoma State team by the same margin), North Carolina ascended to the top ranking. Frank McGuire's Tarheels never fell from number one as they won all 27 of their regular-season contests. McGuire had been the coach at St. John's through the 1952 season, and though the Redmen hadn't been implicated in the point-shaving scandal that had rocked New York City college hoops, McGuire abandoned the Big Apple for Chapel Hill. Once he set up shop at UNC, he proceeded to bring New Yorkers down south to play

for him. His 1957 squad featured a starting five all from the New York metropolitan area, and an ethnic mix—four Catholics and one Jew—that was quite an anomaly below the Mason-Dixon line. The one Semite, All-American Lenny

Kansas' Wilt Chamberlain goes up for a shot from close range against North Carolina in the 1957 championship matchup. Notice how Chamberlain is literally surrounded by five Tar Heel players.

Rosenbluth, was the most talented Tarheel, a six-foot-five-inch (196cm) center who led the team in scoring. Rosenbluth hailed from the Bronx, Bob Cunningham from Manhattan, Joe Quigg and Pete Brennan from Brooklyn, and Tommy Kearns from metro New Jersey.

Both the Jayhawks and Tarheels made it through their regionals to the Final Four in Kansas City, where they were joined by the Russell-less Dons of San Francisco (who were looking for an unlikely and unprecedented third straight title) and the Michigan State Spartans, who had squeaked by Notre Dame and upset fourth-ranked Kentucky. The Dons had an excellent season, all things considered: they won their first few games, extending their record winning streak to 60. Then they lost to Illinois by the astounding score of 62–33. The game was played in Illinois, and perhaps as a ploy by the home team,

there was no heat in the gymnasium. The boys from sunny California remained, both literally and figuratively, ice cold throughout the game. Despondent over the loss, the Dons lost their next 2 games, but then righted themselves and breezed through the remainder of their schedule. Phil Woolpert guided his troops through the West regional, quite an accomplishment without the likes of Russell, Jones, and Mullins. However, USF could not keep pace with Wilt and the Jayhawks and were crushed 80–56 before a partisan crowd in Kansas City.

In contrast, the other semifinal game, between UNC and Michigan State, was one for the ages. UNC got into foul trouble early and could not find its rhythm; Rosenbluth, in particular, was stifled by the tenacious defense of Spartan sophomore Johnny Greene. The score at intermission was 29–all, and both teams accounted for as many points over the next eighteen minutes. With two minutes left and the game tied 58–58, the Tarheels decided to try to hold for the last shot. They missed, and as time ran down Michigan State's Jack Quiggle grabbed the rebound and hurled the ball the length of the court in a desperation shot. To the astonishment of everyone present, the ball hit nothing but net, but the referees declared that the clock had already expired. In overtime, the Spartans led by 2, 64–62, and with seconds left, UNC's Pete Brennan collected the rebound off a missed free throw and hit a jumper to knot the score again. After the second overtime the score was still knotted up at 66 and the game headed into an unprecedented third OT. After the teams exchanged baskets, UNC finally built a lead and held on for a 74–70 victory.

The 1957 final equaled the drama of the UNC–Michigan State semifinal and had the added dimension of an undefeated number one–ranked team, UNC, playing the role of underdog to the number two–ranked Jayhawks. It marked the first time since 1949 that the nation's two top teams squared off in the finals. To prepare for the showdown against the Jayhawks, McGuire studied the defensive strategies used against Chamberlain during the season and was most impressed with Iowa State's tactics in their 39–37 victory. The Cyclones' game plan called for a very deliberate offense that avoided taking shots that Chamberlain could swat away; on defense, Iowa State assigned one man to shadow Chamberlain at all times and used both forwards to collapse on him whenever he got the ball—essentially a 2–1–2 sliding zone. McGuire's coup de grace was to send tiny Tommy Kearns, only five feet eleven inches (180cm) tall, to jump center versus Chamberlain for the opening tap. The play incited the crowd and sparked the Tarheels, who, remarkably, didn't miss a shot for the first ten minutes of the game. They ended up shooting 65 percent for the first half, containing Chamberlain, and led 29–22 at the midway mark. If not for the Tarheels' failures at the charity stripe (a miserable 27 percent), UNC would have been in control of the game. The second half was a different story, as the Jayhawks came storming back behind Chamberlain and took a 40–37 lead with ten minutes left. But coach Dick Harp, who had replaced Phog Allen before the beginning of the season, made what turned out to be a tactical error in calling for a stall to try to freeze the lead (which Jayhawk opponents had tried all year in their efforts to contain Chamberlain). But the strategy destroyed the Jayhawks' momentum and alleviated the pressure on the Tarheels, who had fallen into severe foul trouble. On top of that it allowed the UNC players, who had played fifty-five excruciating minutes the night before, an opportunity to rest on the court. Kansas controlled the ball for the next five minutes; then all hell broke loose when Chamberlain collided with Pete Brennan and a fight broke out. Both benches cleared, and the

Seattle's Elgin Baylor swoops in on the hoop against Gonzaga, leaping over the shoulder of Dennis Vermillion (35) and avoiding the long reach of seven-foot-three-inch (221cm) Jean Lefebre (wearing the knee pads). Baylor scored 42 points in the February 1958 contest, leading Seattle to a 83–67 victory.

fans were delirious. When order was finally restored, the Tarheels were revitalized and scratched their way back into the game, although Rosenbluth, who had paced the Tarheels with 20 points, fouled out with two minutes remaining. As time was running down, UNC senior Bob Young tied the game, 46–46. The pace was slow from there on out, but the tension was immeasurable. Both teams added a basket in the first overtime and neither managed to score in the second.

For the second straight night, the Tarheels were headed to triple overtime. And once again, the third time seemed the charm as Tommy Kearns took control, scoring 4 points to lift UNC to a 52–48 advantage. However, Chamberlain responded on the other end with a

3-point play, on a basket and a free throw, giving the giant a game-high 23 points to go with his 14 rebounds. Then Jayhawk Gene Elston buried 2 free throws with thirty-one seconds left to give Kansas a 1-point lead. But UNC set up a play for Jack Quigg, which landed him on the free throw line with six seconds left. With the frenzied crowd against him, the New Yorker calmly buried both shots, making the score 54–53, advantage UNC. Kansas called time-out to get the ball at half court and set up a play. The Tarheels were waiting for one thing, the lob into Chamberlain, and Kansas did not disappoint them. Quigg jumped up and intercepted the pass, and UNC ran out the clock to preserve their perfect season and claim the national title.

After the game, the media held Chamberlain responsible for the loss, but the sophomore center had played excellently even though North Carolina's defense was designed specifically to frustrate him. In fact, it was Wilt's normally dependable teammates who had let him down. All game long, the other Jayhawks were stone cold despite being open for medium-range shots that they normally made. Other than Chamberlain, the usually accurate Jayhawks shot a miserable 9 of 34 from the floor. Sadly, the 1957 NCAA title game would come to haunt Chamberlain because it was the first in a series of close losses in championship games throughout Chamberlain's otherwise brilliant career.

The 1958 final repeated the scenario of a team of perceived overachievers, in this case the Kentucky Wildcats, battling a team led by one transcendent superstar, high-flying Elgin Baylor of Seattle University. During the season, the legendary Rupp said, in reference to his Kentucky team, "To play in Carnegie Hall you have to have violinists and I have fiddlers." Thus, the 1958 Wildcats were dubbed the "Fiddlin' Five," a moniker that implied an unfavorable comparison to the "Fabulous Five,"

West Virginia's Jerry West (44) in action against William and Mary in the 1958 Southern Conference championship game. Sophomore West, from tiny Cabin Creek, West Virginia, propelled the Mountaineers to the top of the wire service polls with his uncanny jump shooting and brilliant all-around game.

Rupp's glorious squad from the late forties. Yet this team prospered in a season rife with master violinists.

For the balance of the 1957–1958 season, college basketball fans were mesmerized by the accomplishments of four spectacular superstars. First, of course, was Kansas' Wilt Chamberlain, who averaged more than 30 points per game in his junior year. The Jayhawks were virtually unstoppable with "the Big Dipper" in the line-up; however, Chamberlain got injured early in the Big Eight regular season, and before he returned to full strength, Kansas had lost enough games to finish second in the conference and miss the NCAA tournament. Chamberlain, frustrated by the brutal collapsing defenses (often five-on-one) that he faced almost every night, left Kansas after his junior year to play one season with the Harlem Globetrotters before moving on to the NBA. The second most celebrated of the great college basketball players across the nation was Cincinnati sophomore Oscar Robertson, who led the nation in scoring with a 35.1 average, including a 56-point outburst in his debut at Madison Square Garden that set a scoring record for that hallowed arena. Behind Robertson, who controlled the flow of the game like no player before or since (by keeping the ball in his own hands as much as possible), the Bearcats marched to a 24–2 record, a berth in the NCAA tournament, and a number two ranking.

The top-ranked team in the nation, West Virginia, was also led by a phenomenal sophomore, Jerry West, perhaps the greatest jump shooter ever. On the West Coast, Seattle's Elgin Baylor was mesmerizing audiences by doing things unheard of in organized ball. Over the course of the season, Baylor introduced the Northwest, and during the NCAA

tournament, the rest of the nation to "hang time." Fans watched in awe as Baylor beat opposing defenders by leaping into the air while driving the basket and, still airborne, moving past his defenders to position himself for the shot he wanted. In other words, Baylor brought the fancy moves of urban, black street ball he had learned in Washington,

The starting five for the 1958 West Virginia Mountaineers were Don Vincent, Joey Gardner, Lloyd Sharrar, Jerry West, and Bob Smith. The next season the Mountaineers, with the same nucleus of players, came within one basket of the national championship.

D.C., to organized ball and proved that they had a place in the disciplined college game. Few men had Elgin's in-flight body control, and among those who did, none possessed Baylor's overall sense of the game; thus it was Elgin who brought hang time to the big time. Elgin paved the way for the likes of Julius "Dr. J" Erving, David Thompson, the Louisville Cardinals' "Doctors of Dunk," a Houston fraternity known as "Phi Slamma Jamma," and "His Airness" himself, Michael Jordan.

In the tournament, Elgin led Seattle through the West regional to a birth in the Final Four. Number one–ranked West Virginia, however, did not get past its first game, where the Mountaineers were stunned by Manhattan College. Temple then defeated Manhattan to advance to Louisville. Cincinnati reached the Midwest regional finals, but fell to Kansas State in a game played before a home crowd in Kansas City.

Kentucky took advantage of a Mideastern regional played in Lexington to reach the Final Four. And home court advantage remained a key for Kentucky the rest of the way in Louisville. The Wildcats of 1957–1958 were undistinguished compared to most of Rupp's teams; their 12–2 conference record and overall 19–6 regular-season mark were some of the worst records posted by Wildcat teams in recent memory. But this group of Wildcats was disciplined, had cohesion, and, throughout the tournament, had the home court advantage in a state crazy for Wildcat basketball. The enthusiastic crowd helped lift Kentucky over Temple in a tight semifinal, 61–60. Seattle topped K State easily and an intriguing matchup was set for the finals.

A record crowd of 18,803 jammed into Louisville's Freedom Hall for the 1958 finals to see if Rupp could find a way to contain the spectacular star of Seattle, Elgin Baylor. Indeed, the key to the game turned out to be Rupp's skill as a strategist, as he outcoached Seattle's John Castellani, who probably felt confident that Baylor would run and leap past the less athletic Wildcats. Rupp saw that Baylor was prone to foul when the man he was guarding drove to the basket, so he had John Crigler drive on Baylor and sure enough, Seattle's star picked up early fouls. However, Seattle held a 39–36 halftime lead, and even with Baylor playing cautiously, they led 61–60 with ten minutes to play. But then the Wildcats took over and raced to an 84–72 victory, which Rupp would later deem one of his most satisfying ever. The title gave Rupp's Wildcats an unprecedented fourth national championship.

If the 1958 title confirmed Rupp's status as college hoops' greatest active coach, the 1959 tournament brought to the fore California head coach Pete Newell, a new coaching mastermind who would have an inestimable influence on the game over the next five years. Whereas Rupp was an advocate of a fast-tempo, high-scoring game, Newell was the prophet extraordinaire of defensive basketball. While Bill Russell had reminded the world that defense could win not only games, but national championships, Newell developed a style of aggressive defense that could be used by all teams, even those without a Bill Russell. Newell, like USF coach Phil Woolpert, was a product of a West Coast style of play that eschewed the run-and-gun style of the early fifties. Thus Newell advocated a controlled offense to complement an airtight defense. While Newell's influence would spread over the next five seasons, numerous top programs remained committed to an uptempo style of play; in fact, every NCAA final for the next five seasons would pit an offensive-minded team. against a Newell-led or Newell-inspired defensive team.

However, Newell and his Cal Bears remained in obscurity throughout the 1958–1959 regular season as the headlines belonged to two junior scoring machines, Cincinnati's Oscar Robertson and West Virginia's Jerry West. Robertson led the nation in scoring for the second consecutive season and his Bearcats went 24–3 and entered the tournament ranked fourth. Cincinnati had a daunting task in

the Midwest regional finals, when they squared off against number one–ranked Kansas State, which had eliminated the Bearcats the previous year. The Wildcats focused on stopping Robertson, but Oscar's teammates picked up the slack and the Bearcats avenged the previous year's defeat with a 85–75 victory and headed to Louisville for the Final Four. West Virginia did not finish atop the wire service polls as they had in 1958, but they won 25 games against 4 defeats and had high hopes entering the NCAAs.

The "Big O," Oscar Robertson, displays his patented one-handed jump shot against Texas Christian. Robertson twice led his Bearcats to the Final Four (in 1958 and 1959) and is the only player in NCAA history to win three consecutive national scoring titles (1957–1959), one for each year he was eligible.

This time around, the Mountaineers did not let down their fans, as they passed through the East regional to the Final Four. Meanwhile, Newell's ninth-ranked Bears fought their way through the West region, and upstart Louisville, only 16–10 in the regular season, shocked second-ranked Kentucky and squeaked by Michigan State to earn a spot in the Final Four, to be played on their home court.

Both semifinal matchups promised great drama. Jerry West and the sharpshooting Mountaineers would have been heavy favorites over hometown Louisville on any other court. The Cardinals gave the local crowd more than a glimmer of hope as they stayed with West Virginia through most of the first half. But then with West leading the way, the Mountaineers went on a 22–5 run and never looked back. The second game matched Oscar Robertson and the high-scoring Bearcats against California's iron curtain defense, which featured six-foot-ten-inch (208cm) center Darrall Imhoff and forwards Bob Dalton and Jack Grout. The Bears succeeded in slowing down Robertson, but shot poorly themselves in the first half, and Cincinnati led 33–29 at intermission. But Cal relied on its defense, not its offense, to win games, and so in the second half, the Bears simply tightened the screws further and virtually shut Cincinnati down for eight straight minutes to take the lead—and then kept it. The Bears held Robertson to 19 points and won 64–58.

In the finals, California's great defense went up against West Virginia's potent offense, led by Jerry West. Just as in the Cal-Cincinnati semifinal, the offensive team grabbed the lead, but when California clamped down, West and the Mountaineers were forced into numerous turnovers. At intermission the Bears led 39–33. The Bears extended their lead to 12 with ten minutes remaining and looked in control, but the Mountaineers fought their way back into the game by using a pressure defense of their own. Creating turnovers, which they converted into easy baskets, the Mountaineers closed to within 1 point, 69–68, with less than a minute to play. California moved the ball deliberately, perhaps trying to run out the clock, but when Imhoff found himself virtually alone under the basket, he put up a shot. The ball bounced out, but luckily for the Bears, Imhoff put back the rebound. The Mountaineers raced down the court and quickly cut the deficit back to 1 point, but with only five seconds left Cal was able to run out the clock and claim the national championship.

Many of the same faces that had played prominent roles in the 1958–1959 season were back in the spotlight the following year. Robertson and West were seniors and were both trying desperately to capture that elusive national crown. Newell's Bears figured to be strong again, as Imhoff returned to anchor the defense. But there was a new and exciting powerhouse as well, the Ohio State Buckeyes, led by sophomore sensation Jerry Lucas. These four teams were distributed among the four NCAA regionals, and the nation's fans anticipated that the teams would convene for a star-studded Final Four at San Francisco's Cow Palace.

But in the first round of the East regional, West Virginia was stunned by NYU. For the second time in three years West and the Mountaineers' season was ended abruptly by an upstart team from New York City. The NYU Violets, who had gone 19–3 during the regular season,

Ohio State's Larry Siegfried banks in a shot past the reach of the Cal Bears' Darrall Imhoff during the 1960 finals. The photo perfectly illustrates the defensive intensity of Pete Newell's Bears and the ferocity of the OSU offense.

then proceeded to win the East regional. Meanwhile, the other three number one seeds fulfilled expectations and advanced to San Francisco.

In the first national semifinal, Ohio State completely outclassed NYU 79–54. Lucas and junior Larry Siegfried led the way with 19 points each. The Buckeyes were a well-balanced group that featured two other sophomores in addition to Lucas, forward John Havlicek and guard Mel Noel. The other starting forward was the only key senior on the squad, Joe Roberts. Future coaching great Bobby Knight was a backup guard on the team. Given the team's youth, Buckeyes fans assumed that Ohio State would reclaim

its status as the preeminent team in the state once Robertson graduated from Cincinnati.

Nevertheless, all basketball fans in Ohio had to be rooting for the Bearcats in the second national semifinal, in the hope of producing the first-ever inter-state final. In the way stood defending national champion and number one–ranked California, whom number two–ranked Cincinnati met in a rematch of the previous season's semifinal. Cincinnati once again moved in front early, this time by 9 points in the first

half, but not because of Robertson, who did not score his first basket until just before halftime. But just like the previous season, Cal used its defense to storm back, score 9 straight points, and then move ahead for good. The final score was 77–69; as with West, Robertson's brilliant college career (which included an unprecedented three consecutive scoring titles) ended without a national title.

For the second straight season, the final matched the nation's top defensive team, once again Pete Newell's Cal Bears, who had given up less than 50 points per game, against the top offensive team, Ohio State, who had averaged 90 points. Something had to give. Usually in such a contest the defensive-minded team can succeed in dictating the pace of the game, and Pete Newell's kids were especially adept at controlling a game's rhythm. A partisan crowd packed San Francisco's Cow Palace

expecting to see their beloved Bears stifle the Buckeyes and capture their second straight title. But on this day the Buckeyes were red hot, making 16 of 19 shots in the first half. And the Bears were ice cold, shooting a meager 29 percent. Ohio State led 37–19 at intermission. In the second half the Bears tried to climb back into the game with their patented pressure defense, but Fred Taylor's Buckeyes were too disciplined a bunch for such a ploy. Ohio State maintained a healthy lead throughout and breezed to a 75–55 victory to capture the national title.

Following the Buckeyes' resounding victory in the spring of 1960, basketball fans expected Lucas and his teammates to dominate college ball in the coming years. Probably the last thing people expected was the reemergence of the Cincinnati Bearcats after Oscar Robertson's graduation. But Robertson's presence had attracted a new generation

of excellent players to Cincinnati. And the school's new coach, Ed Jucker, decided to mold these excellent athletes into a Pete Newell–type defensive team. "You don't have to teach today's kids how to shoot," Jucker said. "They do it naturally. So you have plenty of time to teach them how to play defense." Jucker built his team around wide-bodied center Paul Hogue and 220-pound (100kg) forward Bob Wiesenhahn, and a pair of speedy sophomores, small forward Tony Yates and guard Tom Thacker. These Bearcats didn't shoot exceptionally well, but they rebounded ferociously and played defense with an iron fist. Their prevailing offensive strategy was patience, precision, and crashing the boards. To the surprise of a nation that had marvelled at Robertson's smooth brilliance for three years, these gritty Bearcats had an excellent season and once again advanced to the Final Four.

Ohio State began the 1960–1961 season ranked number one and held on to that ranking throughout the regular season. They swept through the Big Ten by an average margin of 22 points. *Sports Illustrated* deemed Ohio State "the best basketball team of all time." The Buckeyes entered the tournament looking to become the third undefeated national champion and only the second to do so (along with the 1956 San Francisco Dons) while maintaining the number one ranking all season long. To no one's surprise Ohio State advanced to the Final Four, but not before the Louisville Cardinals almost pulled off one of the great upsets of all time in the regional semifinals. Ohio State took the lead 56–54 on a Havlicek jump shot with six seconds left. But only five seconds later, Louisville's John Turner stepped up to the free throw line for a 1-and-1. Turner made the first but missed the second. The Buckeyes played more to form the next night, advancing past Kentucky, 87–74. Skyline Conference champion Utah won the West regional, while St. Joseph's of Philadelphia (a team whose accomplishments were later scratched from the official records because its players were implicated in yet another point-shaving scandal) won the East.

The two Ohio teams trounced their opponents in the semifinals in Kansas City. The Bearcats downed Utah 82–67 while the Buckeyes annihilated St. Joseph's 95–69. Never before had two teams from the same state met in the finals. The interstate showdown proved to be a thriller. The heavily favored Buckeyes shot better than the Bearcats, but Hogue and Wiesenhahn were able to control the boards and contain Lucas. At halftime the Buckeyes led by 1, 39–38. Rarely did more than 2 points separate the two teams. Cincinnati held a 61–59 advantage with less than a minute left when Bobby Knight scored his only bucket of the game to tie the score. The Bearcats tried to hold for the last shot, but when Tom Thacker missed from short range, Lucas grabbed the rebound

The Buckeyes' John Havlicek elevates for 2 points versus USC in a 76–66 Ohio State victory during the 1961–1962 season. Havlicek was a key player for the Buckeyes, though like the rest of his teammates he performed in the shadow of Jerry Lucas. However, of this great generation of Buckeye players, it was Havlicek, not Lucas, who went on to have a brilliant career in the NBA.

and called time-out with five seconds still remaining. Ohio State passed the ball the length of the court and called another time-out. Then with the final seconds of the game ticking off, Havlicek tried an alley-oop pass to Lucas, but the pass went astray. In overtime, Cincinnati led all the way, as Hogue and Yates converted pressure free throws down the stretch. Defense had triumphed over offense and the Bearcats pulled off the amazing upset, 70–65, to win the 1961 national title.

Twelve months later in Louisville the same two teams squared off in a rematch for the national title. While some significant players had graduated, most notably Ohio State's Larry Siegfried, plenty of talent and experience remained on both of the Ohio teams. Once again,

Ohio State entered the tournament ranked number one, though they did lose 1 game, to Wisconsin by 19 points, an amazingly lopsided upset. Cincinnati, who lost 2 regular-season games, was the number two seed. The Bearcats cruised through the Midwest regional, winning by an average of 23 points. The Buckeyes weren't quite as dominant in the Mideast, but had relatively little trouble winning the region.

The winners of the East and West regionals were expected to be little more than sacrificial offerings at 1962's Final

Four. ACC champ Wake Forest was
blown out by Ohio State. However, the
West regional champion, UCLA, which
had never before won a tournament
game, proved a difficult foe for the
Bearcats. John Wooden's troops stormed
out to a 18–4 lead and led much of the
way behind the superfast Johnny Green.
Paul Hogue tied the score at 70 with 3:20
left, and when neither team could score
over the next two minutes, Jucker told his
Bearcats to hold for the final shot. The
tactic worked: Tom Thacker buried a
hook shot with two seconds left, and the
rematch was set for the next night.

Unfortunately for Ohio State, Lucas
had badly bruised his side when he fell to
the hardwood with eight minutes left in
the semifinal. Without their star center
at full strength, the Buckeyes were in

trouble. Still, the Lucas-era Buckeyes had
already established themselves as one of
the great teams in the annals of college
hoops; previously, no college had ever
appeared in three consecutive finals. It
was also the first time in history that the
same two teams played in the finals in
consecutive years. And the first twelve
minutes of the final game seemed like a
repeat of last year's nip-and-tuck affair.
But with the score tied 21–all, the
Bearcats took command. By halftime the
tally was Cincinnati 37, Ohio State 29.
Hogue had his way in the middle against
a hobbled Lucas, who wore a brace on
his knee. The Buckeyes never mounted a
serious comeback against the Bearcats'
stingy defense. The final score was
71–59. Cincinnati became the fourth
team, alongside the Bill Russell–led San

Francisco Dons, Kentucky's Fabulous
Five, and the Oklahoma A&M Aggies
with Bob Kurland, to repeat as national
champions. In Dayton, Ohio, they were
celebrating as well, for the Dayton Fliers
had won the NIT. In the spring of 1962
the state of Ohio ruled the college basketball universe.

Twelve months later Cincinnati was
back at it again, playing in the final and
trying to become the first team to win
the national title three years running.
Coach Jucker's defense-minded tactics
had paid great dividends. Hogue graduated in the spring of 1962, so Jucker
moved six-foot-eight-inch (203cm) junior

forward George Wilson to center and guard Tom Thacker to forward. Super-quick Larry Shingleton moved into the starting lineup at guard. Junior Ron Bonham held his place at forward and Yates remained a fixture at the other guard position. The Bearcats lost only once in the regular season, by 1 point to Wichita in overtime, which snapped a 37-game winning streak. In the Midwest regional, Texas and Colorado took their best shots at the Bearcats, but Cincinnati downed both teams by 7 points and marched on to the Final Four for a record fifth consecutive time.

Ohio State had another excellent season, even without the likes of Lucas, Havlicek, and Newell, but the Buckeyes tied for the Big Ten title with Illinois and the conference rules stated that the team which had most recently been to the tournament must step aside and let their cochampions participate. Illinois only made it as far as the regional final where they ran into the Loyola (of Chicago) Ramblers, the highest-scoring team in the country. Led by scoring machine Jerry Harkness, who scored 33 points, the Ramblers toppled the Illini. In the East regionals, the formidable Duke Blue Devils were the winners, coached by Vic Bubas and led by All-American senior Art Heyman and deadeye shooters Jay Buckley and Jeff Mullins. Oregon State captured the West regional behind low-post star Mel Counts and the legendary Terry Baker, who had won not only college football's most prestigious award, the Heisman Trophy, but also the Maxwell Trophy for the country's most outstanding amateur athlete, and was named *Sports Illustrated*'s sportsman of the year.

Once again the Final Four convened in Louisville's Freedom Hall. The pundits claimed that all the pressure was on the Bearcats, who were top-ranked and trying for a record-breaking championship. But Cincinnati certainly seemed unflappable in the semifinals against Oregon State. The Beavers played well in the first half and trailed by only 3 points at intermission. But when Counts got into foul trouble in the second half, the Bearcats tallied 16 consecutive points and the rout was on. Cincinnati showed

no mercy and hightailed their way to a 80–46 blowout. The other semifinal offered only slightly more drama. High-scoring Loyola ran out to a 17-point lead, but Duke kicked and scratched its way back into the game and, with less than four minutes to play, trailed only 74–71. In an amazing display of their offensive power, the Ramblers woke up in time to pour in 20 more points before the final whistle for a resounding 94–75 win.

For the fifth straight year the final was a matchup between one of the nation's highest-scoring teams and a first-rate defensive squad. Previously, the only time the offense had prevailed was in Ohio State's victory in 1960. The other three years the immovable object had suffocated the unstoppable force. With Ron Bonham leading the way, Cincinnati appeared headed for another title; the Bearcats held a commanding 45–30 lead well into the second half. But just when the Bearcats seemed in total control, things began to crumble. Center Wilson picked up his fourth foul. (When Coach Jucker responded by bringing in a substitute, it was the first for either team.) Cincinnati tried to freeze the ball, but the Ramblers responded with their own pressure defense, forcing numerous turnovers. Slowly Loyola climbed back into the game. Jerry Harkness hit his first field goal of the game with less than five minutes left, and soon he had the hot hand. The Bearcats' lead was down to 3 with less than a minute left. Loyola continued the pressure and closed to within 1. But with twelve seconds left, Larry Shingleton stepped to the line for a 1-and-1; the score was 53–52 and both free throws would ice the game for the Bearcats. Shingleton made the first, but he missed the second. Harkness grabbed the rebound, raced downcourt, and buried a jumper, and miraculously the game was headed for overtime. Needless to say, Loyola had the momentum at this point. Cincinnati had had its third straight title in its grasp and let it slip away. Still the Bearcats managed to trade baskets with the Ramblers for the next four minutes. With the game tied at 58, Loyola's five-foot-ten-inch (178cm) John Egan won a jump ball against Shingleton and the Ramblers held for the final shot.

When the Ramblers began to attack the basket, Harkness found six-foot-seven-inch (201cm) Leslie Hunter open at the free throw line. The big man's shot hit the rim and bounced out. However, six-foot-six-inch (198cm) Vic Rouse was there to leap up, grab the ball, and bank it off the glass for the game-winning shot. Loyola of Chicago, not the Bearcats of Cincinnati, were the 1963 national champions.

The 1963 final marked the end of the offense versus defense era of college basketball. The next era was dominated by one team, the UCLA Bruins. Under coach John Wooden's masterful tutelage, the 1964 and 1965 Bruins represented a perfect synthesis of the offense versus defense era. The Bruins used their scintillating, full-court pressure defense to key their explosive, fast-paced offense. The result was the beginning of college basketball's greatest dynasty.

Loyola's Vic Rouse skys to control a rebound in the 1963 finals versus two-time defending champion Cincinnati. With seconds left in overtime and the score knotted at 58-all, Rouse grabbed an offensive rebound and put it up and in for the game winner.

Chapter 3

The UCLA Dynasty: 1964–1975

In the annals of major American sports there are a handful of "mini-dynasties" that have lasted about five years, but only four truly great dynasties that have dominated their sport for a decade or more. Three of these are professional: the Montreal Canadiens of the National Hockey League (NHL) from 1951 to 1960, Major League Baseball's New York Yankees from 1947 to 1964, and the NBA's Boston Celtics from 1957 to 1969. And one of them is collegiate: the 1964–1975 UCLA basketball Bruins. As great as the Canadiens, Yankees, and Celtics accomplishments were, UCLA's were more astounding. The three pro dynasties were all built around a core of players who played their entire careers on the championship squad. A college program has no such consistency; this was especially true in the sixties, when varsity basketball careers lasted only three years. So the UCLA program had to continually replenish its talent pool; indeed, UCLA mastermind coach John Wooden won titles with, as it worked out, five distinct generations of players during the twelve-year dynasty. The Bruins also had to dominate a much larger field of opponents than did the pro dynasties—the NHL had only six teams during the Canadiens' era, the Celtics topped a league made up of only eight to ten teams (until the final year of the team's tenure), and baseball's American League had only eight teams until 1961. In contrast, there were more than one hundred schools playing big-time college basketball by the sixties, and at least twenty-five schools had established formidable winning traditions. So a strong argument

can be made that the UCLA Bruins' ten national championships in the twelve years from 1964 to 1975 represent the most impressive dynasty in the history of American sports to date.

One man, and one man alone, is synonymous with the UCLA dynasty: John Wooden, the Wizard of Westwood. John Robert Wooden was born on October 14, 1910, on his family's small farm in basketball-obsessed Indiana. John's parents were modest, churchgoing people who taught their son to value sincerity and hard work. John loved sports, especially baseball, but it was basketball that he excelled at. Already a stickler for self-discipline, he practiced every day after finishing his chores. The hard work paid off when John led Martinsville High to three straight state finals and one title. In an era when basketball was played at a much slower pace than it is today, Wooden used his lightning quickness to slash past defenders for layups. Wooden attended college at Purdue, where he found a kindred spirit in coach Ward "Piggy" Lambert, one of the first architects of fast-break basketball. A solid five feet ten and a half inches (179cm) and 178 pounds (81kg), Wooden used his unparalleled dribbling skills, speed, and stamina to run circles around opponents, earning him the nickname "Rubber Man." He also shot a remarkable 50 percent from the floor. When he led Purdue to its mythical national championship in 1932, he became a folk hero in Indiana. Many consider the three-time All-American to be the greatest player of his era. In 1960, Wooden was inducted into the Basketball Hall of Fame as a player. (Ten years later,

he was elected to the Hall of Fame again, as a coach.)

Professional basketball was virtually nonexistent in the thirties (the NBA formed in 1947), so Wooden took a job as a high school English teacher, doubling as the basketball coach. In his eleven years coaching high school, Wooden compiled a 218–42 record. Following a three-year hiatus for WWII, Wooden got his first college coaching position at Indiana State Teachers College, where he compiled a 47–14 record over two seasons before UCLA lured him to the West Coast. The Bruins were perennial losers, but Wooden turned things around instantly, guiding the 1948–1949 team, predicted to finish last, to a 22–7 record and a first-place finish in the PCC. Wooden proceeded to build a winning tradition in Westwood. In his first fifteen seasons there, the Bruins always finished above .500 and collected five conference crowns. However, the Bruins floundered in the postseason, losing in the first round in four of their five appearances in the NCAA tournament. That all changed in the spring of 1964: Wooden's Bruins would win their next 37 tournament games, 41 of the next 42 after that, and capture ten national championships in the process.

Wooden's coaching philosophy was simple: he trained his teams to win on

Seven-foot (213cm) sophomore Lew Alcindor slams the ball home in his first game on the UCLA varsity. "Big Lew" poured in 56 points to shatter the school scoring record in the 105–90 victory over crosstown rival USC. Alcindor would lead the Bruins to three national championships in his three years of eligibility, an unprecedented feat in the annals of college basketball.

Princeton forward Bill Bradley prepares to drain a short jumper versus Providence in the 1965 Eastern regional final, won by Princeton in resounding fashion, 109–69. Bradley established a new scoring record during the 1965 tourney, with 177 points.

their own terms, to play their game as best they could. The cardinal sin was allowing an opponent to take you out of your game. Wooden would change defensive tactics or adjust his fast-paced offense to suit the talents of his players, but one thing was consistent: year in and year out, his Bruins were the model of efficiency. Coach Wooden possessed an uncanny ability to get his players to execute his strategy flawlessly. How did he do it? Conditioning and practice were the keys. Wooden demanded that every player be in tip-top shape so that they could play his fast-paced, full-court style aggressively. Then at often-grueling practices, the coach worked the team into a well-oiled machine ready to be put in motion at game time. Whenever Wooden introduced a new play to the Bruin repertoire, he waited until he was certain that the team had perfected it before calling for it in a game. Kareem Abdul-Jabbar summarized the UCLA credo, which Coach Wooden instilled in his players: "Let others try to raise to our level; we would be there to begin with."

UCLA had never won a tournament game before 1962, when the Bruins reached the Final Four before losing by 2 points to Cincinnati. The following year

UCLA repeated as conference champs, but the Bruins were eliminated in the first round of the NCAAs. Nevertheless, expectations were high for the 1963–1964 season because the entire Bruin starting five, including All-American candidate Walt Hazzard and shooting sensation Gail Goodrich, was returning. In the spring of 1963 Coach Wooden wrote down a little rhyme, as he was wont to do: "With every starter coming back/Yes, Walt and Gail and Keith and Jack/And Fred and Freddie and some more/We could be champs in sixty-four."

Indeed, the 1963–1964 UCLA Bruins had an abundance of talent and speed. Their fast break, led by All-World playmaker Walt Hazzard, was something to behold, but the tallest player on the team was only six feet five inches (196cm). Wooden needed to devise a strategy so that taller, stronger teams would not overwhelm them. Assistant coach Jerry Norman suggested a full-court press. Wooden was skeptical, but decided to try out a 2-2-1 zone press, which he had used as an Indiana high school coach.

The Bruins' two guards would pick up the other team's backcourt players near their basket and harass them, trying to force mistakes as the other team attempted to move the ball upcourt. The Bruins' two forwards would be waiting like vultures near center court to run down errant passes or trap an unsuspecting foe, while the UCLA center was stationed as a lone defender beneath the Bruin basket to protect against long passes. In the hands of the super-quick Bruins, the 2-2-1 zone press was a lethal weapon. Against the slower, taller teams that it was designed to target, the press generated turnover after turnover, which UCLA converted into an avalanche of points. Wooden was initially incredulous: "It was difficult to believe that college teams could not handle it. I thought we'd be using it needlessly—that is, until I realized we had the type of players who could make it work." In one game against Washington State, the Bruins trailed 15–14 when Wooden called for the press. The Cougars immediately lost their composure, and by the half, UCLA led 61–28. Armed with their new defense, the Bruins served notice to the nation when they upset second-ranked Michigan in December. They proceeded to win all of their regular-season games and not sur-

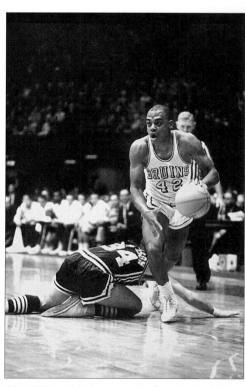

The UCLA Bruins' super-quick floor leader, Walt Hazzard, eludes a foe and heads for the basket. Hazzard led the Bruins to their first national championship as a senior in 1964.

prisingly entered the tournament ranked number one.

In the West regional the Bruins seemed sluggish but, courtesy of the zone press, they managed to squeak by Seattle 95–90 after trailing late. In the second round the Bruins fell behind USF by 12 in the first half, but Hazzard and Goodrich rallied their team into the lead just after intermission and they maintained a slim advantage until the final whistle. The Bruins headed to Kansas City for the Final Four matchup with Kansas State. In the other semifinal, Michigan's marvelous rookie Cazzie Russell gave the Wolverines an early lead against Duke. However, the Blue Devils responded quickly with a flurry of fast-break points, built a double-digit lead before halftime, and cruised to victory. The UCLA–Kansas State semifinal included one of the most bizarre incidents in tournament history. UCLA struggled throughout the game, seemingly unable to find its rhythm. Only Hazzard, with his astonishing array of dribble-drive moves, was able to penetrate Kansas State's 1–3–1 zone. The Bruins trailed late in the game when the press bailed them out again, producing 5 quick points to tie the game. Disoriented, K State called time-out. Just as the teams reached their benches, the UCLA partisans in the crowd burst into a frenzy. Out of nowhere the UCLA cheerleading squad, which had missed its flight to Kansas City, appeared in the arena, ran onto the court, ripped off their street clothes, and led the cheers of the Bruin faithful. The Bruins eventually added another 6 straight points and coasted to a 90–84 win.

Led by tall forward Jay Buckley and guard Jeff Mullin, Duke was almost as quick as UCLA and had a considerable height advantage; the Bruins would have to improve their play to win the title. The beginning of the game was nip and tuck until Coach Wooden called time-out with Duke leading 30–27, in order to implement the zone press. Two and a half minutes after play resumed, the Bruins had scored 16 consecutive points, generated some vintage mayhem, and demoralized the Blue Demons. For all intents and purposes the game was over.

The Bruins won 98–83 and senior Walt Hazzard, who scored only 11 points in the final but controlled the flow of the game, was named MVP. The Bruins finished the season 30–0 and were crowned national champions.

Though the 1965 final featured a dramatic showdown between number

With the graduation of Walt Hazzard following the 1963–1964 season, the Bruins other guard Gail Goodrich stepped up his game. Assuming the role of floor general as well as leading scorer, senior Goodrich carried the Bruins to their second consecutive national title.

one-ranked Michigan (led by Cazzie Russell) and number two UCLA (led by a red-hot Gail Goodrich), in the hearts of the fans the tournament belonged to Bill Bradley. Bradley, the third-leading scorer in the land, led his Princeton Tigers through the East regional in spectacular fashion. In the first round, Bradley got locked in a duel with the whole Penn State team. Four times Penn State took the lead in the closing minutes and four times Bradley tied it back up. The Nittany Lions finally blinked and Bradley put them away in the final minute. Princeton cruised over NC State in round two and annihilated Providence to reach the Final Four in Portland. Princeton figured to have little hope against Michigan in the regional final, but the Tigers had everyone talking when they went twelve minutes in the second half without missing from the line or the field. Princeton led 34–29 when Bradley was whistled for his third foul. Michigan took control of the game while the future Rhodes scholar, New York Knick, and U.S. Senator sat on the

bench with foul trouble. Michigan won, 93–76, but Bradley, who had finished with a mere 29 points, was far from finished. In the consolation game against Wichita, Bradley set new records for points scored in a tournament game, 58, and total points in a tournament, 177. When Bradley left the game, his last as a collegian, he was given the longest ovation in the history of the tournament.

The UCLA Bruins, meanwhile, had lost only 2 games all season on their way to another PCC title. They then ripped Brigham Young, slipped by San Francisco with some late help from their trusty zone press, and pummeled Wichita en route to their showdown with Michigan. The main reason that the Bruins had overcome the loss of Walt Hazzard was the exceptional play of Gail Goodrich. Not only had Goodrich increased his already prodigious scoring (he was a lethal jump shooter), but he became the Bruins' playmaker as well. Also important was Keith Erickson's development into a topflight scorer. And the zone press was as devastating as ever.

The Wolverines moved in front of the Bruins 20–13; then UCLA deployed the 2–2–1. Chaos ensued and soon the

Texas Western's Bobby Joe Hill races past Rupp's Runts in the 1966 NCAA final. This showdown was a landmark event in the history of race relations in U.S. sports. The all-white Kentucky Wildcats, of the segregated Southeastern Conference, squared off against the Texas Western Miners, the first team to reach the national championship game with an all-black starting five.

score was knotted at 24, and eventually the Bruins built a lead that they never relinquished. Goodrich single-handedly kept the Wolverines at bay, scoring a school-record 42 points. UCLA rolled to its second consecutive title, 91–80. However, it was Bill Bradley who was named the tourney MVP.

Shortly after UCLA downed Michigan for the 1965 NCAA title, seven-footer (213cm) Lew Alcindor, the most heavily recruited player of the decade, announced that he would attend UCLA. Alcindor, who lost only 1 game during his high school career in New York City, was already so dominating that many analysts believed he would lead whatever school he attended, let alone a powerful program like UCLA, to a national title or two. Indeed, when Alcindor showed up on the UCLA campus in the fall of 1965, he promptly led the UCLA freshman team to a convincing 75–60 victory over the (then number one–ranked) varsity. Perhaps the best team of collegiates in the nation, the UCLA freshman squad was not eligible for the NCAA title in 1966. The UCLA

varsity had a poor season, failing to win the Pacific Eight, and 1966 came to be known as the year UCLA did not win.

In anticipation of Alcindor's imminent domination, the 1966 tournament was dubbed the "Last Chance Tournament." Indeed, the 1966 NCAA tournament would provide more drama than all of the next seven "Bruin Invitationals" combined. The Final Four consisted of the top three teams in the nation (number four having lost to number three in a thrilling regional final), plus an intriguing upstart. Numbers one and two, Kentucky and Duke, respectively, squared off in one national semifinal at the University of Maryland Fieldhouse, while number three, Texas Western (now University of Texas–El Paso), faced off against Utah, led by their dynamic scoring machine Jerry Chambers. Since Texas Western got little respect in the media because of their weak schedule, the Kentucky-Duke game was viewed by many as the true national title showdown. Without a starter over six feet five inches (196cm) (à la UCLA the past two years), the top-

ranked Wildcats were dubbed "Rupp's Runts." This feisty group had ended Cazzie Russell's brilliant college career with its victory over Michigan in the regional final. The Runts were very quick, passed well, and featured two long-range sharpshooters, forward Pat Riley and guard Louis Dampier. Although Kentucky didn't match up well against the strong rebounding Duke Blue Devils, the scrappy Wildcats found a way to hold their own on the boards and trailed by only 1 at intermission. The second half was tight throughout, but Kentucky moved ahead late, the Blue Devils became unraveled, and Rupp's Runts moved on to the finals.

Texas Western's path to the Final Four had been dramatic. The defense-minded Miners, who led the nation in rebounding, came from behind to knock off Oklahoma City, nipped Cincinnati in overtime, and then survived a classic versus number four, Kansas, and its star, JoJo White. Kansas tied the game on a 3-point play at the end of regulation, and with time running out in the first overtime and the game tied, White launched a thirty-two-foot (9.6m) bomb that hit nothing but net. The KU faithful exploded in triumph. But the referee was pointing to the side of the court where he said White stepped out-of-bounds before releasing the shot, and the game went to a second overtime. Perhaps bolstered by its good fortune, Texas Western burst to a 6-point advantage, but Jayhawk Al Lopes responded with 7 straight points. With time running out on Texas Western, Willie Cager saved his team when he tipped in a missed shot for the game winner, 81–80. The Texas Western–Utah semifinal was considerably less dramatic as the Miners led most of the way, built up a comfortable cushion, and held on to win 88–78 despite Jerry Chambers' 38 points.

Once the two finalists were determined, a striking contrast between the two teams captured everyone's attention. Rupp's Wildcats were all white, while coach Don Haskins' Texas Western Miners were the first NCAA finalists to start five African-Americans (Loyola, the 1963 champions, had four African-American starters). During the 1960s, the civil rights movement had transformed the American landscape, including its sports. Blacks had played an increasingly large role in competitive basketball since World War II, but this particular matchup—between a team of Northern inner-city black youths displaced in Texas and an all-white team from the South (the last bastion of all-white ball and, until the recently passed civil rights bills, the land of Jim Crow)—took on an allegorical significance for the nation. Played in the wake of the Watts riots in the summer of 1965, the game was a signpost in the continuing integration of North American sports.

What was significant for the game itself was that the Miners were not only dominant on the boards but were also as quick as Rupp's Runts. Texas Western's man-to-man pressure defense disrupted the Wildcats. With the score 10–9 the

Miners' Bobby Joe Hill stole the ball and went in for an uncontested layup, then stole the ball again and scored 2 more points. The Miners led the rest of the way. In the critical final moments, the Miners were on target from the free throw line, holding on for a 72–65 victory. While Utah's Chambers, who broke Lovellette's fourteen-year-old tournament scoring record for 4 games with 143 points, was named tournament MVP, the day belonged to a group of black kids from the inner cities of the Northeast who played in west Texas.

But once the season was over, all eyes turned to UCLA. As in 1957, when a few basketball pundits cynically conceded the national title to Kansas before the season began because of the reputed prowess of its sophomore center, Wilt Chamberlain, a landslide of opinion declared the 1966–1967 UCLA Bruins the best team in the country even before the first game. Like the 1957 Jayhawks, the Bruins had a seven-foot (213cm) sophomore sensation, Lew Alcindor, but unlike Chamberlain, young Alcindor was joined by a number of outstanding classmates that included shooting guard Lucius Allen, deadeye forward Lynn Shackleford, and defensive demon Kenny Heitz. As freshmen these players had crushed the defending national champion varsity team and every other opponent who dared step onto the court with them. In 1966–1967 the four aforementioned sophomores teamed with junior point guard Mike Warren to make a young and brilliant starting five, guided by the masterful hand of John Wooden.

The centerpiece of the team was, of course, Ferdinand Lewis Alcindor Jr. "Big Lew" was a New York kid who learned his basketball on the city's playgrounds and was already six feet nine inches (206cm) as a high school freshman. Lew became the most recruited high school player of all-time and a household name. The giant chose to attend UCLA because it fit his criteria: "[I] wanted to play good, winning basketball at an institution that treated its athletes with an element of dignity, under a coach whom I could respect."

After Alcindor and the other super sophs joined the varsity, Coach Wooden

revised the way the Bruins played to fit his new players' strengths. Basically, there was no need to rely on the full-court pressure that the Bruins had used to great effect in their earlier championship seasons. Alcindor's presence at center sufficiently cut off the middle for opposing teams. If the other Bruins played aggressive perimeter defense, the Bruins could stifle opponents with a half-court defense. Similarly, there was no need to overemphasize the running game, though these Bruins did execute fast breaks brilliantly, since Lew's presence vastly improved the half-court offense. Alcindor either drew a double-team, in which case he was brilliant at finding the open man, or he scored easily when defended by only one man. Also, Alcindor could outrebound anyone in the game on either end of the court. Big Lew summarized the very simple system Wooden deployed while he was on the varsity: "Run with the basketball, beat the defense down the court, play good defense yourself, and get the easiest shot you can get." In his debut with the varsity, Alcindor exploded for 56 points and the Bruins rolled over USC. UCLA went undefeated in Lew's rookie year; the Bruins' average margin of victory was 27.4.

The year 1967 began an era in college basketball in which, for better or for worse, it was tacitly understood that the teams across the nation were playing for second place. No team, it seemed, had a realistic chance at ousting the mighty Bruins. Wherever UCLA traveled, fans packed the arenas, teams hoped and prayed for upsets, and come game time opponents were systematically destroyed by the Bruins juggernaut. The one team given a remote chance against the Bruins in the spring of 1967 was the Houston Cougars, led by their talented center Elvin Hayes. The "Big E" had a sizable and talented supporting cast assembled by coach Guy Lewis. The smallest Cougar was six-foot-five-inch (196cm) marksman Don Chaney. The rest of the starting quintet, Melvin Bell, Don Kruse, and Ken Spain, were all at least 235 pounds (107kg). Houston had lost only three times all year, had won the Midwest regional, and hoped to ambush the Bruins at the Final Four in

Louisville. Those who wanted to see the Bruins lose hoped that Houston's big men could contain Alcindor, but it was a pipe dream. Houston nudged ahead 19–18, but the indomitable UCLA Bruins then made 11 straight points and was in command the rest of the way, winning 72–58.

The other Final Four participants were Dayton and third-ranked North Carolina. The Tarheels may have had a fighting chance against the Bruins, but Dayton pulled off an upset, dismissing UNC 76–62 behind Don May's 34 points.

Thus Dayton was sent in as the sacrificial lamb in an anticlimactic final. With five minutes to go, UCLA led 76–47, and Wooden took out his starters. Dayton poured in a bunch of points after the fact to prevent the score, ultimately 79–64, from being the most lopsided ever.

The 1967–1968 college season promised to be more of the same: too much Lew, too much Bruins. The NCAA even tried its hand, to no avail, at slowing down the Alcindor express by outlawing one of Lew's favorite shots, the dunk. Big Lew responded by perfecting another shot, the skyhook, which in time would become the most lethal offensive weapon ever (in the hands of the man whom young Lew would soon become, Kareem Abdul-Jabbar). The Houston Cougars had the balance of their starting lineup back and were still hoping to derail the Bruins in a widely anticipated game scheduled for January 20, 1968.

The number one–ranked Bruins met the number two–ranked Cougars, both undefeated, in what was deemed the "Game of the Decade." The promoters, realizing they were sitting on a gold mine, moved the contest to the newly christened fifty-thousand-seat Astrodome and arranged a national television broadcast through independent networks. As the hype continued to grow, the showdown was renamed the "Game of the Century." In such circumstances, the event itself often turns out to be a letdown, but this time the game lived up to the hype. UCLA, of course, had looked devastating in the early season. But a week before the matchup with Houston, Alcindor landed in the hospital after he was poked in the eye in a game against California.

He lay in bed all week with a scratched cornea. The Bruins won their next 2 games without the big man, and pulled into Houston with a 47-game winning streak. Determined not to miss the Game of the Century, Alcindor came back and tried to play. But Lew's vision was blurry. He shot only 4 of 18 from the field and, in general, was a shadow of his usual self. Elvin Hayes, on the other hand, was brilliant. The Big E scored 29 points in the first half, pacing the Cougars to a 3-point lead. Hayes had success driving the lane, and was just as lethal with his mid-range jump shot. Even with their leader shaken, the Bruins kept fighting back. They tied the game at 54, at 65, and, while they never took the lead, succeeded in knotting the score at 69 in the final minute. But with seconds left and the score still tied, Hayes stepped up to the free throw line. In front of the largest crowd ever to watch a college basketball game, and a nationwide television audience, Elvin buried both free throws to win the game. Hayes was carried from the court to the deafening chant of "E! E! E!"

After the game Elvin talked trash to the media, saying in effect that Alcindor was not so great. The calm and poised Alcindor did not participate in such extracurricular banter. Big Lew simply cut out the *Sports Illustrated* cover that showed Elvin soaring above him to score 2 points, taped it to the inside of his locker for motivation, got himself back in shape, and calmly prepared for the rematch he sensed would take place later in the season. True to form, the two teams swept the rest of their schedules. Houston breezed through the Midwest regional while UCLA swept through the West. The big rematch took place in the national semifinals at the Los Angeles Sports Arena. This time it was an old-fashioned ass-whuppin.' From the start it was all Alcindor and all Bruins. Hayes scored 5 points in the first half and 5 in the second. Every one of the UCLA starters scored 14 or more points. The deficit was 22 at the half and the Bruins pushed it to 44 before the second unit entered. The final was 101–69.

The other two Final Four participants were Ohio State, who upset Kentucky in their regional final, and, once again, North Carolina. The Tarheels, led by Charlie Scott, trounced the Buckeyes 80–66 and hoped for a miracle in the final. But UCLA was too disciplined for any letdown. The Tarheels went into their patented four-corners stall to try to freeze the game early and keep the score close. But Wooden called on Lucius Allen, Mike Warren, and Mike Lynn, who had replaced Keith Heights in the starting lineup, to pressure the ball. The tactic produced a series of turnovers that the Bruins turned into easy baskets and a 32–22 halftime lead. Like so many teams who faced the Bruins, the Tarheels could not generate any interior offense because Alcindor simply swatted their shots away. The second half belonged to the boys from Westwood. Big Lew tallied 34 points, and the final was 78–55. Next year, Alcindor would be a senior; with two championships down, there was just one to go.

As the 1968–1969 season started, fans were already anticipating the following year when, with Alcindor gone, teams other than the Bruins could hope to win the national championship. Beating UCLA while Alcindor was still there seemed almost unthinkable. But at the tail end of the regular season the Bruins showed signs of vulnerability. In their second-to-last game they needed double overtime to defeat crosstown rival USC. The next night the Trojans stunned the Bruins 46–44 on a last-second shot at Pauley Pavilion (UCLA's first home loss in 52 games and only its second defeat during the entire Alcindor era). Still, few doubted that the Bruins would become the first team to win three consecutive NCAA titles. The Bruins had suffered some adversity during the year: Lucius Allen was suspended and replaced by the lesser John Vallely, while Mike Warren and Mike Lynn had graduated and were replaced by Kenny Heitz and six-foot-six-inch (198cm) sophomore Curtis Rowe. But Wooden was a master at inte-

Lew Alcindor lofts his patented skyhook over the reach of Elvin Hayes during the 1968 NCAA semifinals. The third showdown between the Alcindor-led Bruins and the Hayes-led Cougars (who had defeated the Bruins 71–69 during the regular season) was the one for all the marbles. Alcindor and the Bruins proved once and for all who the better team was, crushing Houston 101–69.

grating his players into a cohesive unit. With Alcindor as the constant, the Bruins were as daunting as ever. In the West regional, UCLA systematically decimated all comers—most notably Santa Clara, who had only 1 loss all season, by the score of 90–52.

Big Ten champion Purdue, North Carolina (for the third year in a row), and upstart Drake joined UCLA in Louisville for the Final Four. In the first semifinal Purdue crushed North Carolina 92–65, thanks to Boilermakers Rick Mount and Bill Keller, who poured in a combined 56 points. The Drake Bulldogs seemed like little more than cannon fodder for the Bruins. But Drake did something few teams had the guts to do versus UCLA in the Alcindor era: they played them straight up. UCLA could beat you slow or beat you fast, but they were especially lethal up-tempo. The Bulldogs tried to run with the Bruins. Alcindor was considered unstoppable unless double- or triple-teamed, but Drake played man-to-man defense. It worked brilliantly in the first half. The game was close at intermission and miraculously the Bulldogs stayed with the Bruins through the next ten minutes. Finally, the Bruins took command and tallied 9 unanswered points. But to the astonishment of the crowd, the Bulldogs would not roll over. They made 1 rush, but the Bruins held

them off. With less than thirty seconds left, UCLA led 83–78 when Drake's Willy Carter hit a jump shot, and then, astonishingly, the Bulldogs stole the ball and scored again; there was mayhem in Freedom Hall. There were only nine seconds left. But the Bruins were up to

In the 1970 NCAA finals it was not UCLA but the opposition—Jacksonville—that had the dominant, superstar center, Artis Gilmore. But the Bruins' brilliant forward Sidney Wicks played inspired defense against Gilmore and used his quickness to move around the big man on offense to lead the Bruins to their fourth straight NCAA title. Here, Wicks banks in 2 points past Gilmore.

the challenge; the Bulldogs tried frantically but could not wrestle the ball away. Lynn Shackleford hit 2 free throws and time expired. UCLA had escaped 85–82.

The 1969 final was a welcome return to the familiar for the Bruins, notable for only two reasons: Wooden's troops were squaring off against his alma mater, and it was the great Alcindor's final college game. UCLA jumped out to a 26–10 lead, and the result was never in question after that. The final score was 92–72. Alcindor had 37 points and 20 rebounds and was named tournament MVP for an unprecedented third consecutive year.

The Bruins compiled an 88–2 record with Big Lew, won a record three consecutive national titles, and dominated college basketball like no team in history. The Alcindor age in college basketball was finally over, and it was just beginning in the NBA. Lew was the first player selected in the draft by the second-year Milwaukee Bucks (who had the worst record in the league) and within two years Alcindor led Milwaukee to the NBA title. Lew would change his name to Kareem Abdul-Jabbar, win an unequaled six MVP Awards, and win five more NBA championship rings with the Los Angeles Lakers. He retired after twenty seasons in the NBA as the league's all-time leading scorer, most of his points coming on his patented, and entirely unstoppable, skyhook, which became his signature shot as a pro. Kareem Abdul-Jabbar left a legacy perhaps unrivaled in the history of basketball.

Suffice it to say, the college basketball world (outside of Westwood) gave a collective sigh of relief when Alcindor graduated. Finally, someone besides UCLA could capture the national title! Not so: the Wizard of Westwood was up to the challenge presented by Alcindor's exit. During Lew's reign, Wooden was virtually reduced to a spectator. The Bruins had been so overwhelming that the coach needed to do little besides make sure that the team got to the arena on time. To meet the post-Alcindor challenge, he revived some strategies from the early sixties: full-court pressure and a running offense that emphasized fast breaks and sharp passing. Wooden's new Bruins had to hustle to stay on top, and to the dismay of the rest of the nation's teams, they did just that.

Not that these Bruins were devoid of talent. Returning starter Curtis Rowe, a solidly built yet agile forward, was joined on the front line by the equally brilliant Sidney Wicks. Rowe and Wicks also gave the Bruins more of an aerial and school-yard dimension than they ever had before. Center Steve Patterson rounded out an impressive front line, although in the half-court offense, Wooden deployed a high-post offense, keeping Patterson farther away from the basket than Rowe and Wicks. Returning starter John Vallely gave the Bruins a veteran presence in the backcourt and also had a knack for making shots with the game on the line. Super-quick Henry Bibby added a new dimension with his long-range jump shots; as Wooden noted, "[Bibby] can hit from further out than any player I have ever coached." With this lineup the Bruins won 27 games in 1969–1970 and lost only 3—1 to Oregon and the other 2 to USC, by 1 point. They won the Pac Eight title and entered a weak Western regional ranked number two. They easily dismissed Jerry Tarkanian's Long Beach State squad, 88–65, and then manhandled Utah State, 101–79, to advance to the Final Four.

The other three teams to make it to College Park, Maryland, were New Mexico State, St. Bonaventure, and Jacksonville. Jacksonville emerged from the toughest regional, the Mideast, which included strong teams from Iowa, Western Kentucky, Notre Dame (led by Austin Carr), and number one–ranked Kentucky. In a thrilling regional semifinal, Kentucky's Dan Issel was outscored by Notre Dame's Carr, 52–44, but the Wildcats prevailed. Meanwhile, Jacksonville defeated downtown Freddy Brown and the Iowa Hawkeyes 104–103 on seven-footer (213cm) Pembrook Burrows' tip-in at the buzzer. In the regional final the Dolphins upset Kentucky 106–100. Jacksonville was the talk of the nation as it headed to College Park. Its astounding front line consisted of six-foot-ten-inch (208cm) Rod McIntyre, seven-foot (213cm) Burrows, and the true star of the group, the mighty seven-foot-two-inch (218cm) Artis Gilmore; the Dolphins had perhaps the tallest front line in all of basketball, pro or college.

The first national semifinal promised a showdown between Gilmore and St. Bonaventure's great center, Bob Lanier. However, Lanier was injured in the regional semifinal and could not play. Miraculously, the Bonnies did not give in. They kept the game close throughout but in the end succumbed to the massive Dolphins 91–83. UCLA, meanwhile, romped over the New Mexico State Aggies 93–77. Coach Wooden played his starters the first thirty-eight minutes against the Aggies, but the well-conditioned Bruins never showed any signs of fading. In the final, Wooden chose to put Sidney Wicks on Gilmore and leave center Patterson to guard Burrows. After Jacksonville moved out to a small lead, Wooden made a defensive adjustment and his decision to guard Gilmore with Wicks began to pay off. Wicks used his superior quickness and tremendous leaping ability to frustrate the giant. In one sequence in the first half, Wicks blocked 3 successive shots by Gilmore. UCLA rallied and moved ahead in the final two minutes of the half. Though the final score was only 80–69, the Bruins were in complete control of the game in the sec-

ond half. Wicks finished with 17 points and 18 rebounds, and more significantly, he outplayed Gilmore and was named MVP. After the game, Curtis Rowe boasted, "Every time somebody mentions three in a row, they say Lew did it. Now we just proved four other men from that team could play basketball." UCLA's fourth consecutive title, their sixth in seven years, may have come as a surprise to some, but not to Rowe, Wicks, Patterson, Vallely, Bibby, and, most of all, Coach Wooden.

The next year, Wicks, Rowe, Patterson, and Bibby all returned, the first three as seniors, while Vallely was replaced in the backcourt by two seniors, Kenney Booker and Terry Showfield, who split time. The Bruins started out ranked number one and finished that way, but not without a bit of drama along the way. The Bruins' only loss was at Notre Dame in midseason. Notre Dame scored 89 points, 46 by Austin Carr, while the Bruins managed only 82. Even with just 1 loss, UCLA had not assured themselves a trip to the NCAAs until the final game of the regular season, against crosstown rival USC. The fifth-ranked Trojans had also won all their games but 1, an early-season loss to the Bruins, and if they triumphed against UCLA they would be awarded the Pac Eight title. Many felt it was a showdown between the nation's two top teams. Not lacking any motivation, the Bruins came from behind and sent the Trojans back to the NIT. The Bruins then dismantled Brigham Young in the West regional semifinals. Next up was Long Beach State, which had a 16-game winning streak. The Bruins struggled throughout against the Forty-Niners, falling behind by 11 points at one juncture. Coach Wooden called on his bench to spark the team, and Larry Farmer and John Ecker led them to a 57–55 victory. The Bruins were headed back to the Astrodome, where the Final Four was being held, for the first time since the Game of the Century.

Joining the Bruins in Houston were Villanova, Western Kentucky, and Kansas. Villanova advanced to the Final Four by knocking off undefeated and third-ranked Penn. The ranking was the

highest ever for an Ivy League team, but crosstown rival Villanova ended Penn's season with a horribly one-sided rout, 90–57. Western Kentucky emerged from another Midwest regional loaded with powerful teams. This year five of the region's six schools were ranked in the top ten—Jacksonville, Ohio State, Kentucky, Western Kentucky, and second-ranked Marquette. Ohio State handed Marquette its first loss of the season and then Western Kentucky ousted the

Indiana's Steve Green tries to connect from short range after driving to the basket during the second half of the 1973 NCAA semis, but UCLA's "Big Redhead," Bill Walton, has other ideas. The Hoosiers actually gave the dynastic Bruins a struggle, closing to within 1 point in the second half before UCLA righted itself and cruised to a 70–59 victory.

Buckeyes. At the semifinals in the Astrodome, 31,428 spectators watched Henry Bibby lead the way for the Bruins with his long-range bombs, as UCLA downed Dave Robisch and Kansas 68–60. The other semifinal was a classic. When

Western Kentucky's Jerry Dunn missed a free throw at the end of regulation, the game went into overtime with the score tied at 74. Villanova's six-foot-eight-inch (203cm) All-American Howard Porter tied the score at 85 with a jump shot at the end of the first overtime, and then led the way over the next five minutes as Villanova survived the struggle 98–90.

Of all the championship games that UCLA played in, the 1971 final was the strangest. Villanova was renowned for two things: its exceptionally fast-paced offense and the 2–3 zone that made it difficult for opponents to attack the basket. Coach Wooden had to devise strategies for both of these facets of Villanova's game. To slow down the Wildcats, Wooden called for his handy old zone press. Then he told his team that their offense would revolve around Bibby's zone-breaking jump shot. Both strategies worked in the final; the 2–2–1 zone press forced Villanova into a slower offense, while Showfield and Patterson contributed jumpers along with Bibby to stake the Bruins to an 11-point lead. Then Wooden did something completely out of character; he called for the Bruins to go into a stall, knowing that Villanova coach Jack Kraft was committed to his zone defense. So with the game still in the first half, the Bruins merely held the ball or dribbled it meaninglessly near half court while Villanova remained in their zone—an absurd spectacle. Wooden later claimed that he deployed this tactic to show the NCAA rules committee the inanity of stalling. The game continued this way after halftime until Kraft finally gave in with fifteen minutes left in the game and told his players to abandon the zone defense. UCLA built its lead, which had slipped to 8 points, back up to 12. Then the Wildcats staged a comeback, sparked, oddly enough, by the success of their man-to-man defense. The Wildcats converted some steals into easy baskets and the Bruins' lead went down to 4. Porter succeeded in containing Wicks, who had only 7 points, while the Villanova All-American scored 25 points. However, UCLA's Steve Patterson was having the game of his career. Red hot from medium-range, Patterson tallied a career-high 29 points. With two and a half minutes remaining, the Wildcats crept within 3 points of the Bruins, but they would get no closer. Down the stretch the Bruins had too much experience, composure, and clutch shooting. The final was 68–62 and UCLA had its fifth championship in a row.

As UCLA won its fifth straight national title, they also said goodbye to five seniors, including starters Sidney Wicks, Curtis Rowe, and Steve Patterson. But not many Bruins fans had been worrying about their team's future since the announcement in the spring of 1970 that the nation's most sought-after recruit, Bill Walton, would attend UCLA. Bill Walton hailed from La Mesa, California, just down the road from Westwood. The six-foot-eleven-inch (211 cm) redhead led Helix High to 49 straight victories, averaged 29 points per game, shot 70 percent from the field, and owned the boards. John Wooden got word of Walton's talents and was so impressed that he broke his own rule and visited Walton himself to try to lure him to UCLA. Walton was sufficiently awed. In a scenario eerily similar to when Lew Alcindor showed up at UCLA, the 1970–1971 freshman class included a number of other exceptional basketball players, most notably a sleek six-foot-five-inch (196cm) forward, Keith Wilkes, and a brilliant six-foot-four-inch (193cm) guard, Greg Lee. As sophomores, this trio moved into the Bruins' starting lineup alongside former backup forward Larry Farmer and Bibby. The 1971–1972 Bruins also had a deep bench that included another massive and talented center, Sven Nater, and a pair of quality guards, Tommy Curtis and Larry Hollyfield. Instantly this group began destroying opponents in comparable fashion to Alcindor's squad. Thus was born the "Walton Gang." It would be two and a half seasons before they would lose a game.

During the 1971–1972 season, the Walton Gang made jaws drop wherever they played. They won all 26 of their games by an average margin of 32 points. Oregon State came the closest to posting an upset, 78–72. UCLA thrashed Notre Dame, the only team the Wicks-Rowe Bruins had lost to the previous season, by 58 and 25 points in their two meetings. Long before the NCAA tournament began, coaches and pundits across the country were conceding not just the 1972 title to Walton and company, but the next two after that. In the NCAA's West regional, the Bruins dismissed Weber State and Jerry Tarkanian's Long Beach Forty-Niners and headed back to Los Angeles for their coronation at the Final Four. Their first sacrificial offering was the Louisville Cardinals. Not much was dramatic about the game, though it was interesting that the Cardinals' new coach, Denny Crum, was a former assistant at UCLA and had been instrumental in recruiting Walton to play for the Bruins. Walton showed no mercy, pouring in 33 points and suffocating the Cardinals' interior offense. In the other national semifinal, North Carolina was heavily favored over Florida State. The Tarheels had a player, Bob McAdoo, who was so exceptionally talented that there was a remote possibility that if he faced the Bruins, and had the game of his life, he could lift UNC to the title. But McAdoo was in a funk throughout the tournament, and Florida State, led by their own prodigious scorer Ron King, raced out to a huge lead and held on to earn the right to be annihilated in the finals.

Miraculously, the Seminoles put up a decent fight against UCLA. Florida State had two six-foot-eleven-inch (211 cm) men who successfully denied Walton the ball in the early going and the Seminoles actually built up a 7-point lead (UCLA had not trailed by so many points all year), but then the Bruins scored the next 7 points. Walton found a way to get around the two giants, and UCLA soon had an 11-point lead. However, Florida State was not ready to quit, and when Walton got into foul trouble, the lead began to shrink down. Nater filled in admirably for a spell, then Walton came back and the Bruins held on to win by 5. The gallant Seminoles had come closer than any team all year to upsetting the Bruins. Still, the game was never in doubt down the stretch, nor was the fact that the Walton Gang ruled the roost.

The next season, the Bruins continued to roll over opponents, one after the other, with an efficiency unmatched in the history of

Memphis State's Larry Finch assists a limping Bill Walton (who had sustained a minor injury) off the court near the end of the 1973 championship game. The crowd gave Walton a thundering standing ovation. The junior center had played through foul trouble and scored a finals-record 44 points on 21-for-22 shooting.

the game (or almost any other sport for that matter). Bibby had graduated, so Larry Hollyfield moved into the starting lineup. The UCLA winning streak reached 50 and became the talk of the nation. Sixty straight games was the all-time record, set by Bill Russell's USF Dons. Wooden was already quoted as saying that Walton was like the reincarnation of Russell, except that Walton could also score. The Walton Gang tied the Dons' record, against Loyola, and then broke it against Notre Dame. Heading into the tournament, the streak had reached 71.

What made the Walton Gang so great? First of all, Bill Walton was the consummate team player. He was a brilliant defender, rebounder, and scorer, but his whole way of playing basketball was as one part of a team. Walton provided unparalleled support for the other Bruins in their half-court defense; on offense, he used his tremendous passing skills to feed his teammates whenever opposing defenses collapsed on him. And Walton was a one-man army defending his basket in the Bruins' 2–2–1 zone press, which allowed the other Bruins the luxury to be extra aggressive. Also, Wooden had worked the other Bruins, all multi-talented in their own right, into a thoroughly integrated and efficient supporting cast.

In the 1973 NCAA tournament, the Bruins once again romped through the West regional and headed to St. Louis for the Final Four. The Bruins' semifinal match against Bobby Knight's Indiana Hoosiers seemed like the typical UCLA rout at halftime, 40–22. The game seemed in the Bruins' hands; then, all of a sudden, for virtually the first time in two years, the Walton Gang lost its composure. In a span of less than four minutes, the Hoosiers outscored UCLA 17–0 and Walton collected his fourth foul. With ten minutes remaining, the Bruins regrouped, Wooden made some substitutions, and the team righted itself. The feisty Hoosiers would only score 8 points the rest of the way and the Bruins won 70–59.

In the other semifinal, the favored Providence Friars squared off against the Memphis State Tigers. Coach Gene

Bartow's Tigers were a talented lot led by Larry Finch, Ronnie Robertson, and high-flying Larry Kenon, but the Friars had two exceptional performers in point guard Ernie DiGregorio and the great Marvin Barnes. Like Bob McAdoo the year before, Barnes was so outstanding that fans longed to see him challenge the Walton Gang (even though the Friars had lost earlier in the season to UCLA). Providence jumped out to an early lead, all cylinders clicking, when Barnes fell to floor and was unable to continue. The Friars put up a valiant fight, but the Tigers came back and won, 98–85, to advance to the final.

In college basketball lore, Bill Walton's performance in the 1973 NCAA championship game is the standard against which any exceptional performance is measured. What few people may know is that Walton and UCLA didn't take control of the game against Bartow's Memphis State until the second half. The Big Redhead was on the bench with 3 fouls at the end of the first half while Memphis State erased a 6-point deficit to tie the score. Coach Bartow called for his front line of Kenon, Robinson, and Wes Westfall to all collapse on Walton when he got the ball, and the resultant traffic jam produced a lot of whistles. However, Walton came out like a man possessed in the second half. The UCLA guards tossed the ball up to the side of the hoop, and with his great wingspan, Walton reached up and tapped it in. Using this alley-oop play over and over again, Walton scored 14 of the Bruins' first 20 points as UCLA built a 10-point lead. Playing with passion and control, Walton collected his fourth but not his fifth foul. Guard Greg Lee kept tossing the ball over the hapless Tiger defense and ended up with 14 assists. As the Bruins' lead grew, Walton did not relent. In the end, his statistical line was unreal: 44 points on 21-for-22 shooting. And the Bruins won going away, 87–66. It was UCLA's seventy-fifth straight victory and its seventh consecutive national championship.

The 1973–1974 season was one of the most dramatic and memorable in the history of college basketball. Going into the season were two teams that had gone

undefeated the year before: UCLA and North Carolina, which had finished the regular season ranked number two. But the Wolfpack were prohibited from playing in the 1973 postseason because of a recruiting violation. The playmaker for the talented but slightly surreal-looking group was five-foot-six-inch (168cm) Monte Towe, while the center was stick-thin seven-foot-four-inch (224cm) Rick Burleson. Their superstar was six-foot-four-inch (193cm) David Thompson, who could presumably jump over buildings. With their probation over, the Wolfpack was poised to make a run at the Bruins and the national title in 1974. However, it wouldn't be easy for the Wolfpack even to make it to the NCAA tournament, since to qualify they would have to win the postseason ACC tournament, most likely against a brilliant Maryland Terrapins team. Coach Lefty Driesell's team included two front line gems in Len Elmore and Tom McMillan (a future Congressman), and a brilliant point guard, John Lucas (a future NBA head coach). Both Maryland and NC State wanted to make sure they had a crack at the Walton Gang, so they scheduled the Bruins early in the season.

First up for the Bruins was Maryland. The core of the Walton Gang (the Big Redhead, Wilkes, and Lee) was still intact, of course, and the only change in the starting lineup from the previous season was junior Dave Myers, who replaced graduating senior Larry Farmer. UCLA seemed to have things in hand against Maryland when the Terps scored 7 straight points in the final minutes to close within a point. The Pauley Pavilion crowd held its breath as John Lucas put up a shot, but Myers blocked it to preserve a 65–64 victory and the winning streak. A few days later, UCLA and NC State met on neutral turf in St. Louis. Walton got into deep foul trouble, and as he sat on the bench, the Wolfpack stayed with the Bruins. The score was 54–all when he returned. The final was 81–66, advantage Bruins.

As conference foes, NC State and Maryland met twice during the regular season. After taming the two Eastern title contenders, all seemed well with the Bruins. They pummeled their opponents

The players and coaching staff of the 1972–1973 Bruins pose with the national championship trophy after dismissing Memphis State at the St. Louis Arena for their record-setting seventy-fifth straight win and seventh consecutive title. Still, it looks like just another day at the office for Coach Wooden, in the middle of the pack in a dark suit.

right and left. When they topped Iowa on the road at midseason, their streak was up to 88. One hundred straight wins seemed not only a possibility, but a likelihood. However, UCLA's next opponent was Notre Dame, who had the distinction of being the last school to defeat the Bruins (albeit before the Walton Gang came on the varsity scene). Led by a brilliant, scrappy scorer named Adrian Dantley, center John Shumate, Gary Brokaw, and Dwight Clay, Notre Dame was ranked number two and already had the distinction of snapping Marquette's at-home winning streak at 81 games. Walton was suffering from a back injury that had forced him to miss some games, but he suited up in South Bend. The Bruins raced to a big lead in the first half. And with only three and a half minutes left, UCLA led by 11. Then the Bruins fell apart, committing a series of turnovers that the Irish converted into baskets as the fans grew increasingly delirious. Thirty seconds remained as the Irish

scored their tenth straight point, and twenty seconds later Dwight Clay put Notre Dame ahead. In the final seconds, amid absolute pandemonium, the Bruins attempted a shot and missed. Walton got the rebound, but missed the putback; another Bruin tried to tap it in, but it bounced out; and the buzzer sounded. The Bruins were in disbelief. None of them had ever lost a game in their college careers. The Bruins got a measure of revenge a week later when they beat the Irish 94–75 at Pauley Pavilion, but they were erratic the rest of the season. Three weeks after the loss in South Bend, the Bruins dropped 2 consecutive games in Oregon. It was the first time UCLA had lost back-to-back games since 1966. The Bruins entered the final game of the regular season tied for Pac Eight lead with USC, which was 22–3 and ranked seventh. On that particular night, the Walton Gang was back with a vengeance, leading 47–13 at halftime. The Bruins qualified for the tournament on an up

note but no longer seemed invincible.

UCLA's first opponent in the tournament, Dayton (fresh off an upset of Notre Dame), just about ended the Bruins' seven-year reign. With the score tied at 80, Dayton held for the last shot, but Don Smith's jumper was off the mark and the game went to overtime. Each team managed 8 points in the first overtime. At the end of the second overtime the score was still knotted. Finally, Walton took control in the third extra period and the Bruins survived. The next round was easier as UCLA posted its thirty-eighth consecutive tournament win, against San Francisco, 83–60, and headed to Greensboro, North Carolina, for a showdown with the Wolfpack.

North Carolina State entered the tournament ranked number one and the only scare Norm Sloan's troops suffered in the East regionals, played on their home court in Raleigh, was when David Thompson crashed to the floor in a game against Pitt. The great leaper lay motionless on the floor and was rushed to a hospital, but returned to the arena before the game was over.

The UCLA–North Carolina State semifinal was one of the greatest games in tournament history. After the first half the score was tied at 35. Sloan had Burleson play Walton man-to-man and had Thompson, who was at full strength, shadow Wilkes, hoping in this way to place the burden on the rest of the Bruins. But UCLA opened up an 11-point lead in the second half. The Wolfpack seemed poised to make a run numerous times, but the Bruins kept thwarting their momentum. Then suddenly everything clicked for the Wolfpack; they scored 10 straight points and took a 2-point lead. However, UCLA scored the next 2 baskets. Thompson then tied the score, and when UCLA failed to score on their next possession, the Wolfpack held the ball for the next two minutes for the last shot. Tim Stoddard misfired and the game headed into overtime. The teams traded field goals and once again NC State held for the final shot. This time Thompson drove the lane and as the defense collapsed on him, he dished off to Burleson, who missed from short range. In the second extra period, the Bruins seemed to

North Carolina State's David Thompson skys to swipe a rebound away from UCLA's David Myers during the epic 1974 NCAA semifinal contest. Though only six feet four inches tall (193cm), Thompson played above the rim. Reputed to have a 48-inch (122cm) vertical leap, Thompson went on to become one of the sport's most accomplished dunkers with the Denver Nuggets; unfortunately the dunk was criminalized in the college ranks until the 1976–1977 season.

say enough is enough; Walton tallied 4 points and Wilkes 3 in ninety seconds for a 74–67 lead. The Bruins seemed destined to capture their eighth title in a row. Then, just like at South Bend a few months earlier, the roof caved in on the Bruins. Twice, UCLA missed shots and the Wolfpack converted on the other end, and North Carolina stole a pass which was translated into 2 points. When

Myers missed a 1-and-1 and Thompson scored at the other end, the lead had evaporated and NC State was up by 1. Lee missed a jumper; Thompson hit his free throws, as did Towe (with twelve seconds remaining); and the Wolfpack had dethroned the mighty champions 80–77.

The Walton Gang was history. They had gone out with their heads held high, fighting until the end, unwilling to freeze the ball with a 7-point lead, since Wooden always believed that his teams were superior when the game was played straight up. Because of their struggles in 1974, the Walton Gang, who for two and a half years was heralded as the greatest college team of all-time, finished on a down note and left a legacy comparable but not quite on par with the Bruins teams of the Alcindor era.

The Wolfpack's opponents in the 1974 championship game were the Marquette Warriors coached by the quixotic Al McGuire. Marquette had reached the Final Four from the Mideast regional, where the favored Fighting Irish of Notre Dame were upset by Michigan, who then fell to the Warriors. Kansas rounded out the Final Four. The Jayhawks led the Warriors by a point at the half when McGuire, generally loved by his players despite his short temper, bawled his team out so aggressively in the locker room that his star guard Lloyd Walton called it quits and hit the showers.

Walton's teammates convinced him to keep playing; begrudgingly he redressed and came out for the second half. The Warriors improved their play and advanced to the finals with a 64–51 win. Marquette was a strong team; besides sharpshooting Walton, they had two notable big men in Maurice Lucas and Bo Ellis, a freshman. (The NCAA began allowing freshmen to play on the varsity beginning in 1972–1973.) And the Warriors stayed with the Wolfpack in the first half. They had built up some momentum and taken a 1-point lead, 28–27, when Marquette's Marcus Washington was called for charging. McGuire disagreed and exploded off the bench, screaming at the officials, and was hit with a technical foul. The Wolfpack made all the free throws and kept the ball. On the ensuing possession, Ellis was called for goaltending; McGuire disagreed, exploded again, and earned a second technical. Before this sequence was over, the Wolfpack had a 9-point lead and assumed command of the game, coasting to a 76–64 victory. Dave Thompson was named the MVP. NC State was the national champion.

Heading into the 1974–1975 season, it seemed that UCLA would finally be just one among a number of teams that would compete for the national title—just as it seemed they were in 1969–1970. And just like that year, the Bruins won in the end. In the wake of Walton's graduation, Wooden had a new generation ready to fill out the varsity roster. Foremost among these were forwards Richard Washington and Marques Johnson and point guard Andres McCarter, who would join forward David Myers and former backup Pete Trgovich in the starting lineup. Clearly, no one in this group was a prospective Alcindor or Walton (center Ralph Drollinger, who began the season in the starting lineup, moved to the bench at midseason in favor of a quicker first unit), or even a Wicks or Rowe. But one thing remained a constant. The man with the rolled-up program in his hand, John Wooden, was still the coach. And the venerable one guided these Bruins to a 23–3 season and another Pac Eight title. But Wooden had protected his young team, having them

play all their games at home except for their obligatory conference road games and a game at rival Notre Dame, where they lost again. The Bruins were not allowed such insulation in the NCAA tournament. Right off the bat they faced a challenge. Michigan led at halftime, and the game was tied after regulation, but the Bruins led after five extra minutes. Next they squeaked by unheralded Montana by 3 before finally putting together an impressive performance against Arizona State, earning them a trip down the coast to San Diego for the Final Four.

Joining the Bruins in San Diego were Louisville, led by Wooden protégé Denny Crum; Kentucky, who upset number one–ranked and previously unbeaten Indiana in the regional finals; and Syracuse. For the second time in four years, Louisville and UCLA met in the national semifinals. This '75 showdown would be considerably more memorable than the '72 blowout. The Cardinals moved ahead by 9 early, but the Bruins reduced the difference to 4 by halftime. Louisville remained strong in the second frame. Cardinals star Junior Bridgeman was controlling the boards along with front line mate Wesley Cox, while guard Allen Murphy led the Cardinals in scoring. But the Bruins hung tough. With less than a minute remaining, the Cardinals once again held a 4-point lead. Dave Myers tried to shoot but Louisville's Bill Bunton blocked the shot; Myers tried again—same result. UCLA's Washington gathered the loose ball and tried to score. Once again Bunton was there, but this time the referee ruled that Bunton had gotten a piece of Washington. The UCLA center calmly stepped to the charity stripe and buried both shots. The Bruins then applied full-court pressure. Marques Johnson stepped in to steal the inbounds pass and quickly tied the game. No more scoring occurred in regulation and the game went to an extra period, which had become commonplace for the Bruins in the tournament. The Cardinals' Murphy scored 7 points in the overtime period and staked Louisville to a 74–71 lead. After Myers made 2 free throws to reduce the deficit to 1, Louisville

brought in their designated dribbler, Terry Howard, to try to freeze the game. For thirty tantalizing seconds the Bruins tried to steal the ball from Howard as he weaved among them, but to no avail. So Wooden ordered his players to foul the diminutive guard. Howard had made all 28 of his free throws during the regular season, but amazingly he missed the front end of a 1-and-1. The Bruins controlled the rebound and called time-out. Wooden called for Washington to try a baseline jumper, and with the season on the line, the center hit nothing but net and the Bruins were headed back to the finals. In the press conference after the game, a charged environment became even more dramatic when Coach Wooden announced he would be retiring after the championship game.

The Bruins' opponent in the 1975 final was Kentucky, whose coach Joe B. Hall knew something about the circumstances surrounding the retirement of coaching legends since he had replaced Adolph Rupp only one season earlier. The Wildcats had reached the finals after a rough, 95–79 semifinal contest against Syracuse. The Wildcats featured three freshmen, Jack "Goose" Givens and two six-foot-ten-inch (208cm) wide-bodies, Rick Robey and Mike Phillips, along with All-American Kevin Grevey. The final promised to be a contrast in styles, between Kentucky's strength and size and UCLA's speed and finesse. Of course, UCLA had a special motivating factor on its side. The game was close throughout, and the turning point came when Myers was called for a technical foul with UCLA ahead by a single point late in the game. Wooden then uncharacteristically sprung from his chair and ran out onto the court yelling at the officials. Naturally, no technical was called on the living legend even though his assistants had to restrain him. Kentucky missed the free throw, failed to score on its next possession, and the Bruins took control of the game from there. The final score was 92–85 and the Wooden era came to a glorious close as UCLA won its tenth championship in twelve years.

Chapter

The Big Dance:
1976–1985

The era from the mid-seventies through the mid-eighties was the golden age of college basketball. During this era, college stars like Mark Aguirre, Ralph Sampson, and Patrick Ewing were national celebrities for virtually the entirety of their college careers. The likes of Chris Mullin, Akeem Olajuwon, Clyde Drexler, James Worthy, and a certain Michael Jordan also became household names for a season or two. Never before had college hoops been followed as fervently by so many people, and no era produced greater drama. Although UCLA's undramatic monopoly of power during the '60s and early '70s (with the notable exception of the Game of the Century in 1968 and NC State's 1974 coup) had dampened the media attention paid to the college game, basketball had become more and more popular nationwide. By the mid-seventies the sport was a rite of passage for America's youth, rivaling baseball and football as backyard recreation. The hoop over the garage became as much a suburban archetype as the basket rising out of asphalt was the symbol of America's inner city. As an amazingly broad range of talent graduated from an equally broad range of high schools each spring, and as the Bruins dynasty ended with Coach Wooden's (merciful) retirement, it became evident how evenly dispersed this talent was among America's colleges. Thus, many colleges entertained realistic hopes of snagging a national title.

This increase in parity translated into greater drama come tournament time. The tournament expanded accordingly: from 25 to 32 teams in 1975 (the

first significant increase since 1954), to 40 teams in 1979, to 48 the next year, to 52 in 1983, and finally to 64 in 1985, where it has remained since. In 1976, a new era was about to dawn in which college basketball would become the talk of the nation every March.

The vehicle that would transport the spectacle of college basketball into the hearts and homes of America was television. College hoops had its moments on television before 1975 but these were isolated events, like the Game of the Century. In other words, college hoops only managed to captivate the television-watching public for a few days per year. The NBC television network began to expand its broadcasting of the NCAA tournament by the mid-seventies, including numerous regional matchups; but the big draw was still the Final Four, especially the Monday night championship game.

However, television's relationship with college basketball began to change after the 1977 tournament. That year four teams that were not among the favorites to win the title reached the national semifinals, where they produced some of the most scintillating drama in tournament history. It made for great television. NBC decided to expand its coverage of the tournament. In 1979, the nation's fans watched as NBC tracked the progress of both Michigan State's Magic Johnson and Indiana State's Larry Bird from the first round to their showdown in the finals, a game that attracted a record television audience. CBS outbid NBC for the rights to the tournament in 1982 and continued to expand tournament coverage.

Meanwhile, the growth of cable television in the early eighties led to a tremendous increase in exposure for college basketball. In particular, the all-sports ESPN cable network featured a wide array of regular-season games. Regional showdowns that had not even been broadcast locally a few years earlier were beamed to every corner of the country every night of the week. And fans seemed to have an insatiable enthusiasm for the exciting college game. Consequently, more fans knew more about more teams than ever before and this generated more interest, especially in the NCAA tournament.

Whereas in 1976 even the NCAA regional finals were not broadcast nationally, only five years later American sports fans recognized that the only thing more exciting than watching the first round of the NCAA tourney was watching the second round, which was only superceded by the third round and so on. The 1970 NCAA tournament generated $550,000 in television revenue; the 1996 tourney garnered $178.3 million.

If college basketball fans hoped that the national championship competition would become wide-open in John Wooden's absence, they would have to wait one more year, for the 1975–1976 season was dominated by one team as thoroughly as the Bruins had dominated the NCAA field in their Alcindor-led

Freshman center Patrick Ewing led the Georgetown Hoyas to the 1982 NCAA finals, where he created a sensation in the game's first five minutes: he exploded above the rim four times to reject North Carolina shots. Although all four were ruled goaltending, the altitude of his efforts only made the feat more impressive and intimidating.

heyday—only this time the team was the Indiana Hoosiers. Coach Bobby Knight's squad maintained the number one ranking from the beginning to the end of the season. The Hoosiers not only won all their games; they were rarely challenged.

The odyssey of the Hoosiers team that was crowned national champions in Philadelphia amid the bicentennial fer-

Renowned for his intimidating demeanor, super-intense Indiana head coach Bobby Knight gives a tip to his star forward, Scott May, who excelled at both ends of the court. Knight has expected and gotten the best out of his Hoosiers for the past twenty years, in particular the teams of the mid-1970s anchored by May.

vor of 1976 actually began during the 1974–1975 season. The Hoosiers ran the table during the 1974–1975 regular season, entering the tournament 29–0 and ranked number one in the nation. The media anointed bulky six-foot-ten-inch (208cm) sophomore center Kent Benson and junior All-American forward Scott May the stars of the team, but perhaps the key to the Hoosiers dominance was the tall, strong, and versatile backcourt duo of Quinn Buckner and Bobby Wilkerson, both juniors. The fifth starter was senior forward Steve Green. In the third game of the season the Hoosiers cemented their place atop the national wire service polls with a resounding 98–74 destruction of regional rival Kentucky. And no team in Big Ten history so dominated the conference like the Hoosiers, whose average margin of victory was 22 points. Indiana entered the tournament as the prohibitive favorite

even though May was only available for limited duty because he broke his left (nonshooting) arm with 4 games left in the regular season. Coach Knight had to decide whether to replace the All-American, who was just as brilliant on offense as defense, with the offense-minded guard John Laskowski or defensive specialist Tom Abernathy, a forward. Knight went with the offense, which he later declared "the biggest mistake I've ever made in coaching." To Knight, the '75 team at full strength was his best ever because of its depth and versatility, but by sacrificing defense for points, Knight felt, in retrospect, that he lost control of the games. With Laskowski in the lineup, Wilkerson moved to forward. This setup backfired in the regional final when Laskowski had to defend Kentucky's sensational Kevin Grevey. The Kentucky guard ate Laskowski for lunch. The Wildcats scored 92 points and pulled off a stunning 2-point upset.

The 1975–1976 Hoosiers were on a mission from day one to get what they thought was rightfully theirs, the national championship. With May back at full strength, Knight inserted Abernathy into the starting lineup and the Hoosiers steamrolled everyone who got in their way. First up was defending champion UCLA in a game at St. Louis, a neutral site. The Bruins still had the core of their championship team— Richard Washington, Marques Johnson, and Andres McCarter— intact, but the Hoosiers annihilated them by 20 points. Then the Hoosiers once again swept through a difficult regular-season schedule undefeated, and they entered the tournament free of injuries, poised to take the title.

It would be no cakewalk as the

Hoosiers were placed in a stacked Mideast regional along with number two Marquette, sixth-ranked North Carolina, and number seven Alabama. In the first round, Indiana dismissed St. John's handily, 90–70. Meanwhile Alabama and North Carolina squared off, and behind Leon Douglas' 35 points, the Crimson Tide rolled over the Tarheels. The Tide met the Hoosiers in the next round and played them tough; with less than four minutes remaining, Alabama led 69–68. The score remained that way for the next two minutes as the Hoosiers went into defensive overdrive. Finally, May made a basket. A few more Indiana free throws followed, and the final score was 74–69.

Next up for the Hoosiers was Marquette, who had had an easier draw in the regional, dismissing Western Kentucky and Western Michigan for their twenty-second and twenty-third consecutive victories. The Warriors had lost only once all season, at Minnesota 77–73. Coach Al McGuire's troops were seasoned and talented; seniors Earl Tatum, a sharpshooter, and Lloyd Walton, the floor leader, combined with talented big man Bo Ellis, a junior, and sophomore guard Butch Lee for a potent mix. The Hoosiers knew they were in for a struggle and desperately wanted to avoid last year's fate. May got in foul trouble early and his absence during the balance of the first half allowed Marquette to close an 11-point deficit to 3 at intermission. In the second half, May was back, but had to relax his defense on Tatum; the brilliant shooter kept the Warriors close. With only twenty-five seconds remaining and the Hoosiers leading by

Michigan's dynamic point guard Ricky Green explodes past Indiana's Bobby Wilkerson for a lay-up during the first half of the 1976 finals, which marked the first year in which two teams from the same conference were allowed to play in the tournament. Of course, the title game turned into an all-Big Ten affair.

only a point, a foul was called that sent Wilkerson to the line for a 1-and-1. The volatile McGuire sprung from his seat with some choice words for the officials, who immediately slapped the Marquette coach with his second technical of the game. This meant Wilkerson got his free throw, and then Indiana got 2 more from the charity stripe and kept the ball. The crowd, and both teams, were stunned. Indiana scored 8 points in those final twenty-five seconds to advance to the Final Four.

The East regional sent another undefeated team, though one with considerably less national distinction, to the Final Four: the Scarlett Knights of Rutgers, led by All-American Phil Sellers. The year 1976 was the first in which second-place teams from major conferences could be granted at-large invitations to the Big Dance (a stipulation with devastating consequences for the NIT). Big Ten runner-up Michigan took full advantage of this rule change, winning the Midwest regional over Big Eight champion Missouri, despite a spectacular 43-point effort by the Tigers' Willie Smith. The West regional was won by none other than the UCLA Bruins, who had regrouped after their season-opening defeat to Indiana and, motivated by a desire for a rematch, looked strong heading to Philadelphia under the guidance of coach Gene Bartow, the man who had the unenviable position of replacing John Wooden.

In the first semifinal game, the Wolverines were too much for the Scarlett Knights. Paced by their star point guard Ricky Green, Michigan raced to a 46–29 halftime lead and coasted to victory from there. In the second game, the Bruins did better than in St. Louis some four months earlier, but were still no match for the thoroughly solid Hoosiers. Coach Knight took no chances—he played his five starters almost the entire game and came away with a convincing 65–51 victory. Of course, Indiana had already twice defeated the Wolverines in the regular season, so the Hoosiers were expected to romp in the final (which was the first inter-conference NCAA title game). But these Wolverines were nobody's pushover;

freshman center Phil Hubbard, talented at all aspects of the game, was a quick player bound to cause problems for Benson, and Green's backcourt mate Steve Grote was a world-class outside shooter. Indeed, Michigan came out strong and took a 35–29 lead to the locker room at halftime. Knight's words to his troops at intermission were simple:

Indiana's hulky center with the soft shooting touch, Kent Benson, lofts a short-range jumper over a Michigan defender during the 1976 title game. Michigan shocked the undefeated Hoosiers by taking a 35–29 lead into the intermission, but Indiana overwhelmed the Wolverines in the second half.

"You've got to try harder." They did just that and stormed past Michigan. The Hoosiers outscored the Wolverines 57–33 in the final period to claim the national title in a rout worthy of their excellence.

No team since has posted an undefeated national championship season. The 1975–1976 Hoosiers can easily be considered one of college basketball's all-time greatest teams.

The next season there was no such prohibitive favorite and the wide-open tournament was as thrilling as any to date. In fact, many consider the 1977 NCAAs to be the beginning of what by the mid-eighties had become known as March Madness, a national sporting spectacle of the first order, on par with the professional football and baseball playoffs and, for all intents and purposes, surpassing the NBA and NHL playoffs (though the popularity of the NBA would soar dramatically in the late eighties and early nineties). Exactly when the NCAA tournament became such a huge deal is open to interpretation. Some say that the seminal moment was the 1979 final between Magic Johnson's Michigan State Spartans and Larry Bird's Indiana State Sycamores; others say the transformative moment was the dramatic demise of the Walton Gang in 1974, or Wooden's championship victory in the last game of his career in 1975. But most point to the thrilling 1977 tournament, which was without a distinct favorite but nonetheless rife with upsets, heroic efforts by underdogs, and colorful characters. The tournament truly captured the public's imagination. Indeed, during the UCLA dynasty (1964–1975) fans across the country had bemoaned how the sport had been

UNC's brilliant point guard Phil Ford drives to the basket as UNLV's Glen Gondrezick blocks his path and airborne Reggie Theus reaches out to swat the shot away during the 1977 semifinals. Ford played despite an injured right elbow and executed the Tarheels notorious four-corners stall to near perfection at the end of the nail-biter, an 84–83 UNC victory.

reduced to a competition for second place; Wooden's retirement had promised a more level playing field, but the '76 Hoosiers were as dominant as any Wooden team (and though the Hoosiers did play some close games in the tournament, there was a sense that unless they were upset, no team could get too excited about their chances of winning it all).

Heading into the 1976–1977 season, the Michigan Wolverines, who had lost only one starter from a team that

reached the national championship game and had all of its stars back, were the consensus number one pick. But the Wolverines had lost 7 games the year before and no one was comparing them to the Hoosier juggernaut. Sure enough, Michigan quickly fell from the top spot in the polls. The number one ranking was grabbed by San Francisco, led by seven-foot (213cm) center Bill Cartwright and guard Winford Boynes. But Michigan did have an excellent season, losing only 3 games, and when the previously undefeated Dons lost their last regular-season game, the Wolverines entered the tournament ranked number one. The number two team was UCLA, who became junior Marques Johnson's team when Richard Washington skipped his senior year to turn pro; the Bruins lost only 4 games all year. Another highly ranked team out West was the University of Las Vegas (UNLV), which like USF was largely unproven against topflight competition. Coach Jerry Tarkanian's Runnin' Rebels ran (appropriately) a high-powered offense keyed by forward Eddie Owens and guard Reggie Theus. In the East regional fourth-ranked North Carolina seemed like the top team, though sixth-ranked Kentucky was also strong. The Midwest regional had no clear favorite, though Arkansas was ranked eighth.

Once the tournament began, the upsets came fast and furious. First USF, in an unfortunate draw, was run out of the building by UNLV, 121–95. Then, in a real shocker, UCLA, fresh off a convincing win over Louisville, was defeated by Idaho State, 76–75. With the Bruins eliminated, the Runnin' Rebels raced straight through to Atlanta and the Final Four. The only favorite to survive the other three regionals was North Carolina. In the Mideast, Michigan made it to the regional finals, where they met the University of North Carolina Charlotte (UNCC), who had reached the finals of the NIT the previous season (where they fell to Kentucky). Unfortunately for the Wolverines, the Forty-Niners' Cedric "Cornbread" Maxwell was a player to be reckoned with. UNCC stunned the Wolverines by opening up a 13-point halftime lead, and then showed astounding composure after Michigan stormed back to take the lead. The Forty-Niners regrouped and regained control of the game, winning 75–68. Great things were not expected from Al McGuire's Marquette team, who lost Earl Tatum and Lloyd Walton to graduation, but the Warriors finished the regular season 20–7 and earned an at-large bid to the tournament. Once there, the Marquette Warriors came together and rolled through the relatively weak Midwest regional. Marquette players had a special motivation since their beloved, though controversial, coach, Al McGuire, had announced he was retiring after the season, despite the fact that he was just forty-five years old.

The 1977 semifinal games were both classics. In the first game, coach Dean Smith's Tarheels, led by three brilliant stars—point guard Phil Ford (who was injured during the Final Four and only saw limited action) and forwards Walter Davis and Mike O'Koren—trailed UNLV most of the game, but fought back to grab a slight lead with just over four minutes left and then went into their notorious four-corners stall. UNLV fouled the Tarheels rather than let them freeze the ball, but UNC made enough foul shots to hold on to the win, 84–83. The second game was even more suspenseful. Marquette tore out to a 23–9 lead, but UNCC outscored the warriors 23–2 over the last seven minutes of the

first half to trail by only 3 at intermission. The Forty-Niners then took the lead early in the second half and the two teams stayed close the rest of the way; both played deliberately, recognizing the significance of each possession. With less than two minutes, UNCC led by 3 and McGuire's career seemed destined to end in frustration. But the Warriors' star guard Butch Lee drained a jumper to make the score 47–46. Then the "Mean Green," as the Forty-Niners were also known, tried to stall and as time wound down the Warriors had to foul. They sent Maxwell, one of the great free throw shooters of all time, to the line. Unbelievably, Cornbread, who was rapidly becoming a folk hero across the nation, missed the front end of the 1-and-1. Marquette controlled the rebound, and on the other end, Lee connected on another jumper for a 1-point lead. When UNCC's Lew Massey missed and the Warriors got the rebound, Gary Rosenberger was fouled trying to make a layup with thirteen seconds left and had a chance to ice the game for Marquette from the free throw line. But Rosenberger only made 1 of 2 free throws and Maxwell collected the rebound, drove straight down-court, and tied the game on a layup. Four seconds still remained. In the din of the arena, McGuire huddled his team at midcourt, a clear rules violation, but the referees were not going to determine the outcome of the game on a technicality. Lee then took the ball out-of-bounds underneath his own basket and lobbed a pass the full length of the court (sailing just underneath the scoreboard at center court, the height of which Lee assessed during the time-out) in the

direction of center Jerome Whitehead, who was running the equivalent of a football "post pattern." However, there were two Forty-Niners covering Whitehead; all three players jumped for the ball, but the Warrior big man wrestled it away from the others and placed it in the hoop. The Marquette players and fans stormed the court, celebrating the apparent victory, but the officials had not yet scored the basket. The refs were unsure whether Whitehead had scored before the buzzer. They convened at the scorers' table with both coaches—still no verdict. Finally, they referred to the television replay, and it revealed that Whitehead had just beaten the buzzer. Marquette had won 51–49.

The two coaches in the final, Dean Smith and Al McGuire, were hungry for a national title, both having come close to winning it in the past. But the sentimental favorite was clearly the retiring McGuire. McGuire had turned Marquette into a perennial championship contender in recent years and was known for his ability to communicate with players from disadvantaged inner-city environments.

One of the most dramatic moments in NCAA tournament history: after Marquette's Jerome Whitehead had scored at the buzzer of a tied game versus UNC Charlotte in the 1977 semis, the referees could not decide whether Whitehead had made the shot before time expired. The always emotional McGuire, seeing the refs' indecision, rushed onto the court to register his opinion (as did the Warriors' Bernard Toone). After considerable deliberation, the referees consulted a television replay and ruled in favor of Marquette.

Still, the adoration bestowed on McGuire in his final season, by people other than his players, was something new for the volatile coach, who often jeopardized his team's chances with his outbursts at referees (most memorably in the previous year's regional final against Indiana). But in the spring of 1977, the public embraced the otherwise charming younger brother of the legendary Dick McGuire, who, as it turned out, had led the Tarheels to their only previous title, in 1957.

Coming off its dramatic victory, Marquette was sky-high and played brilliantly in the first half of the final, taking a 12-point lead by intermission. However, UNC stormed back and took the lead 45–43 with more than ten minutes still remaining. It was four-corners time. For once, though, the strategy backfired; Marquette chose not to foul but to hound the ball while stationing their two big men, Ellis and Whitehead, near the basket to cut off easy baskets. They created the necessary turnovers and took a 47–45

joy in his eyes. And a nation watched in wonder.

After the thrilling 1977 tournament, more people than ever tuned in to watch the 1978 spring spectacle (television coverage was ever-expanding). However, the 1978 NCAAs were more like the 1976 tourney than 1977, for once again there was an overpowering, prohibitive favorite, only this time it was the Kentucky Wildcats. Three years earlier the Wildcats had reached the finals with a team that featured two outstanding

there was one burning question: could anyone beat Kentucky?

At halftime of the Wildcats' first-round game it seemed like a distinct possibility, as Florida State led the Wildcats 39–32. Kentucky coach Joe Hall made a daring maneuver at the start of the second half, benching his two All-Americans and going with backups. The move was symbolic of Coach Hall's strategic mind-set. The young coach was an excellent tactician and a crafty psychologist, although he was not getting the credit he deserved for continuing the Wildcats' winning tradition following Adolph Rupp's retirement in 1973. In the second half against the Seminoles, the Kentucky second unit proved better at slowing the Florida State fast break and kept the Wildcats in the game. Then when Robey and Givens, fresh from their time on the bench, returned, Kentucky rolled over the outmanned Seminoles to an 85–76 victory. The Wildcats' momentum continued through the next round, as they outclassed Miami of Ohio, who had upset defending champion and third-ranked Marquette, still led by All-American Butch Lee but now coached by Hank Raymonds. Kentucky's foes in the regional finals were the exciting fifth-ranked Michigan State Spartans led by Jay Vincent, Greg Kelser, and a six-foot-nine-inch (206cm) point guard, Earvin "Magic" Johnson. Magic was the most talked-about freshman in the land, a fiery competitor who was also a first-rate showman specializing in spectacular passes. However, the star of the early part of the Kentucky–Michigan State matchup was the Spartans 2–1–2 zone, which the Wildcats could not solve; at intermission, Michigan State led 27–22. At the half, Coach Hall made his key adjustment on defense, calling for a 1–3–1 zone that could keep Johnson and the Spartans from penetrating. On offense, he called for the wide-bodied Robey to set picks for sharpshooting sophomore guard Kyle Macy. Both moves worked. Michigan State's offense ground to a halt as the Spartans passed up open outside shots and got clogged in the middle, while Macy got hot and carried the Wildcats on to the Final Four in St. Louis.

Kentucky's Jack Givens buries a mid-range jumper for 2 of his 41 points against Duke during the 1978 finals at the St. Louis Arena. Givens' performance lifted the heavily favored Wildcats over the scrappy Blue Devils for their first national title in twenty years.

lead. Then Marquette went into a stall of its own and Butch Lee handled the ball brilliantly. Lee was on a special mission since Coach Smith had snubbed him when he selected the 1976 U.S. Olympic Team (Lee, who had dual citizenship, then joined the Puerto Rican national team and almost single-handedly defeated the U.S.A.). With Lee running the show, the Warriors pulled away from the Heels for a 67–59 victory. The Warrior players stormed the court, but Coach McGuire remained seated with tears of

freshmen, forward Jack Givens and big man Rick Robey. As sophomores the two had played on an NIT championship team, and as juniors they had lost to North Carolina in the regional finals. Now both were All-Americans and the leaders of a team that held the number one ranking all season long (despite losing twice). Heading into the tournament

The three other teams who made it to St. Louis to challenge the heavily-favored Wildcats were Duke, Notre Dame, and the high-flying Razorbacks of Arkansas. The dunk, which had been outlawed since the days of Lew Alcindor (1967) until 1976–77, had come back into vogue in college basketball. During the 1978 tournament no team used this spectacular, emotional weapon with more effect than the Razorbacks, who were led by the "Triplets," three players of almost identical build (six feet four inches [193cm], agile, and strong) and leaping ability—Sidney Moncrief, Ron Brewer, and Marvin Delph. The sixth-ranked Hogs made it to St. Louis from a stacked Western regional where second-ranked UCLA, led by consensus All-American Marques Johnson, was once again favored. Arkansas faced off against the Bruins in the regional final and won a thriller, 74–70, in which the Triplets accounted for 61 points. Notre Dame emerged from the Midwest regional behind stars Kelly Tripucka and Bill Laimbeer. The Fighting Irish had a storied basketball history: they had qualified for the tournament fifteen times, but had never before reached the Final Four. Coach Digger Phelps' team was therefore the sentimental favorite in St. Louis. A young Duke squad, led by a trio of players—junior guard Jim Spanarkel, sophomore center Mike Gminski, and freshman power forward Gene Banks—rounded out the Final Four. These Blue Devils had revived a once-great program and came to the "Gateway to the West" as the underdogs.

However, Duke dominated Notre Dame in the first half of their semifinal, building a commanding 43–29 lead and then holding on in a high-scoring second half for a 90–86 vic-

Marquette's Butch Lee scoops in 2 points versus South Carolina during the 1977–1978 regular season. A fierce competitor and a brilliant slashing point guard, Lee guided Marquette to the national title in 1977, a year in which the Warriors figured to be weaker than previous seasons, when such stars as Lloyd Walton, Earl Tatum, and Maurice Lucas had made Marquette one of the nation's top teams.

tory. The Arkansas-Kentucky matchup was close throughout. Although it was Kentucky senior James Lee who provided the game's most memorable high-flying acrobatics, the Wildcats played a controlled, conservatively paced game. In fact, the Wildcats contained the Arkansas running game so thoroughly that the Hogs' fans never had an opportunity to erupt over a spectacular dunk. Kentucky maintained a slight advantage down the stretch and won 64–59.

The championship game figured to be a mismatch between Kentucky's seasoned veterans and Duke's inexperienced upstarts. The four Kentucky seniors, Robey, Givens, Lee, and center Mike Phillips, had all been to the finals four years earlier. This time they were all business, refusing to participate in any of the pregame hype, while the young Blue Devils behaved like the Wildcats had in 1975 and soaked up the media spotlight. Once the game got under way, Jack Givens took complete control. Behind Givens' onslaught, the Wildcats led 45–38 at intermission. He did not relent in the second half. In the end, Givens had accumulated 41 points, 3 fewer than Bill Walton had tallied five years earlier

De Paul's Mark Aguirre glides past Georgetown's Fred Brown during a 1980–1981 regular season matchup. Aguirre was a college superstar from March 1979 to 1982. After leading De Paul to the Final Four his freshman year, Aguirre's Blue Demons held the number one ranking for much of the next three seasons, though each year they were (amazingly) upset in the first round of the NCAA tournament.

in the same building. Givens' performance ranks besides Walton's and Gail Goodrich's in 1965 as among the greatest ever in the history of the finals. Kentucky rolled to an 11-point lead with a minute and a half to play, and the stoic seniors finally showed some emotion as Hall pulled them from the court. Duke, however, scored 7 quick points and Hall had to reinsert his starters to secure the victory. The Wildcats won their fifth NCAA title, second only to UCLA, with a 94–88 score. For the seniors it was their 102nd victory in their four years at Kentucky.

In the hearts of basketball fans everywhere, one phrase summarizes the 1979 NCAA tournament: Magic versus Larry. Occasionally in the history of college basketball a player emerges who, virtually single-handedly, lifts his team into contention for the national title; examples include Bill Russell, Wilt Chamberlain, Elgin Baylor, and Oscar Robertson. Rarely do two such players emerge at the same time, and when they do, circumstances have always conspired to keep them from meeting in the national championship game—but not in 1979. To the delight of the nation's fans, two of the most brilliant and charismatic college players of all time—Larry Bird and Magic Johnson—carried their teams all the way to a showdown in the NCAA finals. In terms of media attention and television viewership, the contest became the most hyped and watched college basketball game to date.

By any measure, the 1979 NCAA tournament was a classic. The field, which had expanded to forty teams, was wide-open and the four teams that

emerged from the pack to reach Salt Lake City—De Paul, Penn, Indiana State, and Michigan State—were all equally fascinating and improbable. The De Paul Blue Demons had lost four starters from the previous season. In their first game of the season, UCLA annihilated the boys from Chicago by 23 points. But as the season progressed, the young troops jelled under the guidance of Ray Meyer, who had coached De Paul since 1942. Leading the way for the new breed of Blue Demons was a brilliant freshman, Mark Aguirre, and the flashy backcourt tandem of Clyde Bradshaw and Gary Garland. (Garland was also an accomplished singer, who occasionally warmed up the home crowd by singing the national anthem. He came by his talent naturally: his aunt was Dionne Warwick and his little sister became Whitney Houston.) The Blue Demons earned themselves a bid to the Western regional, where they ousted USC and their nearby rival Marquette (from Milwaukee), setting up a rematch with UCLA. The Bruins, led by senior David Greenwood, had compiled the highest single-season shooting percentage in college basketball history, 0.555. Undaunted, De Paul jumped out to a 17-point lead at halftime. The Bruins mounted a furious comeback as the Blue Demons, who had a thin bench, tired. Greenwood tallied 37 points, but it wasn't enough; De Paul held on for the upset and captured the West regional.

However, the true Cinderella story of the tournament (and the decade) involved Ivy League champion University of Pennsylvania. Seeded ninth among the ten teams in the East, Penn snuck by Iona. Then, in Raleigh, North Carolina, the Quakers pulled one of the great upsets of all time. Using a deliberate game plan, Penn stunned the third-ranked team in the country, North Carolina, by 1 point. Next they ousted Syracuse and in the regional finals eked out a victory over St. John's. In two

And he can slam, too! Michigan State's sensational six-foot-nine-inch (206cm) point guard (!) Earvin "Magic" Johnson uses his long reach to dunk the ball over a set defender. A brilliant ball handler and an unrivaled passer, Magic single-handedly revolutionized basketball by shattering the conventional wisdom that guards were small, quick players.

weeks' time, the Quakers' cast of disciplined team players had emerged from obscurity to become folk heroes.

The Indiana State University (ISU) Sycamores entered the tournament as the nation's only undefeated team. The Sycamores consisted of a group of hard-nosed, hard-working Indiana ballplayers and an uncanny six-foot-nine-inch (206cm) senior forward named Larry Bird, who merely averaged 29 points, 14.8 rebounds, 6 assists, and 2.4 steals per game. Bird had been in the national spotlight since the autumn of 1977 when *Sports Illustrated* put him on the cover of its college basketball preview issue alongside a caption that declared Bird "College Basketball's Secret Weapon." Bird had earned the fame with a brilliant sophomore season in which he averaged 32.8 points and 13.3 rebounds, shot 54 percent from the floor, and led ISU to a 25–2 record. Shunned by the NCAA that spring, the Sycamores accepted an NIT bid, where they lost in the first round. The next season, Indiana State won its first 13 games and ascended to number four in the polls, but the team closed out the season 9–9, including another early exit from the NIT. Before his senior year, Bird was drafted by the Boston Celtics, but chose to return to Terre Haute to finish his college career. Bird was eligible for the draft after his junior season because he had actually begun college at the University of Indiana in the fall of 1974 (Bird lasted only twenty-four days in Bloomington before he felt intimidated by the big-town atmosphere and returned home to tiny French Lick to reevaluate his life.

Magic Johnson corrals a loose ball in front of Indiana State's Larry Bird during the 1979 NCAA finals. The Salt Lake City showdown between the two midwestern folk heroes was, of course, only chapter one in the Larry and Magic odyssey, which continued in the NBA with the decade-long rivalry between Bird's Celtics and Magic's Lakers.

Nevertheless, when Bobby Knight was asked who was the greatest player he ever had at Indiana, he replied, "Larry Bird," without hesitating, even though Bird never suited up for the Hoosiers. After a year back in French Lick, the local high school legend decided to attend ISU in low-key Terre Haute.) NBA rules at the time stated that a player could be drafted four years after he initially entered college. They also stated that if a player returned to school after being drafted, the team that drafted him retained his rights, at least until the next draft. So when Larry returned for his senior year, the Celtics and their fans held their breath and hoped their prized prospect would avoid injury. (Actually, Bird did injure himself twice; he broke his left thumb in the Missouri Valley Conference championship game, which

didn't sideline him even for a moment, and he mangled the index finger on his right hand in a softball game after the season. The softball mishap left Larry with a crooked finger, which, miraculously, did not affect his brilliant outside shooting.)

Of course, Bird and the Sycamores had a dream season in 1978–1979. On countless occasions, Larry's teammates stepped up to knock down big shots when opposing teams double- and triple-teamed the superstar. Indiana State finished the regular season 28–0 and then cruised past Virginia Tech and Big Eight champ Oklahoma. Next up was powerful Arkansas, led by its brilliant swingman Sidney Moncrief. The game was tight throughout. Bird was unstoppable until Arkansas coach Eddie Sutton called on Moncrief to guard "Larry the Legend." Moncrief succeeded in denying Bird the ball. With the game tied 71–all, Arkansas fumbled away a chance to hold for the last shot and the Sycamores gained possession. As the clock wound down, ISU got the ball in Bird's hands, but Moncrief was on him like a glove, so Bird passed off to guard Steve Reed, who found sixth man Bob Heaton. Against New Mexico State in the regular season, Heaton had hit the season's most dramatic shot, when he connected from fifty feet (15m) to send the game into overtime and preserve the Sycamores' perfect season. With their perfect season on the line in a game against Arkansas, Heaton connected again, and the Sycamores were headed for Salt Lake City.

Compared to the likes of Penn and Indiana State, Michigan State

University (MSU) had a big-time basketball program. But since losing in triple overtime versus North Carolina in the national semifinals twenty-two years earlier, the Spartans were perennial also-rans in the Big Ten. All that changed when Lansing's own Earvin "Magic" Johnson decided to stay at home and attend Michigan State after leading Everett High in South Lansing (a predominantly white high school across town that Earvin attended via court-ordered busing) to an undefeated season and the state title in his junior year. Earvin was a truly unique talent. Six feet nine inches (206cm) tall, with a powerful, agile body and tremendous ball-handling skills, Johnson could (and did) play any position on the court. But what set Earvin apart from everyone else was his passing. No-look, behind-the-back, triple-pump, pinpoint-precision, and thread-the-needle passes were all staples of his inexhaustible array of tricks. Magic! His teammates learned to expect the unexpected; opponents and audiences were awed. In his freshman year at Michigan State he turned a decent team, led by forward Greg Kelser and guard Jay Vincent, into a contender for the Big Ten and national titles. The Spartans made the tournament and in the regional finals gave the great Kentucky Wildcats a run for their money. Michigan State actually

The Michigan State strategy against Indiana State for the 1979 title game was simple: suffocate Larry Bird. Every time Larry touched the ball, two or three Spartans encircled him; consequently, the Sycamore superhero shot an uncharacteristic 33 percent and Michigan State cruised to the national title. Here, Jay Vincent closes down the baseline while Magic eyes the ball like a hawk from behind.

led the Wildcats at halftime before losing out to Kyle Macy's long-range bombs.

Expectations ran high for the 1978–1979 season. Magic graced the cover of *Sports Illustrated's* college hoops preview edition, just as Larry Bird had the year before. And like the Sycamores in 1977–1978, the Spartans began the season

on a roll, winning their first 13 games and ascending to number one in the wire service polls. Then, just like ISU the season before, MSU hit a midseason snag, suffering 5 defeats in a 9-game stretch. Fans grumbled that Magic and the Spartans had fallen victim to the legendary *Sports Illustrated* cover jinx. But the Spartans called a team meeting and decided to run a more open, freewheelin' offense in order to take full advantage of Magic's gifts. The strategy worked brilliantly. The Spartans won 13 of their remaining 14 games to take a share of the Big Ten title and head into the tournament, on a roll once again. They cruised through the Mideast regional with victories over Lamar, Louisiana State, and a tough Notre Dame team by margins of 31, 26, and 12 points, respectively.

Unfortunately for the Penn Quakers, they were the next obstacle in the path of the Michigan State juggernaut. Only one week after their crowning glory in the East regional, the Quakers were humiliated in front of a national audience. The score at halftime was 50–17. The Johnson-to-Kelser express was nonstop. Magic tallied 29 points, and Greg added 28, many of which came on spectacular slam dunks off alley-oops from Earvin. The final score was 101–67.

The De Paul–Indiana State semifinal matchup was a sharp contrast to the blowout that preceded it; from the opening tip-off it had the feel of a game that would go down to the wire. When the Sycamores, led by Bird's astonishing shooting, built an 11-point lead in the second half, the Blue Demons increased their defensive intensity, actually forced Bird into a series of turnovers, and, with less than five minutes remaining, moved ahead 73–71. From there, De Paul tried to freeze the game, but soon turned the ball over. Bird found Heaton for a layup. De Paul regained the lead, hitting 1 of 2 free throws, but another Heaton layup made the score 75–74, Indiana State. De Paul worked for the last shot, but Aguirre misfired with four seconds remaining. The Sycamores were headed to the final with an unblemished record of 33–0.

Larry Bird had made 16 of 19 shots for 35 points (all of which proved necessary), to go with 16 rebounds and 9 assists against De Paul. Magic had collected 10 rebounds and 10 assists to go with his 29 points, for a triple-double, in the Spartans' semifinal romp. The showdown was set; the nation was on the edge of its seat. It promised to be a match made in heaven, and aired during prime time.

Unfortunately, the game itself failed to live up to expectations. The Spartans kept two men on Bird at virtually all times, suffocating Larry's ability to score or even get into the offensive flow. Bird misfired on 14 of his 21 shots, finishing with 19 points and, even more alarming, only 2 assists. All season long, Bird's teammates had picked up the slack when opponents had focused on Larry, but the Sycamores couldn't keep pace with the Spartans. Michigan State built a 37–28 lead by intermission and coasted to victory. The Spartans were never seriously challenged throughout the tournament, winning their 5 games by an average of 22.8 points. Magic led all scorers in the final with 24 points and was named MVP. Magic and Larry would meet again, including three times in the NBA finals, but Magic won round one.

In 1967 the NCAA outlawed the dunk shot, presumably in an effort to contain the dominance of UCLA's Lew Alcindor, who had made a habit of effortlessly slamming the ball down opponents' throats. While Alcindor, undaunted, led the Bruins to the NCAA crown his remaining two seasons, the dunk was not decriminalized by the college game's governing body until before the 1976–1977 season. The reason for this rule reversal was the play's plainly telegenic appeal. In the interim between 1967 and 1977, the dunk became the signature shot of the most spectacular players in the professional ranks, most notably Julius Erving, alias Dr. J, who played first for the New York Nets and then for the Philadelphia 76ers. The influence of the fine Doctor and his slam-dunkin' brethren on the game of basketball can not be overestimated. Heirs to the tradition of African-American schoolyard ball with its emphasis on improvisation, one-upmanship, and aerial acrobatics, these seventies showmen expanded on the tradition established by Elgin Baylor. Fans who never made it to an American Basketball Association (ABA) game marveled at Dr. J's moves on the highlight reels of the nightly news. Kids across the nation knew that Darryl Dawkins, the Philadelphia 76ers' backboard-shattering behemoth known as "Chocolate Thunder" (who skipped college to go straight from high school to the NBA), named each of his monster jams. On playgrounds across the U.S.A., the same kids tried to emulate the in-flight gyrations of Denver's David "Skywalker" Thompson. During the seventies, both college and professional basketball became increasingly dominated by black players, whose flamboyant style of play was a reflection of seventies black culture, and nothing reflected this more than the dunk shot.

When dunking finally returned to college basketball there was, not surprisingly, an unprecedented outpouring of aerial creativity. And in the spring of 1980, the Louisville Cardinals, nicknamed the Doctors of Dunk, in homage to Erving, slammed and jammed their way to the national title led by a six-foot-three-inch (191cm) senior guard with a forty-eight-inch (122cm) vertical

Louisville's hometown hero, Darryl Griffith, elevates for an easy bucket. Of the greaest dunkers in basketball history, Griffith was the shortest, at only six feet three inches (191cm). Perhaps nothing in the sport is as astonishing as seeing a smaller man use his extraordinary athletic gifts to sky over taller men and slam the ball home. Griffith put on an exhibition of such moves during the Cardinals' drive for the national title in March 1980.

leap—Darryl Griffith, a.k.a. "Dr. Dunkenstein."

Following the climactic Larry/Magic showdown in 1979 there figured to be a power (and star) void at the top of college basketball in 1979–1980, but this space was quickly filled (appropriately enough) by the previous season's third-place finisher, De Paul. Led by the sensational Mark Aguirre, the Blue Demons completed the regular season with only 1 loss (though they played numerous close games) and entered the tournament ranked number one, poised to reward venerable coach Ray Meyer (the same man who tutored George Mikan to superstardom a few millennia earlier) with his first NCAA crown. However, the Blue Demons didn't make it past their first tournament game, losing to a UCLA team who had 9 regular-season losses and finished fourth in the Pac Eight. Larry Brown had succeeded Gary Cunningham as the Bruins coach, the third since John Wooden's triumphant retirement in the spring of 1975. The Bruins struggled early in the season but improved dramatically after midseason, when Brown inserted two freshmen guards, Rod Foster and Michael Holton, into the starting lineup. These two young men joined senior star forward Kiki Vandeweighe, defensive stalwart James (brother of Keith, a.k.a. Jamaal) Wilkes, and power forward–turned-center, six-foot-six-inch (198cm) Michael Sanders. Proving that their upset of De Paul was no fluke, the Bruins squeaked by a talent-laden Ohio State team with Clark Kellogg, Kelvin Ramsey, and Herb Williams, 72–68, and then ousted Clemson 84–75 to reach the Final Four for the first time since 1976.

The NCAA tourney expanded in 1980 to include forty-eight teams; for the first time in the history of the tournament, up to four teams were allowed from any conference (the old limit was two). Thus, when Purdue and Iowa, the third- and fourth-place finishers in the Big Ten, respectively, survived their regionals to advance to Indianapolis, there was the strange circumstance that three of the four national semifinalists would not have even qualified for the tournament in the previous year. This came as no shock to many observers, since the 1979–1980 season reflected the increasing parity in college basketball. During one midseason week, nine of the top twenty teams lost. The new equality in college hoops was attributed in part to a recent rule change that limited the number of basketball scholarships per school to fifteen, which meant that top-rung talent was spread among more schools.

At any rate, the Purdue Boilermakers and the Iowa Hawkeyes made the most of their tournament bid just like UCLA did. Purdue was led by their dominant All-American seven-foot-one-inch (216cm) center Joe Barry Carroll and was coached by Lee Rose, who had led UNCC to its unexpected (and dramatic) appearance in the Final Four only three years earlier. The Boilermakers dismissed La Salle and St. John's in a subregional played on their home court. They then traveled to Lexington, Kentucky, for the regionals. While most expected a showdown in the finals between Indiana and Kentucky, the two regional dynasties who rarely met, Duke stunned heavily favored Kentucky, and Purdue upset its interstate rival, despite the fact that Carroll was held to just 11 points. In the regional finals Joe Barry busted loose with 28 points as Purdue dismissed Duke to reach the Final Four. Iowa, meanwhile, consisted of a very talented group that had been hampered by injuries all year long. Star guard Ronnie Lester, the team's second-leading light, had midseason knee surgery (the Hawkeyes lost 7 of 15 games in his absence). Kenny Arnold played through a broken thumb, while two other prominent Hawkeyes, Vince Brookins and Mark Gannon, fought through injuries all season long. Once in the tournament, this torn and tattered crew caught fire, knocking off Virginia Commonwealth, NC State, and Syracuse before squeaking by Georgetown and sensational shooting guard Eric "Sleepy" Floyd, on center Steve Waite's 3-point play in the final seconds. Iowa had trailed by as many as 14 points early in

Louisville's Denny Crum stands alongside Indiana's Bobby Knight and UNC's Dean Smith as the most successful head coach of the post-Wooden era. While Crum's calm demeanor at game time and his friendly relationships with his players contrasts sharply with disciplinarians like Knight, it is often misinterpreted as a hands-off approach. In fact, Coach Crum, like his mentor John Wooden, makes his primary mark at practice time, emphasizing preparation and execution.

the second half but then stormed back, hitting 71 percent from the floor and 15 straight free throws in the second half to eke out the 81–80 victory and move on to Indianapolis.

The only pretournament favorite to make it to Indianapolis was Louisville. Since Denny Crum left John Wooden's side to take the reins in Louisville, the Cardinals had experienced unprecedented success mixed with adversity. Twice, in 1973 and in 1975, the Cardinals reached the Final Four only to lose to Wooden's Bruins in the semifinals, the second time in heartbreaking fashion. In 1976 the Cardinals had cause to celebrate when Louisville's own Darryl Griffith agreed to stay home and join the Cardinals along with his sidekick, Bobby Turner, who with Griffith had led Male High to a two-year reign atop Kentucky high school basketball. But things didn't go as planned during the Griffith era. Turner dropped out because of academic problems and the Cardinals failed to make it back to the Final Four. Griffith's junior year ended in ignominy as the star was badly outplayed by Arkansas' Sidney Moncrief in the 1979 regional semifinal, in which Louisville was eliminated.

Griffith entered his senior year with the entire weight of four years of expectations on his shoulders. To complicate things further, not only did Griffith have to struggle with switching from guard to forward, but his supporting cast was severely depleted. And not only was Turner gone, but starting center Scooter McCray's season ended with a knee injury before Christmas. With the team struggling, Crum shook things up, moving last year's floor leader, Tony Branch, to the bench in favor of sophomore Jerry Eaves and inserting six-foot-seven-inch (201 cm) freshman Rodney McCray, Scooter's younger brother, into the starting lineup at center. Filling out the starting five were two underclass forwards, six-foot-eight-inch (203 cm) Wiley Brown and six-foot-six-inch (198 cm) Derek Smith. Crum called upon this relatively short but tremendously athletic bunch to make up for their height deficiency by utilizing a full-court press throughout each game. The young Cardinals responded brilliantly, wreaking havoc on opposing teams' offenses (their secret weapon here was reserve guard Roger Burkman, who was perhaps the leading defender in the country) and generating countless turnovers that translated into easy buckets, often in the form of high-flying, crowd-thrilling, gasp-inducing slam dunks. All of the Cardinals could slam impressively, but the unrivaled master was Dr. Dunkenstein himself, Darryl Griffith. One poor soul given the unenviable task of having to guard Griffith echoed the words spoken of Elgin Baylor, David Thompson, Dr. J, and, in a few years, Michael Jordan, when he said, "I've guarded other players who could leap as high as Griffith. But all of them came down." Indeed, audiences were mesmerized at the sight of the six-foot-three-inch (191 cm) Griffith soaring over centers. And Griffith was not all show; he was also a brilliant defender, passer, and rebounder. Prospering under Crum's new system, Griffith averaged 22.9 points a game, was a consensus All-American, and led the Cardinals to a 28–3 record heading into the tournament.

The Cardinals' road to the Final Four was bumpy, to say the least. In their first game, Kansas State extended the Cardinals to overtime and Griffith fouled out early in the extra period. Off the bench came senior Tony Branch, who had taken only 29 shots all year, but he buried a long-range jumper at the buzzer to give Louisville a 71–69 victory. In the next round, against Texas A&M, Louisville was again forced into overtime. The Cardinals' defensive pressure at the end proved too much for the Aggies, however, and Louisville won

Louisville's Rodney McCray rises above the fray for a short jumper against UCLA in the 1980 championship finals. Freshman McCray became the Cardinals' starting center when his older brother Scooter was sidelined with an injury before midseason. Only six feet seven inches (201 cm) tall, Rodney used his superior leaping ability (as did so many of the Cardinals, also known as the Doctors of Dunk) to hold his own in the middle.

going away. In the regional final, Louisville finally had a breather, trouncing highly ranked LSU, and headed to Indianapolis as the favorite alongside three underdogs. After the regional final, Coach Crum said, "There is something about this team, they love each other, they play hard and they play together." Reserve swingman Pancho Wright summed things up a little differently: "The Ville [Louisville] is going to the Nap [Indianapolis]."

In the national semifinals, Iowa fell behind Louisville early and things looked bleak for the Hawkeyes when Ronnie Lester limped off the court with a knee injury. But Iowa hung tough without their leader and kept the game close throughout. However, Griffith was too much: red hot from the outside, the All-American hit 14 of 21 shots from the field and finished with 34 points. Louisville won 80–72 and headed to its first championship game. There the Cardinals

faced their old nemesis UCLA, who had contained Purdue's Carroll in the matchup between John Wooden's alma mater and the school he had coached to ten national titles. Kiki Vandeweighe led all scorers with 24, the Bruins were ahead most of the way, and made their free throws down the stretch to claim a 67–62 victory.

The 1980 final was a rematch of the dramatic 1975 national semifinal, in which Louisville had an opportunity to close out the eventual national champions but misfired from the free throw line at the crucial moment. Of course, the Wizard of Westwood was gone from the Bruins bench in 1980, but Coach Brown

An airborne James Worthy tries to manuever past a Ralph Sampson roadblock during the 1981 NCAA semifinals, one of the many legendary Virginia-UNC showdowns of this era. The seven-foot-four-inch (224cm) Sampson was, along with Patrick Ewing, a dominant figure during the college basketball boom of the early 1980s, though Sampson's failure to lead his Cavaliers to a national crown (and his brief, injury-plagued NBA career) severely tarnished his legacy.

(who would develop a reputation as a coaching genius himself over the next decade, eventually winning a national title at Kansas in 1988) captured some of the old UCLA mystique when he reintroduced Wooden's favored high-post offense at midseason. So Crum, himself a disciple of John Wooden, couldn't have asked for a better opportunity to exorcise some old demons.

But with just four minutes to go in the final game, it must have seemed like déjà vu to Crum as the Bruins led 54–50. Kiki Vandeweighe stole the ball and raced downcourt for a bucket that would have given the Bruins a commanding 6-point lead. But Louisville's Jerry Eaves raced back, caught up to Vandeweighe,

and disrupted the shot. Wiley Brown corralled the rebound, fed an outlet pass to Griffith who brought the ball upcourt, and found Eaves, who, having hustled back on offense, buried a jumper. It was the turning point of a tightly fought game in which both teams shot poorly. UCLA hit only 36 percent from the field; Louisville canned 46 percent, but struggled, 11–20, from the charity stripe. When UCLA held a 28–26 halftime lead,

Coach Crum told his players they were choking, but then apologized for his uncharacteristic accusation and, perhaps realizing the best way to motivate such a freewheelin' bunch, told the Cardinals "he loved 'em and to go out and have some fun." But UCLA played well, refusing to be undone by the Cardinals' unrelenting defensive pressure, and led until, with 2:52 remaining, Eaves scored his second straight basket, a layup off a feed from Griffith. After another defensive stop, the Cardinals finally took the lead on a long-range bomb from Griffith, who with 23 points was the only Cardinal in double digits and would be named tournament MVP. UCLA didn't score again, and Louisville closed the game on a 9–0 run for a 59–54 victory. It remains UCLA's only loss in twelve appearances in the finals and perhaps appropriately it came at the hands of one of John Wooden's greatest disciples, Denny Crum. Like Wooden, Crum proved he was able to adjust his coaching to fit the strengths of his players. In the case of the 1980 Louisville Cardinals, this meant devising a system in which the flamboyant athleticism of the Doctors of Dunk could flourish.

As in 1979–1980, parity remained a central theme of the 1980–1981 Division I men's basketball scene. And perhaps the season's most memorable event (or series of events) was the avalanche of upsets in the early rounds of the NCAA tournament. The NBC television network had recently expanded its coverage of the tournament to include an assortment of early-round games, and when two or more games were happening simultaneously the network showed frequent highlights of other games in action. This let the viewing audience keep abreast of many games simultaneously. Rarely before had a televised sporting event produced as much heart-stopping drama as did the first weekend of the 1981 NCAA tourney. Kansas State upset the top seed in the West, Oregon State; James Madison ousted powerful Georgetown; and for the second straight year De Paul entered the tournament ranked number one and fell prey in the first round, this time to tiny St. Joseph's of Philadelphia, 49–48. But the most astonishing moment came when defending champion Louisville was eliminated on a fifty-foot (15m) buzzer-beater by Arkansas' U.S. Reed. The nation's sports fans were riveted to their television sets. When CBS purchased the television rights to the tournament in the offseason, it knew it had a winner.

Of course, the flurry of first-round excitement was a product of the increasingly even field in college basketball. By 1981, it seemed remarkable that college hoops was only six years removed from the dominance of the Wooden dynasty. Commentators frequently credited the 1973 rule that limited the number of full basketball scholarships a school could award with decreasing the advantage of the top schools. (The ceiling was set at eighteen scholarships per school in 1973 and lowered again to fifteen in 1977; it's now at thirteen.) However, something else was also occurring: basketball's popularity was growing exponentially. Over the past few decades, roundball had become the staple of high school winter athletics. By the 1970s every American boy who was at all athletically inclined played basketball. And in black American culture the sport had found a central role; it was more widely played than either football or baseball. By the late seventies there was an increasingly large pool of talent from which Division I college basketball programs could draw.

prominence. Indiana still had Bobby Knight, who was brilliant at teaching disciplined, fundamentally sound basketball. Coach Knight's basic strategy went like this: play airtight, unrelenting defense, and on offense have the patience to work for a high, very high, percentage shot. The strategy was simple and to the point, and in the hands of Bobby Knight, deadly.

In 1981, Knight faced a unique challenge. He had perhaps the most brilliant and creative point guard in the nation in sophomore Isiah Thomas, but Thomas was prone to bouts of spontaneous improvisation and spectacular creativity—not exactly Bobby Knight basketball. So Knight took some drastic measures to school his star pupil in the ways of

But the new world order, where basketball was played with equal fervor across the nation, did not mean that a traditional power like Indiana, who in its storied past had drawn its players exclusively from its basketball-crazy region, would lose its

Indiana's brilliant point guard Isiah Thomas beats North Carolina's King Rice (21) downcourt for a layup during the 1981 NCAA finals. While many considered Thomas the antithesis of a Bobby Knight player—spontaneously creative and flashy—the sophomore point guard proved beyond a doubt during the Hoosiers 1981 title run that he could discipline his skills for the good of the team (as he did during his legendary NBA career with the Detroit Pistons).

Indiana basketball. With the team off to a shaky start, Knight got so frustrated by Thomas' overly creative playmaking that he threw Isiah out of practice. A little while later, in a showdown with North Carolina at Chapel Hill, Thomas threw 2 errant passes and Knight benched his floor leader for the remainder of the reasonably close game (a 9-point loss). With the Hoosiers a disappointing 7–5, Knight then turned around and named Thomas cocaptain of the team and gave him free rein to run the team within Knight's system. This peculiar brand of psychologizing by Knight worked wonders as the team came together for the Big Ten season. Alongside Thomas, the Hoosiers started their one senior, six-foot-nine-inch (206cm) Ray Tolbert, sharpshooting guard Randy Wittman, and a solid role-playing forward, Ted Kitchel. In February, six-foot-ten-inch (208cm) junior Landon Turner, who had been so erratic in his career at Indiana that Knight had once declared that Turner would never again play for the varsity, worked his way into the starting lineup. Complementing this starting five was six-foot-three-inch (191cm) sixth man Jim Thomas. This Hoosier squad kept getting stronger as the season progressed. They won the Big Ten title and entered the tournament on a roll despite a 21–9 record. The Hoosiers didn't relent in the postseason, sweeping into the Final Four with resounding victories (by an average of 27 points) over Maryland, Alabama-Birmingham, and Cinderella-like St. Joseph's.

Joining the Hoosiers at the Philadelphia Spectrum, where Bobby Knight's troops had capped off their undefeated season with the NCAA title in 1976, were two teams from the ACC, Virginia and North Carolina, and LSU, of the Southeastern Conference. Dale

Putting up a soft jump hook, Georgetown's freshman center Patrick Ewing unveils his "winter collection," the signature all-cotton, gray T-shirt worn beneath his Hoya uniform. While Ewing's play at Georgetown rightly earned him a place among the college game's all-time great centers, he also had an impact on basketball fashion, introducing the layered-jersey look that has been the rage ever since.

Brown's LSU Tigers won the Midwest regional behind the strong play of guard Howard Carter and forward Durand Macklin. The Tigers routed Lamar and Arkansas and then handled a strong Wichita State team led by Antoine Carr and Cliff Levingston rather easily. Against Knight's Hoosiers, LSU got the

better of the play in the first half, leading 30–27 at intermission. Indiana returned to score the first 11 points of the second frame, 7 by Landon Turner. But it was Indiana's defense that turned the game into a lopsided affair. LSU scored only 19 points in the second half of the 67–49 contest, the Tigers' lowest point total in seventeen years.

The other semifinal featured the two marquee teams of the ACC season. North Carolina had lost four starters from the previous season, but coach Dean Smith surrounded Al Wood, his senior star forward, with a talented cast of youngsters: sophomore forward James Worthy, freshman center Sam Perkins, junior guard Jimmy Black, and freshman sixth man Matt Doherty. This troupe finished the season 25–7 after a slow start and downed Pittsburgh, Utah (on the Utes' home court), and Kansas State to emerge from the West regional. Virginia was led by the national player of the year, seven-foot-four-inch (224cm) center Ralph Sampson. Sampson averaged 17.7 points and 11.5 rebounds per game, and was a dominating defensive presence and the talk of the basketball world in the winter and spring of 1981. A competent cast of role players joined Sampson on the Cavaliers, including deadeye shooting guard Jeff Lamp, who was the team's leading scorer with an 18.2 average. The Cavs marched through the regular season to an ACC title and a 25–3 record and earned a number one seed in the

East regional. Despite Sampson's poor play in the first two rounds, Virginia defeated Villanova and Tennessee; then the big man came to life against a Brigham Young team led by Fred Roberts and Danny Ainge (who had knocked off Notre Dame by dribbling the length of the court for a buzzer-beating, game-winning basket), scoring 22 points in the 74–60 Virginia victory.

With its win over BYU, Virginia earned its third meeting with UNC in the national semifinals, Virginia having won the previous two contests. In both earlier games, North Carolina had held big leads (of 12 and 16 points, each in the second half) only to see Virginia storm back to win. This time the teams played to a draw in the first half, 27–27. But the second half belonged to the Tarheels and Al Wood. While the UNC defense was busy collapsing on a frustrated Sampson, Wood registered a performance for the ages, shooting 14 of 19 from the field for 39 points, to pace a 78–65 UNC victory. Virginia coach Terry Holland, who tried every conceivable strategy to try to contain Wood (who had scored 51 points in the 2 Tarheel losses to Virginia), said after the game, "You almost had to stand up and cheer even if you're on the opposite bench."

The 1981 final brought together two coaching legends and two red-hot teams (with less-than-impressive overall records) in a rematch of an early season contest won by North Carolina. However, the atmosphere surrounding the game was transformed dramatically when an assassin shot and wounded President Reagan early in the day. The NCAA governing committee, the CBS television network, and representatives of the two schools discussed whether to postpone the game. The consolation game was played (the last such contest ever held in the tournament) and won by Virginia, but the decision to play the final was not made until thirty minutes before tip-off. The decisive factor was the news that the president was no longer in danger, that he would survive the injury. Once the game began, the sense of crisis lifted and basketball moved to center stage. The Tarheels were quick out of the gate, building a

16–8 lead behind the scoring of Perkins and Wood. Knight made some adjustments, putting defensive stalwart Jim Thomas into the game to shadow Wood, and switching Turner over to defend Perkins. Randy Wittman got hot, and his outside jumper at the halftime buzzer gave the Hoosiers their first lead, 27–26. Isiah set the tone for the second half when he stole the ball and cruised in for a layup for the first score after intermission. Indiana quickly built an 11-point lead and coasted to a 63–50 victory. The Indiana defense smothered Wood, Perkins, and Worthy, whose totals in the second half combined for only 5 points. Offensively, Isiah Thomas led the way, scoring 19 of his 23 points after intermission, and was named tournament MVP.

The decisive Indiana victory handed Bobby Knight his second NCAA title in six years (he would win his third six years later). The immediate future looked bright for the Hoosiers; in fact, it seemed they would have a good chance to repeat, losing only Tolbert among their key contributors. However, Isiah followed his friend Magic Johnson's lead and headed for the NBA after winning the national title in his sophomore year, and, tragically, Landon Turner was paralyzed in an automobile accident in the off-season.

With the national champion hobbled by its player losses, the 1981–1982 season had no dominant team and, indeed, was packed with drama from start to finish. In the ACC, Virginia and North Carolina continued their epic battle for supremacy; the two superteams split the season series, and then UNC won an absurd grudge match in the ACC tournament title game in which Smith had his team play a four-corners stall throughout the entire contest (a game that went a long way towards inspiring the establishment of shot clocks throughout college basketball). Every game Sampson played on the road was a big event, recalling the days of Alcindor or Walton. John Thompson's Georgetown Hoyas became the focus of national media attention as Patrick Ewing, the seven-foot (213cm) freshman sensation with an eight-foot (244cm) wingspan (who single-handedly spawned a new

look in college basketball by wearing a gray T-shirt underneath his tank top jersey), joined an already strong team led by All-American shooting guard Eric "Sleepy" Floyd. A midseason showdown between Ewing's Hoyas and high-ranked Missouri, led by their own seven-foot (213cm) star, Steve Steponovich, produced tremendous excitement. Meanwhile, Mark Aguirre and De Paul were on their way to another tremendous regular season and another stunning first-round elimination from the tournament. Likewise, Alabama-Birmingham shocked Sampson and Virginia in the regional semifinals.

The four survivors who made it to New Orleans were top-ranked North Carolina, Louisville, Houston, and Georgetown. Georgetown had won the first rounds of the NCAAs by trouncing Wyoming and Fresno State, and then handily dismantled fourth-ranked Oregon State by shooting a tournament record 74.4 percent from the field. Louisville started four players from the 1980 championship team—Rodney McCray, Jerry Eaves, Derek Smith, and Poncho Wright—alongside sophomore guard Lancaster Gordon. The Cardinals finished the regular season only 20–9, but made the most of their bid to the tournament by dismissing Middle Tennessee State (who had upset Kentucky, thus preventing the long-awaited "Bluegrass State Showdown"), high-ranked Minnesota, and Alabama-Birmingham. Houston, meanwhile, entered the tournament virtually unnoticed and proceeded to capture the public's imagination. The leader of the '82 Cougars was guard Rob Williams, who averaged 21.1 points per game. Williams' young supporting cast included high-flying forward Clyde Drexler, solidly built Larry Micheaux, outside threat Michael Young, and a seven-foot (213cm) reserve center with unbelievable physical gifts but very unrefined basketball skills, Akeem "The Dream" Olajuwon. The Cougars got by Alcorn State and Tulsa, upset favored Missouri (in St. Louis), and downed Boston College to reach New Orleans. Meanwhile the top-ranked Tarheels had to hold their breath in their first game as they squeaked by James

Madison, 52–50, and then warded off a challenge from a feisty Alabama team before solidly beating Villanova in the regional finals.

Both national semifinals produced close contests. North Carolina jumped out to a 14–0 lead on Houston, but the Cougars battled back to trail by only 2 at intermission. However, the Tarheels were never headed, and the story of the game was the defense played by UNC senior guard Jimmy Black against Rob Williams. The Houston star failed to score from the field in the 68–63 North Carolina victory. The Georgetown-Louisville battle was also heavy on defense. The Hoyas outscored the Cardinals by 2 points in each half and escaped with a hard-fought 50–46 victory.

Thus the stage was set for one of the great games in college basketball history: Georgetown versus UNC, John Thompson versus Dean Smith, and Patrick Ewing and Sleepy Floyd versus James Worthy, Sam Perkins, and Michael Jordan. It was a brilliant game at the time and has only grown in stature since. Thompson kept his troops far away from the media, as was his policy, and even had his Hoyas staying in a hotel in Biloxi, Mississippi, some sixty miles (96.5km) from New Orleans. When reminded that he was the first black coach to guide his team to the finals, Thompson retorted, "I don't want to be the first black nothing." Smith for his part played down the significance of failing to capture a national title in any of his six previous trips to the Final Four and three finals. The media also had a field day with the fact that All-Americans Floyd and Worthy both came from the same small hometown of Gastonia, North Carolina. The excitement was tangible as a record-breaking crowd of 61,612 packed into the Superdome for the final. North Carolina had an impeccable starting five with center Perkins, forward Worthy, and freshman phenom Jordan at guard, complemented by textbook role players Jimmy Black and Matt Doherty. For Georgetown, Ewing and Floyd were joined by senior swingman Eric Smith, power forward Mike Hancock, and a freshman point guard, Fred Brown. All the Hoyas played suffocating defense.

The game got off to a scintillating start as Ewing swatted away everything North Carolina threw at the basket. Four times the freshman was called for goaltending, accounting for the Tarheels' first 8 points; nevertheless it was one of the most intimidating displays of defense in tournament history. Ewing had sent a message all the way to Carolina: don't even think about penetrating to the hoop—the middle is mine. In fact, during Ewing's first thirteen and a half minutes on the court, Carolina was unable to put the ball in the basket for a field goal. Behind this defensive display, the Hoyas catapulted to an early 6-point lead, but after UNC fought back to tie the game at 18, neither team would ever lead by more than 4 points. Worthy caught fire midway through the first half, while Ewing and Floyd responded for Georgetown, giving the Hoyas a 32–31 lead at intermission. A master strategist, Smith devised plays for Worthy along the baseline, below Ewing, and he called on his team to beat the Georgetown defense downcourt whenever possible. Still, Georgetown kept a slight advantage, but when Sleepy Floyd missed a breakaway layup with his team ahead 47–43, the Tarheels responded with a flourish to take the lead. But the game stayed close and the tension mounted. Jordan gave the Tarheels a 3-point advantage, 61–58, but Ewing hit a turnaround and with just less than a minute remaining the Hoyas seized the lead when Floyd buried a difficult jumper. The Tarheels moved the ball upcourt, passed it around the perimeter, and then called time-out with thirty-two seconds remaining and Georgetown leading 62–61. The next sequence is among the most memorable in college basketball history.

In the huddle, Smith told his players that Georgetown would be expecting them to try to get the ball to either Perkins or Worthy, so he wanted them to work for a good medium-range jumper. He singled out freshman Jordan for the shot. As the team took the floor, the coaching legend, who was looking for his long-awaited first title, whispered to the high-flyin' frosh, "Knock it in, Michael." The Tarheels proceeded to work the ball around the perimeter, faking passes into the low post; with seventeen seconds remaining, Jordan came open on the left wing, received the ball, and smoothly buried a high-arcing jumper. Georgetown quickly passed the ball inbounds and, without hesitating or even considering a time-out, moved the ball upcourt for one last shot at the title. As freshman point guard Fred Brown dribbled over half court, the massive crowd was riveted by the drama. Then Brown picked up his dribble and looked to pass to his teammate Eric Smith, but Smith thought he had seen a seam in the Tarheels' defense and had moved toward the hoop, while James Worthy, misreading Brown's actions, jumped into the passing lane behind Brown. As Smith moved toward the North Carolina basket, Brown, in one of the most memorable gaffes in sports history, passed the ball directly to Worthy. The Tarheel junior dribbled the ball downcourt into a corner where he was caught and fouled with two seconds left. Though Worthy missed both foul shots, Georgetown failed to get off another shot. As the final whistle sounded, the Tarheels and their fans erupted in celebration while Coach Thompson consoled Fred Brown. In the most improbable and dramatic fashion, Dean Smith's North Carolina Tarheels were finally NCAA champions.

It seemed unlikely that the 1983 championship game could equal the dramatic intensity of the previous year's final. The high-flying Houston Cougars, alias Phi Slamma Jamma, were heavily favored over the Cinderella-story North Carolina State Wolfpack. Throughout the game, fans anticipated the seemingly inevitable rout; the only question was how long NC State could hold on. But the game stayed close and the tension continued to grow, building to one of the most exciting climaxes in NCAA history.

The road to Albuquerque was packed with teams more heralded than Jim Valvano's Wolfpack. The top-ranked team in the nation was Houston, who had opened up its offense once Rob Williams had moved on to the pros. Venerable coach Guy Lewis could sit back, relax, and watch his team trounce opponent after opponent with spectacular displays of aerial acrobatics led by the likes of Clyde Drexler, Larry Micheaux, Michael Young, and the ever-improving Akeem Olajuwon. The team entered the tournament with a 27–2 record and by the time they erased Maryland, Memphis State, and Villanova and headed to the Final Four, commentators were openly speculating about whether the Cougars could compete in the NBA (an interesting thought, since twelve years later Drexler and Olajuwon would be reunited on the Houston Rockets and storm to the NBA championship).

The Cougars' opponent on semifinal Saturday was the second-ranked University of Louisville, who was making its third appearance in the Final Four in four years. Back were the McCray brothers, Lancaster Gordon, sophomore guard Milt Wagner (who had emerged as the team's leading scorer), and junior Charles Jones, the starting center. Also coming off the bench was a highly touted freshman forward, Billy Thompson. The Cardinals reached the NCAAs with a 29–3 record, knocked out Tennessee, snuck by Arkansas and Joe Klein, and finally encountered their in-state rivals, the University of Kentucky. For years Louisville had been longing to square off against its Bluegrass State rivals, but the athletic directors of the Kentucky program had shied away from the encounter; after all, Kentucky had perhaps the greatest of all college basketball traditions, relative to which Louisville was a mere upstart. In 1982, the Wildcats featured a powerful interior duo of sevenfoot (213 cm) Sam Bowie and six-foot-eleven-inch (211 cm) Melvin Turpin. The showdown was no letdown. Jim Master pulled the Wildcats even at 62 to send the game to overtime. But in the extra period, Louisville was too much, outscoring the Wildcats 18–6, and the Cardinals were on their way to a showdown in Albuquerque with the Houston Cougars.

Freshman Michael Jordan knocks down a mid-range jumper to lift North Carolina over Georgetown for the national title. Besides the obvious, the picture captures the pre-endorsement Airness: notice Mike is wearing Converse All-Stars, while Georgetown's Eric Smith has the (not-yet-popular) Nikes. Jordan credited this shot with providing him with the confidence to take a game over. Jordan did just that time and again during his next two seasons at UNC, blossoming into a superstar.

The single most stunning moment in NCAA tournament history: North Carolina State's Lorenzo Charles drops the ball in the hoop just before the buzzer sounds (having caught Derrick Wittenberg's desperation shot at the side of the basket) to topple overwhelmingly favored Houston and capture the 1983 national title, 64–62. Charles' unforgettable moment of glory unfolded so suddenly and unexpectedly that its significance has yet to register on the faces of teammate Thurl Bailey and Houston's Akeem Olajuwon and Michael Young, who are positioned under the basket expecting a rebound.

While the top two teams in the nation survived the Midwest and Southeast regionals, the East and West regionals were Cinderella brackets. In the East, the University of Georgia, perennial cellar dwellers in the Southeastern Conference, compiled a 21–9 regular-season record and earned an at-large tournament bid. Coach Hugh Durham had built a strong basketball team in recent years at a school known for its football. However, expectations for the 1982–1983 Bulldogs were not high since they had lost superforward Dominique Wilkins, who had left the team a year early for the NBA. The on-floor leadership of the team was handed over to smooth guard Vern Fleming. With Fleming playing brilliantly, the Bulldogs got hot at the right time, eliminating Virginia Commonwealth and then pulling off two amazing upsets to reach the Final Four; they first downed third-ranked St. John's, led by brilliant shooting

forward Chris Mullin, and then upset defending champion North Carolina with its pair of All-Americans, Michael Jordan and Sam Perkins.

North Carolina State's string of upsets was even more amazing—perhaps the most improbable run in college basketball history. Jim Valvano's troops finished the regular season with a mere 17–10 record and probably realized that an at-large bid to the NCAA tournament was unlikely. But in the ACC, the automatic bid for the conference champion has always been determined by the conference tournament. In the first round of

the ACC tourney, the Wolfpack, who finished fourth during the regular season, trailed Wake Forest in the second half, but a spirited comeback gave them a 71–70 victory. They were on their way. Next up was North Carolina with Jordan and Perkins. The Pack played its in-state rival tough but found itself down by 6 with just over two minutes remaining. Coach Valvano ordered his troops to foul intentionally and the strategy worked to a T. UNC misfired from the free throw line and NC State closed the game on a 17–4 run. In the final against fourth-ranked Virginia and Ralph Sampson, who had already beaten NC State twice during the season, the Wolfpack once again came from behind in the second frame to take the conference title and win a trip to the NCAA tournament.

NC State was a mature bunch, led by a trio of seniors, lithe six-foot-eleven-inch (211 cm) Thurl Bailey and two rotund, long-range bombing guards,

Sidney Lowe and Dereck Wittenberg. Complementing this trio were sophomores Lorenzo Charles, a rock-solid six-foot-seven-inch (201 cm) forward, and six-foot-eleven-inch (211 cm) center Cozell McQueen, plus two key backups, swingman Ernie Myers and sharpshooting guard Terry Gannon. The Wolfpack competed in the West regional where they proceeded to fall behind Pepperdine in the first round. With twenty-four seconds remaining, Pepperdine was at the foul line, and leading by 6. Miraculously, Pepperdine missed 3 consecutive free throws and the Wolfpack scored 3 quick baskets to force overtime. Two extra periods later, NC State advanced 69–67. In the next round, UNLV led the Pack by 12 with eleven minutes remaining. But NC State scratched its way back and with four seconds left, Thurl Bailey tapped in a missed Dereck Wittenberg jumper for a 71–70 victory. Gaining confidence as they went along, and with Wittenberg and Lowe shooting with consistency from extremely long range (well beyond the NBA's old 3-point line, making it seem sometimes as if the jumpers were flying from half court), the Wolfpack quickly became the darlings of the tournament. After an uncharacteristic blowout of Utah, the Wolfpack squared off against a familiar opponent, Virginia, who was bloodthirsty for revenge after losing to NC State in the ACC finals. Not surprisingly, Virginia led in the second half, but Lorenzo Charles' 2 free throws in the final minute put the Pack ahead 63–62. The Cavs had two chances to win the game in the closing seconds, but both shots misfired. Ralph Sampson's brilliant college career came to an abrupt and disappointing end, while the Wolfpack headed to the Pit in Albuquerque.

The NC State–Georgia semifinal was close throughout. The Wolfpack built a small lead and held on down the stretch for a relatively comfortable 67–60 victory. Wittenberg and Bailey led the way with 20 points each. Despite the Wolfpack's heroics, most analysts considered the showdown between number one Houston and number two Louisville to be the true national championship game. From start to finish, the game did not

lack for high-flying excitement; rarely have two teams with such awesome athletic ability met in the Final Four. Louisville played a solid first half and led 41–36 at intermission. With thirteen minutes to play, the Cardinals had extended their lead to 8 points. Then the Cougars turned on the afterburners and went on a devastating 21–1 run, highlighted by a series of breathtaking slam dunks. Keying the Houston charge was the young Nigerian Akeem Olajuwon, who had begun playing basketball only four years earlier. In the second half alone, Olajuwon had 13 points (of a game-high 21), 4 blocks, and 15 rebounds. With less than eight minutes to play, Houston held a commanding 12-point lead and cruised to a 94–81 victory.

Heading into the final, NC State's mercurial coach, Jim Valvano, who charmed the media throughout the tournament with his puckish insights, quipped, "If we get the opening tip, we won't take a shot till Tuesday morning." In spite of NC State's heroics and their increasingly strong play throughout the tournament, few people, if any, gave the Wolfpack much of a chance against the likes of Phi Slamma Jamma. However, NC State succeeded in controlling the tempo of the game in the first half and built a 33–25 lead at intermission. Even so, everyone in the Pit was anticipating an outburst by the Cougars like the one that leveled Louisville. So far the keys for NC State were a slow pace on offense that worked for a good shot and the Pack's ability to get back on defense to contain the Cougars' lethal transition game. As predicted, Houston went on a run after the break; Olajuwon dominated on both ends of the court and Houston outscored NC State 17–2 for a 7-point lead. Then, Houston made a tactical error as they tried to play a more contained, controlled style. The Wolfpack regained some momentum as guards Lowe, Wittenberg, and Gannon hit a few of their signature long-range jumpers and forced a couple of turnovers. However, with three minutes left the Wolfpack still trailed 52–46. But the Cougars had an Achilles heel: they were a notoriously bad free throw–shooting team, and Valvano knew it. Indeed, after

NC State moved within 4 points, they fouled Michael Young, who missed his first free throw; Wittenberg then cut the deficit in half. Olajuwon misfired from the charity stripe; Wittenberg tied the score. The invincible Phi Slamma Jamma was on the ropes; all the momentum was with the "Cardiac Kids" from NC State. Valvano told his troops to try for a steal and not to be shy about fouling. The result was Cougar Alvin Franklin missing yet another free throw; the Pack controlled the boards, and with the game still knotted at 52, Valvano ordered his team to hold for the final shot. However, the Wolfpack never got into a flow on offense and as the final seconds ticked away in regulation time, Dereck

Jimmy Valvano, hoisted above the fray, strikes a regal pose and revels in NC State's miraculous 1983 NCAA title. In the course of one month Coach Valvano went from obscurity to become both the clown prince and reigning monarch of college hoops. Overflowing with comic exuberance, Valvano was a brilliant motivator. And as he guided his unlikely cast of underdogs to the promised land in the early spring of 1983, he seemed to personify the very spirit of college basketball.

Wittenberg was so far away from the basket he was even outside of his range. He put up a desperation shot, which fell comically short. But out of nowhere two hands reached up, grabbed the ball, and stuffed it through the hoop as time expired. The hands belonged to Lorenzo Charles. Pandemonium ensued at the Pit. Valvano led the frenzied charge onto the court as the Wolfpack exploded in celebration and the Cougars collapsed to the court in dismay. NC State had pulled off a stunning, thrilling upset, 54–52, and for the second straight year the NCAA final was one for the ages.

The most memorable episode of the 1984 NCAA tournament came in the national semifinal showdown between Kentucky, with its twin towers Sam Bowie and Melvin Turpin, and Georgetown, led by super-intense Patrick Ewing. The Wildcats led by 7 at the intermission, 29–22, but the second half was another story. The Hoyas put on one of the greatest displays of defensive basketball in the history of college hoops. The vaunted Kentucky starting five went 0–21 in the second frame and the team as a whole shot 3–33 from the field. Georgetown blew right by the Wildcats, who scored a total of 11 points for the half, en route to a 53–40 victory that wasn't even that close.

The Georgetown Hoyas, who lost the 1982 final to UNC in heartbreaking fashion and failed to make the Final Four in 1983, were back with a vengeance. The media continued to focus on the dominating seven-foot (213cm) Ewing, but the key to the team was their powerful six-foot-ten-inch (208cm) coach, John Thompson. When Thompson was a pro he had been Bill Russell's backup on the Boston Celtics and apparently was a brilliant understudy. The style of basketball that Thompson preached at Georgetown was pure Russell: defense, intimidation, and intensity (Ewing was his prize pupil). Like Russell, Thompson was as concerned with the intellectual and spiritual growth of his players as with the development of their basketball skills (understanding that the two were intricately intertwined). Thus, Thompson ran his team in a unique fashion; he did not allow his players to talk to the media or converse with opposing players on the court, and he made certain that his players pursued their educations in earnest. For Thompson, these strategies were conducive to the creation of team unity and insulated his players from a lot of unnecessary hype, which allowed them to better pursue their educations, on and off the court. The media felt differently, and coined the phrase "Hoya Paranoia." Oftentimes racist fans of opposing teams, intimidated by a powerful black coach like Thompson with a brilliant all-black team, hurled racial epithets at the Hoyas as they played. But Thompson's troops were unfazed. Under their coach's guidance the Hoyas were as strong mentally as they were physically. In the midst of a whirlwind of hype, the Hoyas blasted their way through the regular season and on into the NCAA tournament.

In spite of Thompson's best efforts to protect his star player, Ewing was the centerpiece of the Hoyas team and the focus of attention. Though the other Georgetown players were standouts, including All-American Sleepy Floyd, in Ewing's freshman year, the Hoyas' dominance was largely attributed to Ewing. Patrick Ewing was born in Jamaica and only moved to Cambridge, Massachusetts, when he was in junior high school. By high school he was seven feet (213cm) tall and a terror on the basketball court. The object of intense recruiting drives by most of the major national basketball programs, Patrick chose Georgetown because he was impressed by Thompson and the coach's commitment to education. A sensation as a freshman, wearing his fashion-setting gray T-shirt under his Georgetown tank top uniform, Ewing was quickly compared to Bill Russell because of his ability to dominate games from the defensive end. By his junior year, Ewing's offensive game was also improving, especially the turnaround jump shot that would mature into an awesome offensive weapon in his professional career with the New York Knicks. The Hoyas fielded an excellent supporting cast for Ewing in his third year. Highly recruited Reggie Williams, a six-foot-seven-inch (201cm) swingman, was impressive in his rookie season. Georgetown's second- and third-leading scorers behind Ewing were a pair of sophomores, six-foot-five-inch (196cm) David Wingate and six-foot-one-inch (185cm) Michael Jackson (not the singer, who, coincidentally, was at the height of his fame in 1983–1984). Guard Gene Smith was a particularly exceptional defender, though all the Hoyas played airtight pressure defense. Forward Bill Martin got ample playing time, but it was the bald-headed, six-foot-nine-inch (206cm) Michael Graham who emerged during the season as an intimidating complement to Ewing beneath the boards. Rounding out the group was veteran Fred Brown, the tragic figure from 1982, who had bounced back from an injury in 1983. It was a deep squad, but Ewing, who led the team in points, rebounds, blocks, and minutes played, was still the man.

The Hoyas captured the Big East title in 1984 and were rewarded with a number one seed—in the West regional. Three time zones away from home, the Hoyas almost fell prey to SMU in the first round. Seven-foot (213cm) Jon Koncak contained Ewing, and the Mustangs slowed the pace to keep the score close. With the score tied at 34, Ewing snuck through to tip in a Gene Smith miss and the Hoyas escaped with a 37–36 victory. Things got easier from there as the Hoyas trounced UNLV despite not scoring during one ten-minute stretch, then crushed Dayton to earn a trip to Seattle. One Dayton player said afterward, "It's frightening. Ewing is very mammoth. He's like an octopus with hands all over the place."

Making their way to Seattle to challenge Ewing and company were Kentucky, Houston, and Virginia. The number one seed in the Mideast, Kentucky, trounced Brigham Young and then, playing on their home court in Lexington, captured the regional with close victories over cross-state rival Louisville and then Illinois. The Houston Cougars were more Akeem Olajuwon's team than ever, and the Nigerian Dream led the Cougars to the Final Four for the third straight year—the first team to do so since UCLA in 1975. The Cougars passed through the Mideast regional with single-digit victories over Louisiana Tech, Memphis State, and Wake Forest. The surprise of the tournament was Virginia. The Cavs figured to slump after the graduation of Ralph Sampson, and the team did lose more regular-season games (9) than they had all of the previous three seasons combined, but they had more success in the tourney than the previous two years. Led by the brilliant play of senior guard Othell Wilson, Virginia got by Iona and then began pulling upsets, over Syracuse, Arkansas, and Indiana. In the regional final versus Virginia, the Hoosiers probably suffered from the aftereffects of an emotional letdown following their astonishing defeat of number one-ranked North Carolina in the regional semifinals. (When Bobby Knight had informed Dan Dakich that he would have the responsibility of guarding UNC's brilliant Michael Jordan, Dakich confessed that "I went right back to my room and threw up." Then Dakich went out and held the All-World guard to 6 points in thirty-five minutes.) Though a star of the game against the Tarheels, Dakich was the goat against Virginia, giving up a key turnover with less than two minutes left in the game that translated into Virginia's go-ahead basket.

The clash of the titans: Georgetown's Patrick Ewing and Houston's Akeem Olajuwon battle for position during the 1984 NCAA final, the first time in NCAA history that two of the college games' all-time dominant centers squared off for the national title. Ewing and Olajuwon balanced each other out, but Patrick's supporting cast outgunned Akeem's and Georgetown won the crown, 84–75. A decade later Hakeem (he added the "H" in the interim) exacted his revenge as his Houston Rockets defeated Ewing's New York Knicks for the 1994 NBA title in the closely contested seven-game series.

The Cavs were heavy underdogs against Houston, but they kept the game close by employing a conservative offense and a diamond-in-one defense designed to contain Olajuwon and Michael Young. With twenty-nine seconds left, Othell Wilson stole the ball and went in for a layup to tie the game. After another Houston turnover, Virginia had a chance to win, and Guy Lewis must have had flashbacks to the conclusion of last year's final. But Virginia failed to score and the game went to overtime, where Houston outscored the Cavs by a pair for a nerve-wracking 49–47 victory.

The final promised to be a matchup of titans, Ewing versus Olajuwon, recalling the legendary battles of Chamberlain and Russell. However, the two big men were both mired in foul trouble and effectively cancelled each other out. Instead, the title was determined by the rank-and-file, and Georgetown's proved superior. Five Hoyas scored in double figures, and the Georgetown bench accounted for 33 points. The Hoyas led 40–30 at halftime and cruised to an 84–75 victory. Akeem Olajuwon's brilliant college career ended without an NCAA title, while Patrick Ewing and Coach

JohnThompson were crowned as national hoops champions.

When Georgetown captured the NCAA title in 1984, many expected Patrick Ewing to bypass his senior year and head for the professional ranks like Michael Jordan, his teammate on the 1984 gold medal-winning U.S. Olympic Team. But Ewing had made a vow to his late mother to stay in school, so to the delight of John Thompson (who himself counseled Ewing to turn pro), Patrick came back for his senior year. The big question during the 1984–1985 NCAA college basketball season was whether the Hoyas could become the first team to repeat as champions since UCLA accomplished the feat in 1972–1973.

Georgetown's arch-rival within the powerful Big East conference, the St. John's Redmen, seemed to be one of the few teams capable of dethroning the Hoyas. Coach Lou Carnesseca's Redmen were led by sharpshooting All-American Chris Mullin, who averaged just under 20 points a game; brilliant junior college transfer, forward Walter Berry; a solid seven-foot (213cm) presence at center, Bill Wennington, who had a nice touch on a short jumper; and a defensive gem in six-foot-six-inch (198cm) Willie Glass. When the Redmen squeaked by Georgetown 66–65 on the Hoyas' home-court in their first meeting of the regular season, St. John's moved briefly to the top of the polls. However, Georgetown enacted its revenge on St. John's in New York City, reclaimed the number one ranking, and held it for the rest of the season. The Hoyas had lost Gene Smith and Fred Brown to graduation and Michael Graham to academic ineligibility, but Horace Broadnax got more playing time in the backcourt, and six-foot-eleven-inch (211cm) Ralph Dalton could be counted on to support Ewing off the bench. More importantly, the maturation of Reggie Williams and the continued

Villanova's Ed Pinckney passes out to an open teammate while Georgetown's Michael Jackson tries to draw the charge during the 1985 title game. One of the keys to shooting a high percentage from the field, as Villanova did in its amazing upset of Georgetown, is to draw the defense to you as you drive the lane and (instead of taking an out-of-control shot) pass to one of your teammates, whose defender has left him to collapse on you, for an easy short-range jumper.

solid play of starters like Wingate, Martin, and Jackson provided the ever-brilliant Ewing with ample support. The Hoyas finished the regular season 30–2, winning both the Big East regular season title and the conference tournament in a grudge match over St. John's 92-80 at the Garden.

The Villanova Wildcats finished fourth in the Big East (Syracuse finished third), losing twice to both St. John's and Georgetown in the process. A solid team steered by six-foot-nine-inch (206cm) center Ed Pinkney, flashy forward guard Dwayne McClain, and point guard Gary McClain, the Wildcats completed the regular season 19–10 and received an invitation to the Big Dance. To many people's surprise, the Wildcats won the Southeast regional and joined St. John's and Georgetown at the Final Four in Lexington, Kentucky. Never before had one conference placed three teams in the Final Four.

The lone representative of the rest of the nation's college basketball teams was Memphis State, who had captured the Midwest regional with narrow 2-point victories over Boston College (of the Big East) and Oklahoma. Coach Dana Kirk's Tigers were led by a pair of giants, soft-shooting six-foot-ten-inch (208cm) Keith Lee and seven-foot (213cm) William Bedford. Rounding out the Tigers' starting lineup were three other quality players: slick guard Andre Turner; a junior forward with a memorable name and a solid game, Baskerville Holmes; and freshman swingman Vincent Askew. However, the talented Tigers were derailed in the national semifinals by a Villanova team that was playing superb team basketball and had begun to believe in itself. The eighth seed from the Southeast overcame Memphis State with a flawless second-

half performance. The game was knotted up 23–all at the half but the Cats won pulling away. Dwayne McClain led all scorers with 19. The surprising Wildcats then sat back and waited to see which of their conference foes they would face in the finals. Georgetown and St. John's had breezed through the East and West regionals respectively. To no one's surprise, Georgetown remained on a roll, defeating St. John's for the third time in

The astonished Villanova Wildcats celebrate their upset of the Hoyas (who had beaten them twice during the regular season) in the second-ever interconference NCAA title game. Villanova coach Rollie Massimino said that his troops would have to, among other things, "shoot in the fifty percent range" to have a chance to win—the Wildcats hit on 78 percent of their shots. Particularly lethal was Harold Jansen (in the center of the photo, who looks like a miniature Kevin McHale and on this night played like the Celtic great), a previously unheralded backup who was perfect from the field, hitting all five of his jumpers.

the season, 77–59. The media prepared for a coronation on Monday night; everyone seemed to expect a championship-game blowout worthy of the Alcindor-led UCLA Bruins. Ewing would take his rightful place alongside Big Lew, Walton, and Mr. Russell.

When asked what his team would have to do to defeat Georgetown, coach Rollie Massimino said, "We're going to have to play a perfect game...And that may not be enough. We can't turn the ball over too much against their various pressure defenses. And we have to shoot

in the fifty percent range." As it turned out, Rollie's troops did better than that. While Georgetown's tenacious defense did force numerous turnovers, Gary McClain succeeded in keeping the Wildcats composed and within their disciplined offense. And Villanova topped 50 percent from the field, connecting on a record-shattering 78 percent of their shots. The "perfect game" indeed: Villanova pulled off the greatest upset ever in an NCAA final, surpassing even NC State's miracle in '83.

How closely fought was the contest? Villanova hit 7 of its first 8 shots but still trailed 20–14. Then Georgetown hit a cold spell and Villanova bounced back to tie the score at 20. The Wildcats raised some eyebrows with a 29–28 halftime lead. In the second half the Wildcats attempted only 10 shots from the floor, and made 9; backup guard Harold Jansen finished 5 for 5. The Hoyas attempted 25 more shots than Villanova during the contest, but to no avail. Georgetown's pressure defense generated turnovers, but also whistles. Villanova tallied 19 points from the charity stripe in the second half, while Georgetown only attempted 8 free throws all game, Ewing none. Villanova led throughout most of the second half, but when the Hoya defense succeeded in flustering the Wildcats, the defending champs scored 6 consecutive points to take a 54–53 lead. When Georgetown forced another turnover, Coach Thompson called for a stall. The strategy backfired on the Hoyas. Villanova regained possession, and a Jansen jumper put the Wildcats on top for good. The Cats scored their final 11 points from the free throw line and, to the astonishment of the crowd and the nation, held on for a 66–64 victory.

Chapter 5

March Madness Marches On: 1986–1996

By the fall of 1985, all of the young men who had been college basketball superstars over the past few years—the likes of Ralph Sampson, Patrick Ewing, Michael Jordan, Chris Mullin, and the cast of Phi Slamma Jamma—had graduated to the NBA. This group was the core of the most popular, and most widely followed, generation of college basketball players in history. In the NBA, they would join Magic Johnson and Larry Bird to become the most celebrated cast of pro players in history—forming the nucleus of the 1992 U.S. Olympic Dream Team that captured the imagination of the entire world. Through the mid-eighties, college basketball's popularity was so great that no one imagined that the public would follow the Jordans and Ewings to the NBA in such record numbers. Within five to seven years the pro league's popularity would equal and then surpass that of college basketball's.

Not that the public's interest in NCAA basketball declined—in fact, it probably even increased overall, but the spectacular rise of the NBA would have a tangible effect on the college game over the next decade. By the mid-nineties, an increasing number of the nation's basketball fans looked at the college game merely as a proving ground for future NBA players, a minor league to be plundered by the major leagues after each season. More and more frequently, the top college stars skipped their final years of eligibility and headed for the big money of the pro ranks, which contributed to the public's perception of the newer generation of stars as greedy. The bond between college stars and their fans seemed more tenuous than ever and anyway, it was difficult for a collegiate to build up the type of mythic stature of an Alcindor, Walton, or Ewing after only one or two seasons in the limelight. The flight of talent from the college ranks to the NBA is undoubtedly the biggest problem facing college basketball in the immediate future. And in what may be the beginning of an even more disturbing trend, Chicago high school star Kevin Garnett skipped college entirely and was drafted in the NBA first round in 1995 by the Minnesota Timberwolves. After Garnett had a reasonably solid rookie season, the trend was furthered when two high school seniors, Kobe Bryant and Jermaine O'Neal, were chosen in the first round of the 1996 draft (though neither was snapped up as early in the draft as Garnett). If any of these three hyper-talented players develops into an NBA superstar, it will set a terrible precedent for college hoops. The NCAA is virtually powerless to stem the talent drain. Colleges had hoped that the rookie salary cap adopted by the NBA, which reined in the astronomical contracts that were commonly given to first-round picks (severely cutting into the salaries of veteran players in the NBA's salary-cap system), would slow down the early exodus of top players from the nation's campuses. In fact, the salary cap had the opposite effect: the budding superstars recognized that the sooner they reached the NBA the sooner the big bucks would come their way; accordingly, the first-round picks in the 1996 draft were by far the youngest ever selected.

After years, even decades, of using roughly the same rules, the NCAA made two major rule changes in the mid-eighties that transformed the game more drastically than at any time since the NCAA tournament began. First, the NCAA adopted a forty-five-second shot clock for the 1986 tournament after an array of different-length shot clocks were experimented with in different conferences (the NCAA changed to a thirty-five-second clock in 1994). Second, and even more significant, the NCAA instituted a 3-point shot, from beyond an arc nineteen feet nine inches (6m) from the basket, at the beginning of the 1986–1987 season. The impact of both rules was tremendous. Gone forever were teams that tried to freeze the ball with two, five, ten, or even thirty minutes left in a game, a (sometimes absurdly abused) strategy that had been prevalent throughout the history of the college game. The 3-point shot not only significantly reduced the ability of big men to dominate a game, or a season; it absolutely transformed the topography of the game. In other words, the presence of the 3-point line changed not only where shots were released from, but how passing patterns developed, the spacing of players on the court (both defensively and offensively), and the significance of possessions down the stretch.

All for one and one for all: the number one-ranked UCLA Bruins close ranks and focus their energy before a 1995 NCAA tournament game. The pressure on every team in the tournament is intense, but the 1995 Bruins carried added weight. No UCLA team had reached the Final Four in fifteen seasons, and the school's unrivaled legacy—ten titles in twelve years, from 1964 to 1975—was ancient history.

In the early and mid-nineties, college basketball experienced another type of shake-up as conference realignments were made. The ancient Southwestern Conference folded, the once-powerful Metro dissolved, the Great Midwestern lasted four seasons before disappearing into the sprawling Conference U.S.A., and the Big Eight became the Big Twelve, while the Big Ten kept its name in spite of adding an eleventh team. The Big East, Southeast, and Western Athletic Conference ballooned into super-conferences. The result of all of these mergers, besides creating greater television revenue, was to marginalize the significance of regular-season titles, since the top four or five teams from each of these super-conferences were all but assured an invitation to the Big Dance, the NCAA tournament. More than ever before, the tournament became the focus of the college basketball season.

In the decade from the mid-eighties to the mid-nineties, college hoops may have had its share of problems, but come tournament time all was well; the nation pulled up a chair, turned on the tube (in record numbers), and took in the most thrilling three weeks in American sports.

Heading into the 1985–1986 season there was a power void in college basketball. Not only was Patrick Ewing no longer around to dominate the scene, but all of the Final Four teams from the previous season had been led by seniors. Appropriately, a freshman would lead his team to the promised land come March.

The four teams that survived the regionals in 1986 were LSU, Duke,

Navy's David Robinson drops in the game-winning basket versus Cleveland State in the 1986 East regional semifinals. Robinson single-handedly turned the Midshipmen into a national power. The Naval Academy has a six-foot-six-inch (198cm) height restriction for incoming students, which, of course, has hampered its basketball program. However, David Robinson experienced an extremely late growth spurt while at Annapolis; suddenly, the nation's best college center was one of the Middies.

Kansas, and Louisville. The biggest surprise of the tournament was LSU. One of the Tigers' top players, Nikita Wilson, was suspended for academic reasons midway through the season. Still, Dale Brown's team fought on and, despite a fifth-place finish in the SEC, earned a place in the newly expanded (to sixty-four teams, the size it remains today) tournament with a 22–11 record. Guided by sophomore forward John Williams and senior guard Derrick Taylor, the Tigers posted 4 comeback victories in the Southeast regional, including a stunning upset over heavily favored Kentucky, who had already defeated the Tigers three times during the season. The 1986 LSU Tigers were colorful Coach Larry Brown's consummate over-achievers. In the late eighties and early nineties, Brown's teams were loaded with talent. Chris Jackson (who would change his name to Makmid Abdul-Rauf and become a star for the Denver Nuggets of the NBA), seven-footer (213cm) Stanley Roberts, and another giant by the name of Shaquille O'Neal all starred for Brown.

The other three teams to reach Dallas were all highly seeded. Kansas made it through the Midwest regional with only one glitch. Against Michigan State, the Jayhawks trailed by 4 with just over two minutes remaining when Kansas star guard Ron Kellogg scored in a sequence that took almost twenty seconds and yet the game clock moved only one second. The controversy seemed to unnerve the Spartans more than the Jayhawks, who survived in overtime.

Duke, the nation's top-ranked team, tiptoed through a dramatic East regional. The Blue Devils struggled early against both Mississippi Valley State and De Paul (who finished the regular season with a meager 16–12 record) before pulling away for victories. But the headlines in the region were reserved for two surprise teams. Upstart Cleveland State ousted Bobby Knight and the Indiana Hoosiers in the first round and then blew by St. Joseph's with their fast-paced "run-and-stun" style to set up a showdown with the other media darling of the tournament, the U.S. Naval Academy. The Midshipmen were led by their towering center, David Robinson. The Academy has strict restrictions on height because of submarine regulations, and no one who is more than six feet six inches (198cm) is admitted to Annapolis, a fact that severely hampered their varsity basketball program (and gave new meaning to their nickname, the Middies). However, Robinson, who was less than six feet six inches when he arrived at Navy, experienced an uncommonly late growth spurt and shot up to six feet eleven inches (211cm) by his sophomore year. In the Cinderella showdown, Navy jumped ahead of Cleveland State. Then the Vikings' breakneck pace caught up with the Midshipmen and Cleveland State pulled ahead. That's when "the Admiral," David Robinson, took things into his own hands, scoring 13 points down the stretch, including the clinching basket with six ticks left on the clock. Next up for the Navy was mighty Duke. Early on, the Middies held their own and actually led 20–16 when Duke went on an 18–2 run. Leaving Navy in their wake, the Blue Devils coasted to their twentieth straight victory.

The 1985–1986 Louisville Cardinals had a nice mix of talented underclassmen and talented upperclassmen. Denny Crum started three seniors, forward Billy Thompson and guards Milt Wagner and Jeff Hall, alongside sophomore forward Herbert Crook and freshman center Pervis Ellison. Louisville's sixth man, forward Tony Kimbro, was also a rookie. The Cardinals struggled early in the season with their new mix of players but came together down the stretch, entering the tournament on an 11-game winning streak. The Cardinals cruised through the first three rounds of the tournament. Crum was counting on veteran leadership from Thompson and Wagner, who both played key roles on the 1982–1983 Cardinals team that reached the Final Four. What Crum couldn't anticipate was the steely nerved composure of freshman Ellison. "Never Nervous" Pervis was simply unflappable as the Cardinals advanced deeper in the tournament. Even in the most tension-laden moments, Ellison, who still had braces on his teeth, wore the same relaxed expression he did before and after the game. Against Auburn in the regional final, Ellison came up big. Auburn was a strong, bruising team that dominated opponents under the boards. With the game on the line in the closing minutes, Ellison snuck between two Auburn players to tip in a missed shot and give the Cardinals a 3-point lead. Pervis then raced downcourt as Auburn went on a fast break. Tigers center Jeff Moore squared up and shot. Ellison came flying in and rejected the ball all the way back to mid-court, where his teammate Jeff Hall picked it up and cruised in for an uncontested dunk. The sequence clinched the game and Louisville advanced to the Final Four for the fourth time in the eighties.

In Dallas, the Cardinals came out tight against LSU and trailed 44–36 at the half. But Louisville turned it up a notch after intermission, shooting 63 percent in the second frame and leaving the boys from the bayou in the dust, 88–77. Cardinal Billy Thompson led the way with 22 points on 10-for-11 shooting. The Kansas-Duke showdown proved more intriguing. Larry Brown's Jayhawks were led by sophomore sensation Danny Manning and junior guard Ron Kellogg. The Blue Devils were an eclectic bunch. Without a starter over six feet eight inches (203cm), they relied on finesse, which they had in abundance. Duke started four seniors: hard-nosed forward Mark Alarie, swingman David Henderson, center Jay Bilas, and the Player of the Year, guard Johnny Dawkins. Complementing this veteran core was junior guard Tommy Amaker

Louisville's Tony Kimbro (44) and Pervis Ellison battle for position under the boards against Duke's Danny Ferry (35) and Mark Alarie during the 1986 NCAA finals. In the closely fought game, Ellison's ability to win key rebounds down the stretch proved to be the decisive factor in the Cardinals victory.

and quickly improving freshman sixth man Danny Ferry. Alarie played the defensive game of his life against the Jayhawks, holding Manning to 4 points. But Kellogg's 22 points took up the slack, and Kansas led 65–61 with time winding down. However, Kansas misfired a few times from close range and the Blue Devils scratched back to tie the game at 67. Johnny Dawkins controlled a loose ball in the final minute and fed Danny Ferry for the go-ahead basket. On the other end, Ferry drew a charging call

against Kellogg with eleven seconds left to clinch the game.

The title game offered a contrast in style, but more off the court than on. Duke University is one of the premier private educational institutions in the country, on a par with the Ivy Leagues. By the mid-eighties the University of

Louisville was mostly known for its stellar basketball teams made up of inner-city youth, rife with character (witness the Doctors of Dunk) but hardly topflight students. The media picked up on this contrast and unfairly cast Duke as the good guys, the exemplars of clean living, who were both athletes and scholars. This journalistic angle was particularly unfair to Coach Crum and his staff, who worked hard to see that his players pursued their educations. On the court, the two teams had quite similar styles. While Duke was roundly applauded for their fundamentally sound approach to the game, the '86 Cardinals were a more disciplined lot than some of their shoot-from-the-hip predecessors. Both teams worked patiently on offense for a good shot, played airtight defense, and were led by dynamic senior guards—Dawkins for Duke and Wagner for Louisville.

For most of the game, Duke had the upper hand. Twice, Dawkins went on a tear, running circles around Wagner. The Duke defense also contained the Cardinals fast break and was generating easy opportunities on the other end. With both Wagner and Thompson in foul trouble, things looked bleak for the Cardinals, though the game was not out of reach. Crum kept emphasizing defense and the strategy paid off. The Cardinals tightened the screws, holding Dawkins to 2 free throws in the final fifteen minutes. Somehow Wagner avoided picking up his fifth foul and got the hot hand. In one sequence, Ellison scored a bucket, the Cardinals held on the defensive end, and Wagner completed a 3-point play to pull

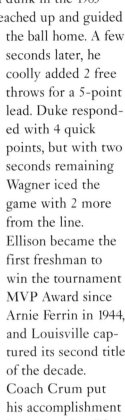

UNLV's Armon Gilliam goes up for a short jumper amid a troika of Hoosiers during the 1987 national semifinals. In a brilliant performance, Gilliam knocked down more than 30 points, while being trailed by half the state of Indiana. However, it was not enough as Bobby Knight's Hoosiers kept pace with the Runnin' Rebels scoring machine and outexecuted UNLV down the stretch to advance to the finals.

Louisville within a point. Down the stretch, Pervis moved to the fore, stifling the Blue Devils' interior offense, controlling the boards, and lighting up the scoreboard. With the Cardinals up 66–65 in the final minute and the shot clock ticking down, Jeff Hall put up an air ball, but in a scene reminiscent of Lorenzo Charles' last-second dunk in the 1983 title game, Ellison reached up and guided the ball home. A few seconds later, he coolly added 2 free throws for a 5-point lead. Duke responded with 4 quick points, but with two seconds remaining Wagner iced the game with 2 more from the line. Ellison became the first freshman to win the tournament MVP Award since Arnie Ferrin in 1944, and Louisville captured its second title of the decade. Coach Crum put his accomplishment in perspective: "I'm really going to enjoy this one....it kind of puts you in select company."

Although it was a freshman who led his team to the national title in 1986, one who would presumably be in strong form in 1987, few prognosticators picked the Louisville Cardinals to repeat as champions. The reason was not that Pervis Ellison had been injured, or that Denny Crum would fail to provide him with a strong supporting cast; rather, the balance of power in college basketball was expected to shift because of a rule change. The NCAA had installed a 3-point line. "Never Nervous" Pervis may have been superb down the stretch of the 1986 tournament, but his game was in the low post, and low-post baskets only counted for 2 points. With the rule

change, a jumper from only nineteen feet nine inches (6m) away from the basket (substantially closer than the NBA's 3-point line and even closer than the international border) and well within range of many of the nation's sharpshooters netted 3 points. The days when big men could dominate college basketball were seemingly over.

The 3-point shot would have a tremendous impact on the college game in its inaugural season, but when the NCAA championship game came down to one dramatic shot it was a good old-fashioned deuce. Once again, a thrilling title game capped off a dramatic season in suitable fashion.

1986–1987 was the season that Indiana coach Bobby Knight stepped into the modern era, with a vengeance. Throughout his tenure in Bloomington, Knight was an advocate of traditional, hardworking, disciplined basketball. Knight frowned on zone defenses and had his teams play aggressive man-to-man; likewise, Knight demanded that his players slow the ball down on offense and work for a good shot from a half-court set rather than running the fast break. Also, Knight had previously refused to recruit junior college players. But Knight's teams had been struggling in recent years and the coach recognized it was time for change. So the 1986–1987 Hoosiers played zone as well as man-to-man defense, and would occasionally push the ball on offense. Two of the Hoosiers' starting five were junior college transfers. And though Knight railed against the 3-point shot, he called on sharpshooting Steve Alford to spot up just outside the arc. The results were sterling: the Hoosiers finished the regular season 24–4 and were seeded first in the Midwest regional.

Then the fun really started in the tournament. After blowing out Fairfield, the Hoosiers trailed Auburn by 14 in the second round. To the delight of a capacity crowd at the Hoosierdome, Indiana native Alford led an exhilarating come-back with 31 points on 7-for-11 shooting from 3-point range. The Midwest regional was held in Cincinnati and forward Rick Calloway, who hailed from the Queen City, led the Hoosiers in a comeback victory over Duke with a season-high 21 points. Next up was LSU. The Tigers had built a double-digit lead midway through the second half when Coach Knight had seen enough and exploded off the bench in one of his signature tantrums. Knight gave a brilliant performance as he lit into the referees, raved like a lunatic, and, in the coup de grace, smashed a telephone at the official scorers' table. When order was restored after the obligatory slap-on-the-wrist technical against Knight, LSU had lost its momentum. Indiana scratched its way back into the game. The Tigers tried to freeze the ball to protect their lead, but faltered at the free throw line when the Hoosiers fouled them. In the final minute, Indiana closed to within a point and LSU once again missed the front end of a 1-and-1. But LSU played tough defense and as the clock ticked down, Hoosiers power forward Daryl Thomas put up a desperation shot. It was an air ball, but hometown hero Rick Calloway managed to catch the ball and lay it in for a miraculous 77–76 victory.

Joining the Hoosiers at the New Orleans Superdome were UNLV and two representatives of the Big East, Providence and Syracuse. Jerry Tarkanian's Runnin' Rebels stormed into the Final Four with a garish 37–1 record. No team in the country had utilized the 3-point shot to greater effect throughout the season. Star guard Fred Banks attempted 358 three-pointers during the season, more than either Indiana (with Alford) or Syracuse attempted all season. Forward Gerald Paddio was also a long-range bomber, but the centerpiece of the UNLV dynamo was a rock-solid power forward with a soft shooting touch, Armon Gilliam. The "Hammer" led the team in rebounding (9.3 per game) and scoring (23.2), and he didn't even attempt a three-pointer all season.

Like the Runnin' Rebels, Rick Pitino's Providence Friars were 3-happy, but unlike Vegas, long-range bombing was the sum total of the Providence game. The Friars finished low in the pack in the Big East, compiling a 21–8 regular-season record, but received an invitation to the Big Dance. Pitino's boys put on the school colors and had a blast

at the ball. Piloted by a diminutive triumvirate of 3-point bombers—six-foot (183cm) Billy Donovan, six-foot-four-inch (193cm) Delray Brooks (a transfer from Indiana), and six-foot-four-inch (193cm) Ernie Lewis—the sixth-seeded Friars swept through the Southeast regional with upset victories over Alabama and Big East champ Georgetown. Donovan, in particular, was on fire, averaging 26.5 points per game in the regional.

However, Providence proved to be no match for its Big East rival, Syracuse, in the national semifinals. Coach Jim Boeheim's Orangemen were a supremely talented lot. Sophomore point guard Sherman Douglas led the way with his eye-popping passing and slick moves to the hoop. Junior center Rony Seikely, a native of Lebanon who grew up in Greece and had the physique and features of a classical statue, was rock-solid in the middle. Senior guard Greg

Monroe was an inside-outside threat, while power forward Derrick Coleman, a six-foot-nine-inch (206cm) freshman, brimmed with potential. And, believe it or not, the Orangemen did not rely on hoisting threes. Against Providence, Syracuse did it with good old-fashioned defense and balanced scoring. The Orangemen held Donovan to 8 points, while every one of their starters scored in double digits. The halftime score was

36–26 and the Orangemen breezed to a 77–63 win.

The second semifinal was a thriller. Bobby Knight had gone against conventional Bobby Knight wisdom all year long with good results, so why not continue? Everyone anticipated that Knight would try to control the pace against Tarkanian's racehorses, but instead he called on his Hoosiers to beat the Runnin' Rebels at their own game. The result was end-to-end action. Gilliam and Banks were unstoppable, tallying 70 points between them on 26-for-49 shooting. Unfortunately, their teammates only hit on 9 of their 33 shots. Meanwhile, the Hoosiers as a team hit on 60 percent of their shots. Steve Alford led the way with 33 points. Alford attempted all of the Hoosiers' 3-point shots (he went 2–4 from downtown), while the Rebels hoisted 35 long-range bombs, making only 13. When the dust settled, the final score

Indiana's Keith Smart takes a jump shot over Syracuse's Rony Seikely in the first half of the thrilling 1987 championship finals. With five seconds left in the game, Smart buried a 16-foot (5m) jumper from the left side to lift the Hoosiers to a 74–73 lead. Then Smart capped off his brilliant clutch performance—he had scored 12 of the Hoosiers' 15 final points—by stealing the ball on Syracuse's inbounds pass to clinch Indiana's fifth NCAA title.

was Indiana 97, UNLV 93. In the national spotlight, the two teams that had lived by the three, UNLV and Providence, had died by the three.

For the fourth time in six years, the final was a classic. The game was tight throughout the first half and 1 point separated the teams at intermission. The second half followed a pattern familiar to Indiana basketball fans: the Hoosiers fell behind and made a spirited comeback led by a local product (must be mom's home cooking). In this case, the unlikely hero was Keith Smart, the Hoosier's other guard, a super-quick six-foot (183cm) junior college transfer who grew up in nearby Baton Rouge, Louisiana. When Knight benched Smart early in the second half after a sloppy play, the Hoosiers had no one to contain Sherman Douglas. The Orangemen quickly built a 10-point lead. Knight reinserted Smart, who sparked a 10-point Hoosier run. But Syracuse rebounded, literally. The Orangemen recaptured the lead as their big men controlled the boards. With the Syracuse lead up to 5 points with less than eight minutes remaining, Smart, who averaged a mere 11 points a game,

The Arizona Wildcats' super-smooth forward Sean Elliot glides in for 2 points past Oklahoma's low-post scoring machine Stacey King at the 1988 Final Four in Kansas City. Elliot single-handedly kept Arizona in the contest with a 31-point performance, but the Sooners' athleticism was too much for the Wildcats in this showdown of number one seeds.

kept the Hoosiers in the game with 4 consecutive field goals. Still, Indiana could not overtake the Orangemen. When Syracuse's Howard Triche stepped up to the free throw line with thirty-eight seconds remaining, his team led 72–70. Triche buried a pressure free throw, but then misfired. Little Keith Smart grabbed the rebound and drove the length of the court for a basket. Then Smart fouled freshman Derrick Coleman with twenty-eight seconds still remaining. Coleman missed the front end of the 1-and-1 and Indiana's Daryl Thomas cleared the boards. The Hoosiers moved into their half-court offense as the seconds ticked away. The Orangemen blanketed Steve Alford. As the clock moved under ten seconds, Smart dribbled the ball on the wing and then fed it to Thomas in the low post, but Coleman and the Syracuse interior defense gave him no room to maneuver. Thomas passed the ball back to Smart; with five seconds remaining, Keith let go of a sixteen-foot (4.9m) jump shot. "What do I remember most?" Smart recalled. "How quiet the arena got when the ball left my hand. And all of a sudden it went in." Smart scored 12 of the Hoosiers' final 15 points and hit the most celebrated jumper in the glorious history of Indiana basketball to clinch the 1987 NCAA championship.

The 1987–1988 NCAA college basketball season was wide open. At the beginning of the year, recent champions Indiana and Louisville were considered top contenders, but both faltered during the season and neither were there at the end. The Kansas Jayhawks were expected to go only as far as their brilliant but oft-injured superstar, Danny Manning, could carry them.

Heading into the tournament Coach John Chaney's Temple Owls, featuring slick freshman guard Mark Macon, were ranked number one in both polls. The Arizona Wildcats, led by smooth forward Sean Elliot and sharpshooting Steve Kerr, were number two, while Big Ten champ Purdue and Big Eight champ Oklahoma were next in line. Kansas, meanwhile, had struggled tremendously through the regular season. At one point its record was a dismal 12–8. The low

point came when rival Kansas State, who had a strong team led by high-scoring swingman Mitch Richmond, snapped the Jayhawks' home game–winning streak at 55. But the Jayhawks righted themselves in time to compile a 23–11 record and earn a bid to the tournament.

The four top-ranked teams were awarded number one seedings in each regional. Meanwhile, four strong teams qualified for the tournament from the Big Eight—Oklahoma, Kansas, Kansas State, and Missouri. The two Kansas teams ended up in the Southeast regional. Fourth-seeded K State encountered Purdue in the regional semifinals and, behind a strong performance by Richmond, upended the Boilermakers 73–70. Next, the Wildcats squared off against the sixth-seeded Jayhawks, who had breezed into the rematch with their interstate rivals, overcoming Vanderbilt 77–64 after Vandy had cleared the way for the rest of their bracket by upsetting number two seed Pittsburgh. The Jayhawks hungered for revenge against Kansas State since the Wildcats had swept the regular-season series. Kansas State had a formidable basketball history, but it was nothing compared to Kansas' virtually unparalleled basketball tradition. This time the stakes were especially high, for the winner would not only win the regional, but have home-court advantage at the Final Four in Kansas City. The Wildcats might have had the better of it during the regular season, but the Jayhawks were peaking at the right time of the year. Manning poured in 20 points, Kansas contained Richmond, and the Jayhawks exacted their revenge, 71–58, to reach the Final Four for the second time in three years.

Joining the Jayhawks in Kansas City's Kemper Arena were number one seeds Arizona and Oklahoma and the number two seed, Duke, who had ousted Temple, 63–53, in the East. The Blue Devils squared off against Kansas in the first semifinal, a rematch of the 1986 national semifinal. The red-hot Jayhawks controlled the game from start to finish. Manning led the way with 25 points, while guard Milt Newton, who was making a name for himself in the tournament, added 20. Danny Ferry led Duke with 19 points but the tight Kansas defense frustrated the Blue Devils, who shot only 34 percent. In the other semifinal Oklahoma used its up-tempo style to race past Arizona 86–76 in spite of Sean Elliot's 31-point performance. Oklahoma's Mookie Blaylock, a brilliant point guard, suffocated Steve Kerr, who hit on only 2 of 13 shots. Big Eight teams had gone thirty-one years without winning a Final Four game (since Wilt Chamberlain!) and on the same day they won two.

Oklahoma, like K State, had prevailed in both of its regular-season encounters with Kansas. However, this was a different Kansas team at the final; coach Larry Brown had whipped the Jayhawks into playing efficient basketball. And Danny Manning was red hot; throughout the tournament opposing teams approached the Jayhawks with one thing in mind—to stop Danny Manning—but to no avail. Whether driving to the basket, squaring up for jumpers, or slipping by defenders with his exquisite low-post pivot moves, Manning was unstoppable. Still, the Oklahoma Sooners were loaded with talent. Junior Stacey King was superb down low and could also run the court in Coach Billy Tubbs' fast-paced style. Mookie Blaylock, who set the tournament record for steals with 23, was a brilliant ball distributor and defender. Power forward Harvey Grant was a force down low, while forward Dave Sieger could be overwhelming from the outside. With

Kansas' Danny Manning rejects a shot by Oklahoma's Harvey Grant during the 1988 championship game. Manning was nothing short of sensational on both ends of the court all night long. His performance ranks alongside Bill Walton's 44-point outburst in 1973, Wildcat Jack Givens' output in 1978, and Bruin Gail Goodrich's in 1964 as one of the four greatest individual performances in the annals of the NCAA title game.

good reason, the Oklahoma Sooners believed that if they played their game as they had been playing it all along there was nothing Danny Manning could do to derail them.

The first half was played at breakneck speed, which would seem to have been to the Sooners' advantage, but the score was tied at 50 at halftime. Oklahoma's Sieger was putting on a

shooting clinic, burying 6 three-pointers, but both Oklahoma guards, Blaylock and Ricky Grace, were in foul trouble. The Jayhawks had kept pace with the Sooners by shooting a blistering 71 percent. At the half, Larry Brown, a masterful game strategist, called for Kansas to slow the tempo, muscle the Sooner big men, and, most importantly, shadow Sieger wherever he went. Sooners coach Billy Tubbs played into Brown's hands by calling off Oklahoma's devastating full-court pressure in order to avoid losing his backcourt to foul trouble. The game stayed close until the end, when Manning stepped to the fore with some clutch baskets. The brilliant Jayhawks forward finished with 31 points, 18 rebounds, 5 steals, 2 blocks, and 2 assists. In his last game as a collegian, Manning unequivocally proved he was the top college player in the nation, leading his team to an 83–79 victory and a national championship.

The 1989 NCAA tournament was topsy-turvy. All of the Final Four teams—Illinois, Michigan, Seton Hall, and Duke—were at-large entries to the tournament; none of them would have even qualified for the field before the 1975 rule change. And in what became the defining story of the tournament, Michigan made an assault on the national title with an interim head coach. At the close of the regular season, in which

Tennessee State to win by a point on a Mookie Blaylock layup. Perhaps the most peculiar story surrounding an upset was that of little Siena College, which downed Stanford 80–78. Siena's team had played under quarantine circumstances all year because of a measles epidemic on the small New York State campus; perhaps Stanford was timid for fear of contagion. Minnesota braved a contest with the Siena Saints and survived, but were ousted by Duke, who downed Georgetown in the East regional to advance to the Final Four for the third time in four years. The Sooners, still led by Stacey King and Mookie Blaylock, had hoped to revenge last year's loss in the finals, but they fell in the round of sixteen to Virginia, 86–80. Michigan then flexed its muscles and demolished the Cavaliers 102–65 to earn a trip to Seattle. The top-ranked team in the nation, Arizona, didn't make it past the third round, as they were knocked off by a young UNLV team 68–67, thus ending Sean Elliot's brilliant college career. Big East runner-up Seton Hall then dismantled the Runnin' Rebels 84–61 to win the West. The only number one seed to make it to Seattle was Lou Henson's Illinois team, which was distinctive for having five starters that were virtually interchangeable. All five were in the six-foot-four-inch (193cm) to six-foot-seven-inch (201cm) range and could jump, shoot, and play great defense—though Nick Anderson and Kenny Battle were the most accomplished of the Illini quintuplets.

Much like the scenario the previous year when Kansas squared off against Kansas State and Oklahoma, Michigan faced a team in the national semifinals that had beaten them twice (convincingly) in the regular season. But riding a crest of exuberance, somehow sparked by the improbable story of interim coach Fisher, Michigan was playing its best basketball of the year. Sharpshooting senior forward Glenn Rice led the talented Wolverine squad, which included center Terry Mills, power forward Loy Vaught, point guard Rumeal Robinson, and sophomore swingman Sean Higgins, all of whom averaged more than 10 points per game. The entire starting five would go on to lengthy careers in the NBA.

the Wolverines finished 24–7 and third in the Big Ten, head coach Bill Frieder announced he had accepted the Arizona State head coaching job for the following season. Later the same day athletic director Bo Schembechler called a press conference, fired Frieder, and handed over the team's reins to assistant coach Steve Fisher.

The early rounds of the tournament were rife with drama. Number one–

Michigan's Glenn Rice slams one down with authority against North Carolina in 1989 regional semifinal action. A sleek and powerful six-foot-nine-inch (206cm) forward who could take it to the hole, Rice was also renowned for his exceptional outside shooting. All tournament long, Rice lit it up from outside.

seeded Georgetown barely escaped a stunning upset in round one against Princeton when Alonzo Mourning blocked 2 shots in the final seconds to preserve a 50–49 victory. Likewise, number one–seeded Oklahoma had to come back from 17 points down against East

The team truly jelled in the second round of the tournament when they eliminated UNC 92–87, avenging losses to the Tarheels in the previous two NCAA tournaments. Rice led the way with an immaculate performance of 13-for-19 shooting, including 8 for 12 from 3-point range. Then Michigan romped over Virginia and headed to Seattle. Illinois' relentless full-court pressure had unnerved the Wolverines in their previous two meetings, but in Seattle the boys in blue maintained their composure. The game was tight throughout; Illinois succeeded with its quickness, while Michigan controlled the boards. With Illinois ahead 79–78 with about a minute left, Wolverines senior Mark Hughes grabbed an offensive rebound, put it up and in, and was fouled. Hughes made the free throw. Battle tied the game at 81 and with thirty seconds left the Wolverines held for the last shot. Terry Mills missed from the corner, but Sean Higgins grabbed the long rebound and tossed up a shot that went in. Michigan would be playing for the NCAA championship for the third time in its history, looking for its first title.

Duke was favored in the other Final Four game. Senior Danny Ferry, in his third Final Four without a victory, brought a veteran's experience and a hunger to win to the tournament, while the Blue Devils' wunderkind, freshman Christian Laettner, who had outplayed Alonzo Mourning in the regional finals, was in his first. But the Seton Hall Pirates had that lucky mix of talent, character, and guts that enables a team to rise to the occasion come tournament time (see NC State in '83 and Villanova in '85). The Seton Hall student body had been calling for P.J. Carlissimo's resignation before the season, even though he had led the Pirates to their first NCAA tournament appearance in 1988. At the beginning of the season, the Pirates were picked to finish where they usually did, near the bottom of the Big East. What people didn't know was that Carlissimo had added a secret weapon to his mix of unheralded but intelligent New York players: a deadeye shooter from down under by the name of Andrew Gaze, known in his homeland as the Australian

Larry Bird. Gaze was already in his mid-twenties, but he had his NCAA eligibility intact, and though many were skeptical about his appearance on the Seton Hall campus in time for the 1988–1989 season, the nation's fans took him to heart as the Pirates made their run through the West regional. However, gut check time came early for the Pirates against Duke as the Blue Devils started the game on top, 26–8. The Pirates fought back and by halftime the deficit was only 5. When Laettner and his replacement Alaa Abdelnabby both collected their fourth fouls early in the second half, the Pirates' big men—Ramon Ramos, Darryl Walker, and Anthony Avent—took control of the boards and, in one of the greatest turnarounds in NCAA history, won going away, 98–78.

The 1989 final in the cavernous Kingdome was extraordinary. Seton Hall once again fell behind, but remained close until Michigan went on a tear early in the second half. With less than nine minutes remaining, the Wolverines led by 10 and seemed to have the game in hand when Pirates senior guard John Morton took over. In one of the great clutch performances in NCAA final history, Morton scored an amazing 17 points in eight minutes, capping it off with a three-pointer to tie the score with only twenty-four seconds left. Rice missed in the final seconds and the NCAA final was headed to overtime for only the fifth time in its history. Unfortunately for the Pirates, Morton's magic ran out when he missed from the lane with Seton Hall up 79–76 and only 1:35 left in OT, but Michigan still had to deliver. Terry Mills pulled the Wolverines within a point. Morton missed again and Michigan grabbed the rebound; Rumeal Robinson drove the lane with time running down and drew a controversial foul that put the talented point guard, a 65 percent free throw shooter, on the line. With the whole world watching, Robinson canned 'em

both with three seconds remaining and Michigan won its first national title, 80–79. Steve Fisher was undefeated, 6–0, as a head coach.

The 1989 final was the last in a string of eight sensational national championship games in which the average margin of victory was less than 3 points. There is no comparable period in the rest of college basketball history, and the prospect of a thrilling showdown helped make the NCAA final a national spectacle of the first order. In contrast, the Super Bowl was decided by an average of 24 points during these eight years (the 1982–1989 seasons). But the run of thrilling NCAA finals would end in 1990 with a blowout.

The two biggest stories of the 1989–1990 college basketball season met face-to-face in Oakland-Alameda Coliseum on March 25 in the NCAA Western regional final when Jerry Tarkanian's superb Runnin' Rebels faced off against Paul Westhead's Loyola Marymount Lions. The Rebels had been a fine team in 1988–1989, when they won 29 and lost only 8 games, then knocked out number one–ranked Arizona in the round of sixteen before losing to Seton Hall in the West regional final. UNLV figured to be even better in 1989–1990 when they added the '89 junior college Player of the Year, Larry Johnson, a six-foot-five-inch (196cm) hulk of a power forward with a soft shooting touch and an unwavering drive to win.

Michigan's steady point guard Rumeal Robinson stepped to center stage at the national championship game versus Seton Hall. With the Wolverines down by 1 point in the final seconds of overtime, Robinson (a 65 percent free throw shooter) stepped to the line. In a scenario envisioned by kids at practice sessions everywhere, Robinson calmly buried both shots, won the championship for the Wolverines, and became a folk hero.

Johnson joined an excellent cast that included high-flying Stacey Augmon, a brilliant defender; a pair of quick 3-point shooting guards, Greg Anthony and Anderson Hunt; and centers David Butler and Moses Scurry. Remarkably, only the two centers were seniors. Tarkanian was convinced he finally had the talent to put him over the top, having been frustrated by close calls in 1977 and 1987 and a number of high-ranking teams that lost early in the postseason. "Tark" entered the 1990 tournament intent on disproving the myth that the Rebels were never as good as their record because they played weak schedules.

Loyola Marymount was a different story altogether. Coach Paul Westhead, who led the Los Angeles Lakers to the 1980 NBA title before resigning in 1982 over a controversial run-in with Magic Johnson (he was succeeded by one of his assistants, Pat Riley), turned the Loyola program into a winner. Before 1988, Loyola Marymount had only reached the tournament twice, in 1961 and 1980. Westhead, who began at LMU before the 1985–1986 season, transformed the Lions into the highest-scoring team in college basketball history. Loyola played both offense and defense at absolutely break-neck speed, a sort of UNLV/Oklahoma hypertext. In '88, Westhead's Lions made the Big Dance and won a game before bowing out to UNC. The following year they made the Big Dance again but lost in the first round. In '89, Lions junior Hank Gathers flourished spectacularly in Westhead's system, becoming only the second player to lead the nation in rebounding (13.7) and scoring (32.7) in the same season (the other player to do so was Wichita State's Xavier McDaniel in 1984–1985). The solidly-built, six-foot-seven-inch (201 cm) Gathers scored almost all of his points from close range; he had an astounding field goal percentage (more than 60 percent) but was a miserable free throw shooter. During the 1989–1990 season, Gathers and coscoring demon forward Bo Kimble were poised to make a run at some all-time scoring records as well as the number one ranking. Indeed, the Lions succeeded in establishing a new mark for team scoring, averaging an amazing 122.4 points

per game. Kimble led the way and the nation with 35.3 points per game, Gathers averaged 29, and sharpshooter Jeff Fryer added 22. However, the Lions' hopes of assaulting the top of the polls were undermined when Gathers fainted on the court in a December 9 game against Santa Barbara. Doctors determined that Gathers had a cardiovascular problem that caused him to have an irregular heartbeat. He sat out 2 games, was put on medication, and was then allowed to continue to play. But Hank wasn't the same. He felt moody and weak, so he persuaded his physicians to lower his dosage. He began to feel and play better. Then in the semifinals of the West Coast Conference tournament, in a game against Portland, with less than fourteen minutes remaining in the first half, Gathers made a spectacular slam dunk on a fast break—vintage Loyola basketball. But as Gathers dropped back to play defense, he collapsed near mid-court. He struggled to his knees, but fell again to the court and his body went into convulsions. He was suffering a massive heart attack. His mother, his team-mates, his coach, and his doctor all rushed to his side, but moments later he was dead.

The WCC tournament was called off after the tragedy, but the Lions were awarded an NCAA bid on the merits of their regular-season conference title. The next time the Lions played, in the first round versus New Mexico, the national media was there. Gathers' buddy Bo Kimble, who was at Hank's side when he died, dedicated his performance to his friend. The right-handed Kimble honored Gathers by taking his first free throw left-handed, as Hank had done. Kimble scored 45 points

and the eleventh-seeded Lions won 111–92. Their next foe was the defending national champion, number three–seeded Michigan. The Wolverines tried to run with the Lions and were eaten alive, 149–115. Loyola's point total was a tournament record. Fryer led the way with 41, and Kimble added 37 and once again shot his first free throw with his left hand (and, for the second straight game, made the free throw). In the next round, Alabama was smart enough to try to slow the game down. The Crimson Tide milked the clock, but the Lions were up to the challenge, emerging with a gutsy 62–60 victory. Next came the showdown with UNLV. Loyola tried to stay with the masters of the run-and-gun, but the Rebels were too strong, too big, and too talented; they rolled over the heroic Lions 131–101 and headed to Denver for the Final Four.

Elsewhere in the tournament, number one–ranked Oklahoma's postseason woes continued. Oklahoma had earned a number one seeding four times since 1985 and in those years made the Final Four once, losing twice in the second round. Once again, the Sooners lost in the second round, to UNC, who in turn lost to the Final Four-bound Arkansas, led by Lee Mayberry and Todd Day. Duke won an East regional held at the Meadowlands in East Rutherford, New Jersey, where they had won it the previous two seasons. The fourth Final Four team was high-scoring Georgia Tech, who featured three exceptional perimeter marksmen—Dennis Scott, Brian Oliver, and Kenny

UNLV's high-flying Stacey Augmon finishes off a fast break with style. The lanky Augmon was one of the greatest defensive forwards in the history of college hoops and was also the Runnin' Rebel most likely to slam home an alley-oop during the early 1990s.

Anderson—all of whom averaged more than 20 points per game and were dubbed "Lethal Weapon 3."

UNLV matched up against Georgia Tech in the semis and overcame a 7-point halftime deficit with its signature pressure defense to win 90–81. In the other semifinal, Duke used its disciplined approach and senior Phil Henderson's 28 points to dismember high-scoring Arkansas 97–83. The final was ugly. With the exception of Henderson, Duke was a young team, featuring sophomore Christian Laettner and freshman point guard Bobby Hurley. The Rebels built a sizable lead and then, in front of a national audience, the Blue Devils unraveled in the second half. After eight straight years of thrilling, nail-biting championship games, the 1990 final was the most lopsided in history, 103–73. Tark finally had his national title. He'd won it in the most convincing fashion, and four of his five starters were coming back.

The 1991 Final Four found Duke and UNLV in a rematch. Almost a year after their first encounter, in the national semifinals, fans expected more of the same. UNLV seemed only stronger; they stormed through the regular season and stood poised to become the first undefeated national champion since the Indiana Hoosiers in 1976 (and only the eighth ever) and, even more significantly, to become the first repeat champions since the Walton Gang in 1973. In an era of supposed parity, the Rebels were about to make an unequivocal statement; they planned to declare their superiority and take their rightful place among the great college teams of all time. The Rebels had four star players—guards Anderson Hunt and Greg Anthony, forward Stacey Augmon, and the centerpiece of the team, the irrepressible Larry Johnson—back from last year's championship squad, and a new face, center George Ackles, who did a more than admirable job of filling up the middle. Duke also returned with many of the same faces, most notably junior forward Christian Laettner and sophomore point guard Bobby Hurley. The Blue Devils seemed to be setting new standards for consistency and frustration at the same time: the boys from Durham, North Carolina, were appearing in their fourth consecutive Final Four, their fifth in six

years, and their ninth overall, and they had yet to claim a national title.

Between them, Duke and UNLV defined college basketball in the early 1990s. While both were basketball powerhouses, the two programs were polar opposites. On the court their respective styles contrasted sharply. Appropriately,

During the UNLV versus Duke "rematch," the 1991 national semis, UNLV's Evric Gray flies toward the basket while Duke's Bobby Hurley tries to draw a charging foul, Christian Laettner positions himself under the boards, and Rebel Anderson Hunt, in typical UNLV fast-break style, calls for the basketball from behind the three-point arc.

the Runnin' Rebels ran, wherever and whenever possible, on defense and offense. Coach Mike Krzyzewski's Blue Devils played a steady-paced, disciplined game: patient offense, zone defense. Off the court, the contrast was even greater. To many, UNLV represented everything that was wrong with big-time college basketball, while Duke symbolized all that was right. UNLV coach Tarkanian was constantly in hot water for alleged NCAA recruiting violations; in fact, he was able to prevent his program from being placed on probation only by bringing a series of lawsuits against the

NCAA. At the center of UNLV's problems was its recruitment of suspect students (most notoriously, Tarkanian's courting of New York schoolyard legend Lloyd "Sweet Pea" Daniels, who never graduated from high school), which gave UNLV its "win at any cost" reputation. In contrast, Duke not only ranked among

the nation's leaders in graduating its players, but the college itself was one of the nation's best. In fact, Duke is as recognized among the intelligentsia for its world-famous professors as it is among sports fans for its great basketball teams. Thus, the UNLV-Duke showdowns were more than mere basketball games—they were symbolic morality plays. But after the thrashing the Blue Devils took in 1990, few gave them a chance against the Runnin' Rebels in the 1991 rematch.

Indeed, few teams were given much of a chance all season against the UNLV juggernaut. The 1991 tournament took on the feel of one of the tournaments at the height of UCLA's dominance—it seemed like a foregone conclusion. The Rebels did not disappoint as they swept through the West regional with 3 lopsided victories and a slight tussle, 62–54, with a Georgetown team led by twin towers Alonzo Mourning and Dikembe Mutombo. Duke, meanwhile, was moved from the East regional since UNC won the ACC title, but with a series of convincing victories made it to the Hoosierdome from the Midwest regional. From the East, North Carolina joined the party, as did Kansas, on the heels of a surprisingly one-sided 93–81 victory over number two-ranked, number one-seeded Arkansas in the Southeast regional final.

Duke and UNLV squared off in the first national semifinal and right away the game felt different from the previous year's final. Duke paced the Rebels throughout the first half, and UNLV led 43–41 at intermission. Fans expected the typical UNLV second-half explosion. But Duke never lost its composure and the Rebels couldn't shed the feisty Devils. Then with 3:51 to play came the turning point. With the Rebels leading 74–71, Greg Anthony penetrated the lane for an apparent basket, but the referee called Anthony for charging into Duke forward Brian Davis. Duke scored 2 points at the other end and instead of a commanding 5-point lead, the difference was only 1. After that, the Rebels knew it was a fight to the finish. With seconds left, Duke led 79–77. UNLV brought the ball downcourt for one last possession; Anderson Hunt squared up for a 3-point shot and misfired;

and by the time Larry Johnson controlled the rebound, the game was over.

Duke had posted the most memorable upset in the tournament since Villanova's victory over mighty Georgetown in the 1985 final. The final sequence typified the whole game. Countless times the Rebels broke downcourt with a two-on-one or three-on-two advantage, and then passed the ball out for an open three-pointer instead of attacking the middle; this strategy had consistently worked for Tarkanian's Rebel troops since the advent of the 3-point shot in 1986–1987, but they shot erratically on March 30, 1991. However, UNLV didn't lose the game by themselves. The Blue Devils played well and were composed down the stretch. A big difference between the 1990 and 1991

Duke's sophomore point guard Bobby Hurley (dribbling the ball) and freshman forward Grant Hill break downcourt against Kansas during the 1991 finals. The Blue Devils had been regulars at the Final Four since 1986 (except in 1987), but had never won it all. After toppling the Runnin' Rebels in the 1991 semis, they weren't about to let it slip away again; they stayed focused and downed the disciplined but outmanned Jayhawks, 72–65, for their first-ever national title.

UNLV-Duke showdowns was the defense of Blue Devil Grant Hill. The lanky freshman forward's quickness and leaping ability gave the Blue Devils an added dimension in 1991, one that made the Rebels less willing to attack the middle after Hill had generated a number of turnovers. So Duke, who had to live all year in the shadow of the 1990 final debacle, came of age in 1991. In the process, the balance of power in college basketball shifted from the bright lights of the Las Vegas desert to the rolling hills and study halls of Durham, North Carolina.

After Duke's victory, the prospect of an all–North Carolina final loomed. Only three weeks earlier, the Tarheels, powered by guard Hubert Davis, forward Rick Fox, and center Pete Chilcutt, had blasted the Blue Devils by 22 in the finals of the ACC tournament. Perhaps Duke would be able to avenge another lopsided loss in the finals. But Kansas pulled an upset, downing the Tarheels, 79–73. Coach Roy Williams' Kansas team was a disciplined bunch with Lee Randall and Mike Maddox in the low post and dynamic swingman Alonzo Jamison and point guard Adonis Jordan playing above the rim. But Duke had come too far to be let down in the finals. It was the Blue Devils' ninth trip to the Final Four, their third final in five years; they had never won the national title, and considering that they had just cleared the biggest hurdle in Duke basketball history, they figured their time had come. Indeed, the Blue Devils maintained a lead throughout virtually the entire game. Kansas stayed close, but the day belonged to Duke. The final was 72–65. The Blue Devils were the national champions and none of their key players was a senior.

During the 1991–1992 season, the Duke Blue Devils assumed the role played the previous season by UNLV, that of the prohibitively favored defending national champion. In retrospect, the Blue Devils' heroic upset of the seemingly invincible Runnin' Rebels in the 1991 national semifinals was like a changing of the guards—the king is dead, long live the Duke! Duke began the season atop both wire service polls and remained there throughout—though, unlike the 1990–1991 Rebels, the Blue Devils did suffer 2 regular-season losses, both on the road, against ACC rivals North Carolina and Wake Forest. The Duke team had hardly changed from the previous year, though sharpshooting guard Bill McCaffrey had transferred to Vanderbilt. Six-foot-ten-inch (208cm) All-American senior Christian Laettner and junior point guard Bobby Hurley remained at the core of the Blue Devils' attack. Their sidekicks consisted of three versatile swingmen, Grant Hill, Thomas Hill (no relation), and Brian Davis, all brilliant defenders, and sophomore sixth man Antonio Lang, who provided quality minutes in the low post. The Blue Devils crushed the Tarheels by 20 points in the finals of the ACC tournament, and then breezed through the first three rounds of the NCAAs with decisive victories over Campbell, Iowa, and Seton Hall. Next up on the road to the Final Four (or, in Duke's case, the expressway to the title) was sixth-ranked, second-seeded Kentucky. The Cats put up a road block.

The Kentucky Wildcats were back in the limelight after the darkest period in their history, even worse than the early fifties when many of the Wildcats' star players were implicated in the point-shaving scandal. A 1988 NCAA investigation into numerous rule violations at Kentucky resulted in the men's varsity basketball team being suspended from postseason play for the next three seasons, devastating the Wildcat program. When it came time to try to revive the hallowed Kentucky tradition, the names of the most respected coaches in the business were mentioned as possibly going to Lexington. But most coaches demurred, too intimidated by the prospect of rebuilding from the ground up. Not Rick Pitino. The former Providence College coach had moved on to the NBA immediately after taking the Friars to the Final Four in 1987, and led Patrick Ewing and the New York Knicks

Duke's Christian Laettner sends perhaps the most dramatic shot in tournament history toward the bottom of the net. Defending champion Duke trailed Kentucky by 1 in overtime at the 1992 East regional final. With just seconds left in the game, Laettner received a long bomb from Grant Hill, faked one way, turned the other, and buried this jumper.

to two consecutive trips to the playoffs. Pitino jumped at the opportunity to follow in the footsteps of the legendary Adolph Rupp. Pitino was given almost total control of the U of K basketball program and began the hard work of rebuilding in 1989–1990. Two seasons later, Pitino had the Wildcats back among the elite teams in the nation (where they have remained ever since). The 1991–1992 Wildcats were a high-scoring, hard-working group that featured pressure defense (which would become Pitino's signature at Kentucky) and 3-point shooting. The team didn't have a certified star, but John Pelphrey and Sean Woods were solid and freshman Jamal Mashburn looked like the real thing. The Wildcats won the Southeastern Conference and breezed past Old Dominion, outscored Iowa State, and outplayed a tough UMass team to reach the regional finals.

The defining moment of the 1991–1992 college basketball season came in the NCAA East regional final matchup between Duke and Kentucky. Indeed, the game has few rivals in NCAA tournament history. From start to finish, the showdown generated end-to-end action. Duke was its usual brilliant, well-disciplined self, and Kentucky matched the Blue Devils, step for step, shot for shot. The teams shot a combined 61 percent over the game's final twenty-five minutes. The game was tied at the end of regulation, 93–93. The teams went

Statistically, O'Neal was as dominant as virtually any center in college basketball history, but this did not translate into any championships. The Tigers' struggles during the O'Neal era (1989–1990 through 1991–1992) reveal how the significance of a talented big man has been diminished in the age of 3-point shooting.

back and forth in overtime, John Pelphrey performing in the clutch for the Wildcats, Christian Laettner—who passed Elvin Hayes as the all-time scorer in NCAA tournament history in the first half—simply sublime for Duke. Laettner proved himself worthy of the all-time record by hitting all 10 of the free throws he attempted in the game and shooting a perfect 10 for 10 from the field, including the spectacular game-winning shot. In

the waning seconds of the overtime period, Kentucky went up 103–102 on an incredible, high-arcing jump shot. Inbounding, Grant Hill hurled a full-court pass to Laettner, who caught the ball at the free throw line, dribbled once, faked both ways to shed both defenders, shot, and hit nothing but net as the buzzer sounded. Afterward Laettner reflected that he didn't "realize what happened. I just caught the ball, turned around and made the shot." Laettner's perfect game, which clearly ranks among the greatest individual performances in basketball history, saved the Blue Devils by the skin of their teeth. An elated and, no doubt, relieved Coach Krzyzewski added, "I think we've all been part of one of the greatest games ever. You hope someday you're a part of something like this. I was just standing around afterwards figuring what a lucky son of a gun I am." Duke's drive to repeat as champions continued.

Joining the Blue Devils in Minnesota for the Final Four were Indiana, Cincinnati, and Michigan. The Hoosiers won the West regional where they overcame two teams expected to contend for the national title at the beginning of the season, LSU and UCLA. Shaquille O'Neal surprised the basketball world by remaining at LSU for his junior season, when the agile seven-foot-one-inch (216cm), 300-pound (136kg) center would have been the consensus number one draft pick in 1991. Shaquille had an excellent season, but the Tigers struggled, finishing the season ranked a mere twenty-five, providing ample evidence that the short 3-point shot meant that even exceptional big men could no longer dominate the college game. Seeded seventh in the West regional, the Tigers fell to second-seeded Indiana, 89–79, in the second round, and that was it for O'Neal who, as expected, bypassed his senior season for the NBA. Bobby Knight's Hoosiers played typical Bobby Knight defense, but on offense they lit up the scoreboard. Led by star forwards Calbert Chaney and Alan Henderson, the Hoosiers moved past Florida State to set up a showdown with fourth-ranked UCLA, who was trying to end a twelve-year Final Four drought. Coach Jim Harrick had rebuilt a winning tradition in Westwood and had a strong team in 1991–1992 led by sharpshooting senior Don McClean. However, the Hoosiers blew right by the Bruins, 106–79, on their way to Minneapolis.

Cincinnati was the surprise team of the tournament. The fourth-seeded Bearcats trounced Delaware, pasted Michigan State, and then squeaked by the University of Texas–El Paso, 69–67. (UTEP had posted the tournament's biggest upset, when they eliminated second-ranked Kansas, 66–60, in the second round.) Cincinnati then manhandled Memphis State, 88–57, and a Bearcat bunch steered by southpaw point guard Nick Van Exel and low-post bruiser Corey Blount was takin' down the twine in Kansas City. It was the first time Cincinnati had qualified for the Final Four since 1963, when a loss to Loyola dashed their dreams of becoming the first school ever to win three consecutive national titles.

If not for Duke's dynastic Blue Devils, the story of the 1992 tournament would certainly have been Michigan's "Fab Five." Coach Steve Fisher had a great recruiting year in 1991, luring five topflight high school seniors to Michigan. The 1990–1991 Wolverines had been a veteran team; thus, no starters returned to Ann Arbor in the fall of '91. So Fisher started his five prize recruits: center Juwan Howard, forward Ray Jackson, six-

foot-seven-inch (201 cm) point guard Jalen Rose, off-guard Jimmy King, and the jewel among jewels, power forward Chris Webber. After some initial growing pains, the Fab Five came together brilliantly. The Wolverines were ranked fifteenth in the final AP regular-season poll and were seeded sixth in the Southeast regional. The Wolverines downed Temple, East Tennessee State (who had shocked third-seeded Arizona), and second-seeded Oklahoma State in a series of close but solid postseason victories. Then the Fab Five squared off against Big Ten champion Ohio State, led by high-scoring senior Jimmy Jackson. When the dust settled after an overtime period, Michigan prevailed 75–71. At an average age of nineteen years and twenty-eight days, the Fab Five were in the Final Four.

Both semifinal games of the 1992 tournament were tight throughout. In the first game Indiana led 42–37 at halftime, but Duke came on strong in the second half for a tight 81–78 victory. In the nightcap, Cincinnati was ahead 41–38 at intermission, but the young Wolverines suffocated the Bearcats down the stretch and, with four starters in double figures, had too many weapons for Cincinnati to contain. Michigan won 76–72. The final was nip and tuck in the first half, the Wolverines holding a 31–30 advantage at the break. But the Blue Devils blew out the Fab Five in the second frame, posting a lopsided 71–51 victory. In the final game of the Laettner era, Duke put on a clinic, playing airtight defense and a brilliantly finessed offense. One year after the Blue Devils earned their first-ever title by upsetting the heavily favored defending national champion, they became the first

team in nineteen years to repeat as national champions.

Many felt that the Blue Devils were able to repeat as champions because Duke players valued their educations more than players at other schools and so were more likely to stay at Duke for four years. While no one posited this theory the previous year when UNLV came close to repeating as champions, it is true that Duke players have, as a rule, stayed

Duke players surround Coach Mike Krzyzewski, alias Coach K, and hoist the NCAA championship trophy following their victory over Michigan's Fab Five in the 1992 title game. This Blue Devils team was the first group since UCLA's Walton Gang (1972–1973) to repeat as national champions. The nineteen-year drought between back-to-back titles was the longest in tournament history.

in Durham for four years. Players that play together longer develop better teamwork and Duke's cohesiveness undoubtedly contributed to its amazing run from 1986 to 1994, in which the Blue Devils reached the Final Four seven times, the finals four times, and captured a pair of national championship banners in consecutive seasons, 1991 and 1992.

The 1992–1993 season promised to be a showcase for the second-year Fab Five, and indeed, come tournament time Michigan made a dramatic march back to the finals. However, the rest of the college basketball universe didn't passively take a backseat to the young mavericks from Michigan. In fact, Indiana, not the Wolverines, captured the Big Ten title and entered the tournament ranked number one. However, the Hoosiers fell in the Midwest regional final to second-seeded Kansas, while the other three top-seeded teams—Kentucky, North Carolina, and Michigan—all advanced to New Orleans.

Not that the early rounds of the tournament were without thrills: second-seeded Arizona's postseason woes continued when the Wildcats were stunned by 20-point underdog Santa Clara in the first round. And Michigan's second-

In a long shot of the 1993 finals, Michigan's Fab Five, now sophomores, attack the basket against North Carolina. Ray Jackson puts up a short jumper from the side, Jimmy King (21) and Juwan Howard crash the boards, Chris Webber boxes out in the paint, and point guard Jalen Rose (5) looks on. Representing the balanced Tarheels squad are Brian Reese (31), George Lynch (34), big man Eric Montross, and two others.

round match against UCLA was a thriller. The Bruins led by as many as 19 in the first half before Chris Webber and Ray Jackson led the Wolverines back. However, the Fab Five continued to hurt themselves at the free throw line and UCLA was able to force an overtime. Michigan did not secure the victory until Jimmy King's tip-in off a Jalen Rose miss—with one and a half seconds left in overtime—produced an 86–84 final. However, the most memorable second-round game was between two-time defending champion Duke (featuring Bobby Hurley, who was on a mission to become the first player ever to start in four consecutive NCAA championship games, and increasingly spectacular junior Grant Hill) and the Cal Bears (led by freshman point guard sensation Jason Kidd). After Cal led the entire game, by as much as 18 early in the second half, the Blue Devils came roaring back and with 2:21 remaining took a 77–76 lead. But just as Kidd had provided the heroics in the first round with a last-second shot that beat LSU, the brilliant point guard came up with the big play against the seasoned Blue Devils. After Hurley deflected one of the Bears' passes, a mad scramble ensued on the floor; somehow Kidd emerged with the ball, raced down-

court, and threw up an unlikely shot that fell down, and Cal regained control of the game. The final was 82–77 and the Blue Devils' two-year reign and string of five consecutive appearances in the Final Four was over. The Bears were the darlings of the tournament for the next few days but couldn't get by the disciplined Kansas Jayhawks—featuring brilliant guard Rex Walters and hulking center Greg Ostertag—in the next round. The Jayhawks then posted a convincing win over an Indiana team weakened by an injury to their star Alan Henderson, who could play only three minutes in the regional final.

The Jayhawks' opponent in the national semifinal in New Orleans, the University of North Carolina, had to scramble to get past Arkansas, 80–74, and then required overtime to defeat a resourceful Cincinnati team led by veterans Corey Blount and point guard Nick Van Exel. However, these Tarheels were a well-balanced team that had four

starters—junior center Eric Montross, senior forward George Lynch, sophomore guard Donald Williams, and junior forward Brian Reese—who averaged double figures in points. UNC rolled over Kansas 78–68 and Dean Smith returned to the finals for the first time in eleven years. The 1982 final versus Georgetown was the single greatest victory of Smith's coaching career and one of the most memorable games played in college basketball history. Coincidentally, the 1993 final was to be played in the Louisiana Superdome, the site of Smith's victory eleven years earlier.

While UNC was a formidable opponent by any measure, the winner of the first national semifinal between Michigan and Kentucky promised to be the favorite in the finals. Kentucky had been nothing short of awesome in advancing to New Orleans, devouring its opponents by an average margin of 30.5 points and scoring a tournament-high 106 points in their blowout of Florida State in the regional finals. Coach Rick Pitino's team was not exceptionally deep (like the Wildcats teams in '95 and '96), but it had a budding superstar in forward Jamal Mashburn. The Wildcats' race-horse style would be in contrast to the controlled but equally physical half-court style of the Fab Five. The game lived up to expectations. Michigan held a 5-point lead at halftime, but Kentucky's full-court pressure bore fruit in the second half and the game was all knotted up at 71 after regulation. Michigan survived the heavyweight slugfest with an 81–78 victory and advanced to the finals for the second straight year.

The championship game was equally dramatic—an ebb-and-flow battle of great surges. First UNC led, then Michigan moved ahead by 10, then the Tarheels blasted back and led by as many as 8; with four and a half minutes remaining, the Wolverines were up by 4. But tournament MVP Donald Williams buried a three-pointer and then senior George Lynch took over, making a steal that was converted into an easy basket, burying a turnaround jumper, and finally lofting a perfect pass to Montross for a dunk. However, the Wolverines stayed close, trailing 73–71 with time running down. Then Webber controlled the boards off a UNC miss, dribbled down-court, and made a gaffe that handed the title to North Carolina and brought to mind painful memories of 1982, when Georgetown's Fred Brown threw away the title by passing to the Heels' James Worthy in the closing seconds with UNC clinging to a 1-point lead. Webber was cornered by two Tarheel defenders with eleven seconds left, and he signaled for a time-out. But the Wolverines had already used all of their allotted time-outs. An automatic technical foul was called, which gave UNC 2 free throws plus the ball. The final score was 77–71 in a thrilling game that will always be remembered for Webber's ill-fated time-out. And for the second time in his career Dean Smith won a national title—both victories were at the Superdome and decided by fatal mistakes by the other team in the final seconds. In a town like New Orleans, with its mystical past and Caribbean flavor, one has to wonder: what voodoo do you do, Dean?

It was a quite a sight—the President of the United States cheering his home state's team to the national championship. But there he was, Bill Clinton, the nation's forty-second chief executive, rooting for the Arkansas Razorbacks at the Final Four in Charlotte, North Carolina. Midway through the season, as the Hogs ascended to the top of the wire service polls, word leaked out from the White House that Georgetown alumnus Clinton had gone "Hog wild." And when the Razorbacks put the finishing touches on Michigan's Fab Five minus one (Webber had turned pro) in the Midwest regional, President Clinton let it be known that next weekend the affairs of state were taking a backseat to the Final Four.

Entering the NCAA tournament, Arkansas and North Carolina were the cofavorites, but the defending champions were stunned in the second round by Boston College 75–72, ending UNC's streak of thirteen consecutive visits to the Sweet Sixteen. B.C. then moved past Indiana (completing a sweep of college basketball's two most accomplished active coaches, Dean Smith and Bobby Knight) before succumbing to Florida in the East regional semifinal. The other two number one seeds were Big Ten champ Purdue, led by Player of the Year and national scoring leader Glenn Robinson (30.3 points per game), and the Missouri Tigers, who were the first team ever to win all their Big Eight regular-season games. However, Purdue and Missouri only got as far as their regional finals before losing to Duke and Arizona, respectively.

The Duke-Florida game matched a Blue Devils team playing traditional Duke basketball—disciplined offense and tight zone defense—versus a Florida team with the interior strength of wide-bodied six-foot-seven-inch (201cm), 300-pound (136kg) Demetrius Hill and six-foot-ten-inch (208cm) center Andrew Declerq and a pesky defense keyed by guards Craig Brown and Dan Cross. However, the ever-seasoned Blue Devils were not likely to be rattled. Forward Andrew Lang and center Cherokee Parks were still around from the '92 champi-onships, but the unquestioned leader of this group of Blue Devils was high-fly-ing forward Grant Hill. The son of foot-ball great Calvin Hill, Grant had been instrumental in lifting Duke over UNLV and on to its first title in 1991 with his superb defense. Since then he had devel-oped his offensive skills to become a great player overall. Still, Florida moved in front of the Blue Devils early and held a 39–32 halftime advantage. But with Hill leading the way with 25 points, Duke rallied for a 70–65 victory and reached the finals for the fourth time in five years.

The other semifinal matched favored Arkansas against Arizona. For the Wildcats, who had suffered so many humiliating defeats in early rounds of the tournament in recent years, just making the Final Four was redemption. However, these Wildcats were unique among Lute Olsen's teams, which usually featured bulky low-post players paired with either one-dimensional jump shooters or a slashing forward like Sean Elliot. The

Michigan's Chris Webber is left to ponder his thoughts after making one of the greatest gaffes in sports history, while North Carolina's seven-foot (213cm) center Eric Montross raises his hands in victory during the closing seconds of the 1993 finals. Moments earlier, with UNC ahead by 1 point in the game's final twenty seconds, Webber had con-trolled the defensive boards, dribbled downcourt, and, hoping to set up for a game-winning shot, called for a time-out. But Michigan had already used up its time-outs, and the call resulted in a technical foul. North Carolina was awarded 2 foul shots, the ball, and, in effect, the national championship.

1993–1994 Arizona Wildcats were led by a pair of spectacular guards, Khalid Reeves and Damon Stoudamire. Arkansas, on the other hand, had it all; the Razorbacks were strong, fast, deep, and talented. The centerpiece of coach Nolan Richardson's crew was bulky power forward Corliss Williamson, who possessed a soft shooting touch and led the team in both scoring (20.4 per game) and rebounding (7.7). Williamson's supporting cast included deadeye shooter Scotty Thurman; guards Cory Beck, Clint Macdaniel, and Al Dillard; and a tandem of centers, Dwight Stewart and freshman Darnell Robinson. All eight of these Hogs were excellently conditioned and primed to play Richardson's favored brand of defense—all-out, all over the floor, all the time (or "forty minutes of hell," as the coach liked to call it, though by tournament time the Razorbacks only unleashed this defensive "hell" at select-ed times). At its best, Arkansas' defensive pressure was an awesome offensive weapon that forced turnovers that led to easy baskets and routs. The Razorbacks, who lost only three times all season, won every home game by more than 10 points except for an 84–83 squeaker over LSU. However, ana-lysts thought that Arizona's brilliant guard tandem might be just the antidote for however many minutes of hell Richardson might throw at the Wildcats. Indeed, Arizona held a 67–62 lead with eight minutes remaining when Reeves was whistled for his fourth foul and took a seat on the bench. Then all hell broke lose. Two minutes and 12 straight points later, Arkansas had the game in hand and cruised to a 91–82 victory.

The Blue Devils–Razorbacks final pitted two teams noted for highly con-trasting styles: Duke's disciplined control game versus Arkansas' all-out, fast-paced frenzy. However, over the course of the season the Hogs had evolved into a team capable of patient and detailed offensive execution. Meanwhile Duke's Grant Hill, who was trying to join Lew Alcindor and his UCLA classmates as the only college players in history to play on three national championship teams, excelled in the open court. The contest was close throughout the first half, which ended 34–33, advantage Hogs. Then Duke went on a 13–0 run to open a 10-point lead with seventeen minutes left. But the next nine minutes were hell; the Razorbacks forced 9 turnovers with their all-out defense and outscored the Blue Devils 21–6 for a 5-point lead. Duke rebounded to take a brief 1-point lead, but the Hogs seemed to regain control and led 70–67 with two minutes left. Richardson called for a stall, but the strategy backfired when Stewart missed a three-pointer and Hill retaliated with a trio to tie the game. With less than a minute left, Arkansas worked the ball around the half court offense, looking for a good shot, but at every turn the Blue Devils were there; with the shot clock winding down, Stewart was poised to try from the top of the key when he fumbled the ball. Luckily, Stewart saw Scotty Thurman open to his right and got him the ball. From far behind the 3-point arc, with Duke's Antonio Lang jumping out at him, Thurman let go of a rainbow just before the shot clock expired—and hit nothing but net. To the delight of the president and Arkansans everywhere, the Hogs held on for their first national championship, 76–72.

The 1995 Final Four in Seattle gathered defending champion Arkansas alongside three of college bas-ketball's most storied schools—UCLA, North Carolina, and Oklahoma State—in a grouping that recalled some of the NCAA tournament's finest moments. UCLA, with a record ten NCAA cham-pionships but none since John Wooden's retirement in 1975, was making its first Final Four appearance in fifteen years. Oklahoma State, formerly Oklahoma A&M, had not been a basketball power-house since coach Hank Iba's heyday in the forties and fifties. The Cowboys were actually making their first Final Four appearance, because the last time the school had reached the national semifinals, 1951, was the year before the inaugural Final Four. Oklahoma State center six-foot-ten-inch (208cm) Bryant "Big Country" Reeves brought to mind the school's greatest star, seven-foot (213cm) Bob "Foothills" Kurland, who led the Aggies to consecutive NCAA crowns in 1945 and 1946. North Carolina repre-sented a more contemporary power-house, having won the tournament as recently as 1993, but the Tarheels had been consistent winners throughout, winning the national title in 1957 and 1982 and appearing in 29 NCAA tour-neys, the third most behind Kentucky (37) and UCLA (31). Also, UNC head coach Dean Smith provided a link to the very beginning of the sport, for Smith played for the legendary Phog Allen at Kansas, who, in turn, was coached by the inventor of basketball himself, Dr. James Naismith. Meanwhile Arkansas was try-ing to join UCLA, Oklahoma State, Kentucky, USF, and Duke as only the sixth school ever to repeat as NCAA champions. Thus, the 1995 Final Four provided a field day for college basket-ball historians.

While *Sports Illustrated* declared UCLA number one at the top of the sea-son, most pundits thought that Arkansas deserved the top ranking since it had all of its starters back from its 1994 champi-onship squad. However, the Hogs quickly fell from the top of the polls when they lost the Hall of Fame "Tip-Off" Classic to a powerful Massachusetts team led by two superb low-post players, Lou Roe and Marcus Camby. UMass had a dis-tinct home-court advantage in the show-down since the Hall of Fame is located in Springfield, Massachusetts, where Dr.

Duke's Grant Hill drives to the basket. By the time Hill was a senior, he was "the man" on the Blue Devils team. As a freshman and sophomore, he was merely a part of the supporting cast, specializing in defense. But Hill worked nonstop on his all-around game (his free throw shooting went from embarrass-ing to consistent, as did his jumper), and by his fourth season in Durham he was a consensus All-American.

Naismith invented the game more than a hundred years earlier and where the University of Massachusetts also happens to be located. However, neither UMass nor any other team was able to hold on to the number one ranking for very long until UCLA got hot at midseason and went on a 13-game winning streak to close out the season 25–2 and enter the tournament atop both polls. A trio of seniors—All-American forward Ed O'Bannon, center George Zidek, and point guard Tyus Edney—guided the Bruins, who also got quality minutes from a younger O'Bannon brother, Charles, and two high-flying freshmen, Toby Bailey and J.R. Henderson. Arkansas seemed sluggish at times throughout the season, compiling a 27–6 record, but at tournament time most analysts felt that the experienced Razorbacks were still the team to beat. One team that fell off considerably was Duke. The Blue Devils actually ascended to a number one ranking early in the season, but then Coach K fell ill and had to take a leave of absence from the team, which fell apart. Duke plummeted to a 13-and-18 record and missed the NCAA tournament (and the NIT as well) for the first time since 1983.

There were few upsets in the early rounds of the tournament but there were many close calls, one of which became the tournament's defining moment. Missouri, behind shooting guard Paul O'Liney's 23 points, led UCLA with 4.8 seconds left when Tyus Edney took the ball near his own basket, dribbled the length of the court weaving through the Tigers defenders at breakneck speed, and, as the buzzer sounded, put up a running one-hander from about six feet (183cm) away, over an outstretched defender six inches (15cm) taller than him. The ball banked off the glass and fell straight through the net. It was another bitter tournament defeat for Norm Stewart's Tigers, who lost in the regional finals the previous year to Arizona and are the most successful team over the past twenty seasons never to make the Final Four. UCLA then went on to dismiss Mississippi State and the University of Connecticut by more comfortable margins. Oklahoma State upset UMass in

Arkansas' Scotty Thurman slams home 2 points during the 1995 Midwest regional final versus Virginia. On a balanced and deep Arkansas team, Williamson stood out as the team's star. The focus of the team's half-court offense, Williamson was a rock-solid low-post force with a soft jumper who also possessed the athleticism to play the Razorbacks' favored style of full-court pressure defense and fast-break offense.

the East regional final. North Carolina dismissed highly touted Georgetown and Kentucky on the road to the Final Four, thanks in great part to two sensational Tarheel sophomores, forward Jerry Stackhouse and center Rasheed Wallace, both of whom, in a sign of the times, would leave UNC for the NBA after the season. Arkansas, meanwhile, escaped a scare against Memphis, when Scotty Thurman buried a jumper in the final seconds of overtime. The Hogs then righted themselves with an easy win over Virginia in the regional finals.

While the historical significance of the foursome in Seattle allowed for fans to reminisce about some of the great moments in tournament history, all the games themselves were decided by comfortable margins. First, Arkansas rolled over North Carolina in the first semifinal matchup, 75–68, which many felt was a pairing of the two best teams. Then UCLA handily dismissed OSU 74–61 to win a meeting with the defending NCAA champs in the final game. UCLA

was a mature and efficient unit with considerable explosiveness, while Arkansas was proving that they deserved consideration as one of the great college units of all time. Indeed, the Razorbacks were favored in the final, especially since Edney was sidelined with a sprained wrist. This meant that the daunting task of running the Bruin offense against Arkansas' legendary pressure defense fell on the shoulders of sophomore defensive standout Cameron Dollar. The game was played at a fast pace and Dollar proved up to the task. Ed O'Bannon was brilliant, racking up 30 points, 17 rebounds, and 3 steals in what *Sports Illustrated* called perhaps the best final game performance since Jack Givens' amazing 41-point outburst in 1978 (though Danny Manning's clutch performance in 1988 should not be overlooked). Behind senior O'Bannon and unlikely hero Dollar, UCLA surged ahead with about six minutes remaining and coasted to an 89–78 victory. Coach Jim Harrick, who in his seventh season had already lasted longer than any post-Wooden UCLA coach, led the Bruins to their first title since the days of the Wizard of Westwood. Wooden himself looked on approvingly from the stands. Twenty years after the Wizard's last hurrah, the Bruins captured their first post-Wooden national championship.

Whereas the 1995 Final Four in Seattle recalled the glorious past of the NCAA tournament on account of the storied traditions of the four participating schools, the 1996 Final Four recalled the darkest moment in the history of the college by virtue of its location. The 1996 Final Four was held at the Meadowlands sports complex, just across the Hudson river from Manhattan. The last time the NCAA held its championship finals in the greater New York City metropolitan area was in 1951, a few months before the infamous point-shaving scandal rocked the world of college basketball. After the scandal the NCAA wanted nothing to do with the Big Apple, where most of the backroom deals between players and gamblers had been made. Before the scandal broke, six out of the previous seven NCAA finals had been held in New York; afterward, New York didn't host the finals for forty-five years.

Coincidentally, the school that captured the 1951 national championship, the University of Kentucky, was the prohibitive favorite in 1996. Much like New York City, the Wildcat basketball program was seeking redemption, though for more recent improprieties. In the late 1980s, the Kentucky basketball program had been rocked by recruiting violations stemming from coach Joe Hall's tenure. For the second time in its glorious history, though for different reasons, the Kentucky basketball program had been laid to rest for an entire season (1988–1989)—as it had been in 1952–1953.

In the summer of 1989, coach Rick Pitino was brought in to revive the moribund Kentucky basketball program.

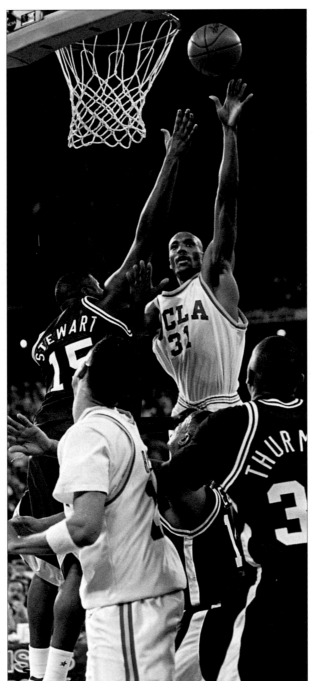

UCLA's Ed O'Bannon tosses in 2 points over a defender while Razorbacks Scotty Thurman and Bruin Toby Bailey position themselves under the boards during the 1995 NCAA finals. O'Bannon, the 1994–1995 Player of the Year, led the Bruins to an 89–78 victory over the defending champions with a spectacular 30-point, 17-rebound performance. It was UCLA's first NCAA crown in twenty years, and the first that was not won during its remarkable twelve-year dynasty (1964–1975).

Pitino had made a national reputation for himself when he led an upstart cast of 3-point-shot-hurling Providence Friars to the 1987 Final Four. In the following off-season, Pitino left the Friars to coach the New York Knicks, Pitino's hometown team (which had yet to win consistently during the Patrick Ewing era). Pitino led the team to an Atlantic division crown in 1988–1989 and the young coach became the toast of the town. Pitino was deemed

a hero even by the New York media—until the summer of 1989, when he stunned everyone by accepting the head coaching job at troubled Kentucky. As part of the lucrative deal, Pitino was given almost complete control over the program.

Once again, Pitino did a brilliant job of rebuilding. By 1992, the Wildcats were back among the nation's top teams, and came within a whisker of dethroning reigning champion Duke in the regional finals. The next season Kentucky returned to the Final Four for the first time in nine years. After 1993, Pitino started stockpiling top recruits and quality transfers (players who began their college careers at other schools) from around the country. However, the Wildcats failed to get by North Carolina in the 1995 regional finals. Thus, entering the 1996 season, Pitino's honeymoon period was coming to a close. The "Blue" faithful wanted nothing less than a national title from Pitino and his talented troops. Fans throughout the Bluegrass State had begun to question Pitino's skill as a strategist because of crucial decisions he had made in the finals of the previous three seasons that many people felt had cost Kentucky championships.

Pitino had done something very radical with his Wildcats over three seasons. Since the departure of Mashburn following the 1992–1993 season (Mashburn's junior season), Pitino deliberately built a team without a dominant star. While he recruited a large group of exceptionally talented young players, he asked his players to sacrifice their desire to excel individually for the good of the team. By 1995–1996, Pitino had structured his team so that it had eight players in heavy rotation; every Wildcat player, even every starter, could expect to sit on the bench for at least ten minutes during each game. Pitino was developing a team that could apply constant, all-out defensive pressure over every inch of the court. Pitino knew he had exceptional depth on his team and that if he rotated his players enough he would always have fresh legs on the court. Since the 1964 UCLA Bruins, teams that have used brilliant full-court pressure defense have had tremendous success in the NCAA tournament. Unlike the great defensive teams of the interim, however, Pitino's Wildcats, going nine deep (or more), pressured the ball whenever possible, all game long. So for most college basketball analysts, the prevailing question about the Kentucky Wildcats of 1995–1996 was not about Pitino's skill as a strategist but whether a team that relied on so many players could stick together and execute down the stretch against more traditionally structured teams (particularly mature teams that played a half-court game).

The Wildcats faced just such a challenge in only their second game of the season, against UMass. The Minutemen were coming off their strongest season in years, but they had lost one of their two frontcourt stars, Lou Roe, to the NBA. Roe's departure left rangy six-foot-eleven-inch (211 cm) Marcus Camby as the team's centerpiece. But Camby's Minutemen teammates—forwards Dana Dingle and Donta Bright and guards Carmelo Travieso and Edgar Padilla. Travieso and Padilla, who also played together on the Puerto Rican national team, worked so smoothly together that it was as if they communicated telepathically. Both were super-quick, exceptional ball-handlers, unrelenting defenders, and good outside shooters, and both knew how to work the ball inside to Camby. This seasoned group of Minutemen was more than ready for the Kentucky onslaught and stunned the Wildcats 92–82, maintaining a 4- to 10- point lead throughout the second half. UMass shot to the top of the polls and Kentucky retreated back to Lexington, licking its wounds. The Minutemen's controlled style had prevailed over the Wildcats' flash.

After Camby inexplicably collapsed before a game with St. Bonaventure's (hospital tests ultimately proved inconclusive) on January 14, the Minutemen shocked the nation by reeling off 4 straight victories without their star center. And when Camby returned, the Minutemen's roll continued. Just when it seemed like UMass would complete the first undefeated regular season since UNLV in 1990–1991 and try to become

the first undefeated national titlist since Indiana in 1975–1976, the Minutemen were upset by in-conference foe George Washington, 86–76, on February 24, after 26 victories to start the season.

Instantly, the Kentucky Wildcats regained the number one ranking (to the dismay of UMass fans). Since their humbling setback to UMass, the Wildcats had been dismantling opponents: against Vanderbilt, the Wildcats tallied 13 points before the Commodores managed to hit the rim with a shot; one night, the Wildcats poured in 86 points against LSU in the first half; and they annihilated Morehead State, 96–32. Their average margin of victory was more than 30 points. The Kentucky "starting nine"—guard Tony Delk, forward Antoine Walker, forward/center Walter McCarty, forward Derek Anderson, guard Anthony Epps, center Mark Pope, swingman (forward/guard) Allen Edwards, shooting guard Jeff Sheppard, and super freshman forward Ron Mercer—and "tenth man" Wayne Turner were a brilliant, seamless unit made up of star-caliber players. In an era when the best players on other teams left school early once they established their reputations in the college ranks, the Kentucky players displayed the selflessness of champions. Kentucky posted 27 consecutive victories following the loss to UMass and seemed poised to rip through the NCAA field when they hit an unexpected snag in the finals of the SEC tournament, against Mississippi State. The Bulldogs, led by center Eric Dampier and sharpshooting forward Dontae Jones, avenged their regular-season loss to the Wildcats with a stunning 84–73 upset. Once again, Kentucky had fallen to a team with a strong, half-court offense. On the eve of the Big Dance, a shudder ran through the Bluegrass State. And UMass recaptured the nation's number one ranking heading into the tournament.

In addition to the UMass-Kentucky conflict atop the wire service polls, a number of other teams entered the postseason with realistic hopes of capturing the national title. Kansas spent the entire season among the nation's top ten teams and dominated play in the Big Eight. The same was true of Conference

U.S.A.'s inaugural champion, Cincinnati. Wake Forest, led by seven-foot (213 cm) center Tim Duncan, and Georgia Tech, led by sensational freshman point guard Stephon Marbury, were the class of the ACC. But the strongest conference seemed to be the Big East, which had three teams—Georgetown, Connecticut, and Villanova—that were ranked in the top ten for most of the season. The Big East tournament final was one of the year's most scintillating games: Georgetown came back from a double-digit deficit in the final five minutes against UConn to take a 1-point lead with just seconds left, but Connecticut All-American Ray Allen, who had been struggling all game long, hit an improbable running jump shot as time expired to lift the Huskies to victory. The tournament selection committee rewarded number one seeding to UMass, Kentucky, UConn, and Purdue, which won its record-tying third straight Big Ten title.

The first two rounds of the tournament provided many thrills but few upsets. The most memorable moment came when defending champion UCLA fell to Ivy League champion Princeton in the first round. Princeton's legendary coach, Pete Carrill, had announced that he was retiring after the tournament; his Tigers sent him out in style. Mississippi State then unceremoniously ousted the Tigers 63–41. Only three of the top sixteen teams failed to advance past the second round. Marquette, a fourth seed, lost to a grossly underrated Arkansas team; Villanova fell to a solid bunch of Louisville Cardinals; and, in the only surprise of any note, number one seed Purdue lost to Georgia. Thus, for the second straight year, no Big Ten teams reached the Sweet Sixteen.

Likewise, the regional semifinals produced some brilliant play but only one upset. UMass and Georgetown advanced to a much-anticipated showdown in the East regional. Second-seeded Wake Forest squeaked by Louisville, 60–59, when the Cardinals failed to connect in the final seconds, setting up a showdown with Kentucky. Out West, Arizona also misfired in the closing seconds, allowing Kansas to advance.

Syracuse's John Wallace came up with the shot of the tournament to defeat Georgia in overtime. The Bulldogs had trailed by 2 with just seconds left in the extra period when Pertha Robinson buried a three-pointer to give Georgia the lead. The Orangemen chose not to call time-out and the ball ended up in the hands of center/power forward Wallace, who dribbled upcourt and pulled up and shot from just outside the 3-point arc, hitting nothing but net as time ran out. Meanwhile in the

Marcus Camby, 1995–1996 Player of the Year, slams home 2 points for UMass versus Kentucky at the 1996 Final Four. The six-foot-eleven-inch (211m) junior was dominant on both ends of the court, using his long arms to block shots and clear the boards near his own basket, pouring in the points with hole with a wide array of low-post moves.

Mideast, red-hot Mississippi State ousted top-seeded Connecticut, 60-55, in a game that was not as close as the score suggests. Number two Cincinnati downed number three Georgia Tech handily, 87-70.

The marquee matchup of the regional finals was UMass versus Georgetown. Many analysts across the country, both at the beginning of the season and at the start of the tournament, had predicted that Georgetown

would take the national title. Led by sensational sophomore point guard Allen Iverson, the Hoyas featured their signature pressure defense and aggressive style of play. Heading into the regional final showdown, many critics said that Georgetown would simply be too physical for the Minutemen. But UMass was sharper than the Hoyas on both ends of the court, and even though Marcus Camby had to contend with foul trouble, the Minutemen led the entire game and coasted to an 86–62 romp. In contrast, the Western regional final was a close game. Syracuse beat Kansas in a nip-and-tuck Western regional final, 60–57; in a year when three other Big East teams had been heralded all season long, Syracuse managed to become the first Big East team to reach the Final Four in seven seasons (since Seton Hall in 1989). In the Southeast regional, Mississippi State continued its brilliant postseason run with a convincing victory over Cincinnati, 73–63. In the Midwest, Kentucky devastated its fourth straight opponent, Wake Forest, 83–63. The Wildcats' average margin of victory in the first four rounds of the tournament was 28.25 points.

So as Pitino's troops rolled into the coach's hometown for the Final Four, the stage was set for redemption, Bluegrass style. A national championship for the Wildcats would exorcise the ghosts from Kentucky's distant (1951), not-so-distant (1988), and recent past (the only two teams to tarnish the Wildcats' otherwise perfect season were conveniently joining them at the Meadowlands). However, the Wildcats' dream of knocking off UMass in the semis and then crushing the pesky Bulldogs from the Deep South in the finals came to an end when Syracuse toppled Mississippi State in the first national semifinal, 77–69. The main event, the rematch between the two teams that had dominated the wire service polls all season long, followed. UMass, led by consensus Player of the Year Marcus Camby, would take on Kentucky, the pundits' prohibitive favorite to win. Immediately, Kentucky moved in front and, with its unrelenting pressure, seemed on numerous occasions ready to pull away from the Minutemen.

But UMass showed tremendous poise in the face of the Wildcats onslaught, periodically stringing together a series of baskets and raising the possibility that the Minutemen's superior half-court execution would allow them to overtake Kentucky. But the Wildcats never panicked, its own half-court offense produced well, steady shooting guard Tony Delk led the way with 20 points, and its pressure defense sparked a series of runs. In the second half, Kentucky built up a double-digit lead five times, only to see the courageous Minutemen cut it back to single digits each time. But down the stretch it became evident that Kentucky was just too much to handle, even for the disciplined and clutch Minutemen. At the end of the game the UMass players looked as if they had just run a marathon, while the jubilant Wildcats bounced off with fresh legs, only one hurdle from the coveted NCAA crown.

Nobody gave Syracuse much of a chance in the finals. The Orangemen did not have much depth, though their starting five was a talented, veteran unit. Rock-solid Otis Hill complemented the team's star, John Wallace, down low; shooting guard Jason Cipolla was a steady performer; and forward Todd Burgan and point guard Lazarus Sims could both drive to the basket and light up a game when they got hot. Nevertheless, Kentucky was in the habit of blowing teams out, and only powerful UMass had challenged the Wildcats in the tournament thus far; given that anything less than a national title would be construed a disappointment back home, it seemed unlikely that Kentucky would lack focus. Syracuse's best hope was to stay close and hope their 2–3 zone could stymie the Wildcats down the stretch.

Besides Kentucky's surplus of fresh legs and talent, the main worry for the Orangemen was turnovers. Unlike UMass, with its brilliant backcourt tandem, Syracuse had only one certified ball handler, Lazarus Sims. Indeed, the game got under way with a torrent of turnovers, but Syracuse's inability to control the ball was more than balanced out by Kentucky's anemic shooting. If not for Tony Delk, who accounted for 9 of the Wildcats' first 11 points with a triad of threes, Syracuse would have built an early advantage. In fact, Syracuse did lead 21–18 after eleven minutes, but then the wear and tear of Kentucky's system started to take its toll. The Wildcats outscored Syracuse 22–9 over the next seven and a half minutes and took a 9-point lead to the locker room at intermission.

The Orangemen came out composed for the second frame and were within 6 points when point guard Lazarus Sims injured his wrist with less than fourteen minutes left. Without a seasoned ball handler, Syracuse was a sitting duck for the Wildcats; two and a half minutes later the deficit was 13 and the Kentucky faithful were looking for the kill. But Sims taped up his wrist and reentered the game. Behind the brilliant effort of Sims' fellow senior, John Wallace, who led all scorers with 29 points, the Orangemen outscored Kentucky 12–3 over the next four minutes and the lead was down to 4. The play became more controlled, as each possession took on greater meaning for both teams. Then Wallace made 2 free throws with 4:46 remaining and the deficit was down to 2. On the next possession, Kentucky misfired but Walter McCarty tipped the rebound in and

Kentucky's diminutive Tony Delk rises above the big men for a layup during the 1996 title game versus Syracuse. The basket was Delk's only 2-point field goal in the finals; he accounted for 21 of his 24 points from behind the 3-point arc. The senior's record-setting shooting (most treys in a finals) lifted the Wildcats to victory.

Syracuse never got as close again. The play was the final turning point of the game and reflected another of Kentucky's strengths, offensive rebounding; the Wildcats, led by McCarty and Antoine Walker, won the battle of the offensive boards 18–8. Tournament MVP Tony Delk led the Wildcats with 24 points, 21 of which came from behind the 3-point arc, but the key contribution came from freshmen Ron Mercer, who bailed out his cold teammates with a brilliant, and unexpected, 20-point performance. Syracuse put up a gallant effort but fell short 76–67.

In the end, Pitino and his troops—and the Kentucky basketball program as a whole—had redeemed themselves. While UMass and Syracuse both played the Wildcats tough in the Final Four, the Wildcats never trailed in the second half throughout the tournament, a type of dominance that would have made "Baron of the Bluegrass" Adolph Rupp proud. The Wildcats won their sixth NCAA title, which placed them second all-time to UCLA (11), and in the course of the season surpassed North Carolina for the most victories by any school in the history of college basketball. But don't expect Kentucky to rest on its laurels; as the Wildcats fans began their celebration at the Meadowlands, a chant rang out: "Back to Back! Back to Back!"

NCAA Division I Champions

Year	Champion	Coach	Runner-up	Score	Most Valuable Player	Site
1939	Oregon	Howard Hobson	Ohio St.	46-33	None	Evanston, IL
1940	Indiana	Branch McCracken	Kansas	60-42	Marvin Huffman, Indiana	Kansas City, MO
1941	Wisconsin	Harold Foster	Washington St.	39-34	John Kotz, Wisconsin	Kansas City, MO
1942	Stanford	Everett Dean	Dartmouth	53-38	Howard Dallmar, Stanford	Kansas City, MO
1943	Wyoming	Everett Shelton	Georgetown	46-34	Ken Sailors, Wyoming	New York, NY
1944	Utah	Vadal Peterson	Dartmouth	42-40 (1)	Arnold Ferrin, Utah	New York, NY
1945	Oklahoma St. (2)	Henry Iba	NYU	49-45	Bob Kurland, Oklahoma St.	New York, NY
1946	Oklahoma St. (2)	Henry Iba	North Carolina	43-40	Bob Kurland, Oklahoma St.	New York, NY
1947	Holy Cross	Alvin Julian	Oklahoma	58-47	George Kaftan, Holy Cross	New York, NY
1948	Kentucky	Adolph Rupp	Baylor	58-42	Alex Groza, Kentucky	New York, NY
1949	Kentucky	Adolph Rupp	Oklahoma St.	46-36	Alex Groza, Kentucky	Seattle, WA
1950	CCNY	Nat Holman	Bradley	71-68	Irwin Dambrot, CCNY	New York, NY
1951	Kentucky	Adolph Rupp	Kansas St.	68-58	None	Minneapolis, MN
1952	Kansas	Forrest Allen	St. John's	80-63	Clyde Lovelette, Kansas	Seattle, WA
1953	Indiana	Branch McCracken	Kansas	69-68	B.H. Born, Kansas	Kansas City, MO
1954	La Salle	Kenneth Loeffler	Bradley	92-76	Tom Gola, La Salle	Kansas City, MO
1955	San Francisco	Phil Woolpert	La Salle	77-63	Bill Russell, San Francisco	Kansas City, MO
1956	San Francisco	Phil Woolpert	Iowa	83-71	Hal Lear, Temple	Evaston, IL
1957	N. Carolina	Frank McGuire	Kansas	54-53 (3)	Wilt Chamberlain, Kansas	Kansas City, MO
1958	Kentucky	Adolph Rupp	Seattle	84-72	Elgin Baylor, Seattle	Louisville, KY
1959	California	Pete Newell	W. Virginia	71-70	Jerry West, W. Virginia	Louisville, KY
1960	Ohio St.	Fred Taylor	California	75-55	Jerry Lucas, Ohio St.	San Francisco, CA
1961	Cincinnati	Edwin Jucker	Ohio St.	70-65 (1)	Jerry Lucas, Ohio St.	Kansas City, MO
1962	Cincinnati	Edwin Jucker	Ohio St.	71-59	Paul Hogue, Cincinnati	Louisville, KY
1963	Loyola (Ill.)	George Ireland	Cincinnati	60-58 (1)	Art Heyman, Duke	Louisville, KY
1964	UCLA	John Wooden	Duke	98-83	Walt Hazzard, UCLA	Kansas City, MO
1965	UCLA	John Wooden	Michigan	91-80	Bill Bradley, Princeton	Portland, OR
1966	Texas-El Paso (3)	Don Haskins	Kentucky	72-65	Jerry Chambers, Utah	College Park, MD
1967	UCLA	John Wooden	Dayton	79-64	Lew Alcindor, UCLA	Louisville, KY
1968	UCLA	John Wooden	N. Carolina	78-55	Lew Alcindor, UCLA	Los Angeles, CA
1969	UCLA	John Wooden	Purdue	92-72	Lew Alcindor, UCLA	Louisville, KY
1970	UCLA	John Wooden	Jacksonville	80-69	Sidney Wicks, UCLA	College Park, MD
1971	UCLA	John Wooden	Villanova	68-62	Howard Porter, Villanova	Houston, TX
1972	UCLA	John Wooden	Florida St.	81-76	Bill Walton, UCLA	Los Angeles, CA
1973	UCLA	John Wooden	Memphis St.	87-66	Bill Walton, UCLA	St. Louis, MO
1974	N. Carolina St.	Norm Sloan	Marquette	76-64	David Thompson, N.C. St.	Greensboro, NC
1975	UCLA	John Wooden	Kentucky	92-85	Richard Washington, UCLA	San Diego, CA
1976	Indiana	Bob Knight	Michigan	86-68	Kent Benson, Indiana	Philadelphia, PA
1977	Marquette	Al McGuire	N. Carolina	67-59	Butch Lee, Marquette	Atlanta, GA
1978	Kentucky	Joe Hall	Duke	94-88	Jack Givens, Kentucky	St. Louis, MO
1979	Michigan St.	Jud Heathcote	Indiana St.	75-64	Magic Johnson, Michigan St.	Salt Lake City, UT
1980	Louisville	Denny Crum	UCLA	59-54	Darrell Griffith, Louisville	Indianapolis, IN
1981	Indiana	Bob Knight	N. Carolina	63-50	Isiah Thomas, Indiana	Philadelphia, PA
1982	N. Carolina	Dean Smith	Georgetown	63-62	James Worthy, N. Carolina	New Orleans, LA
1983	N. Carolina St.	Jim Valvano	Houston	54-52	Akeem Olajuwon, Houston	Albuquerque, NM
1984	Georgetown	John Thompson	Houston	84-75	Patrick Ewing, Georgetown	Seattle, WA
1985	Villanova	Rollie Massimino	Georgetown	66-64	Ed Pinckney, Villanova	Lexington, KY
1986	Louisville	Denny Crum	Duke	72-69	Pervis Ellison, Louisville	Dallas, TX
1987	Indiana	Bob Knight	Syracuse	74-73	Keith Smart, Indiana	New Orleans, LA
1988	Kansas	Larry Brown	Oklahoma	83-79	Danny Manning, Kansas	Kansas City, MO
1989	Michigan	Steve Fisher	Seton Hall	80-79 (1)	Glen Rice, Michigan	Seattle, WA
1990	UNLV	Jerry Tarkanian	Duke	103-73	Anderson Hunt, UNLV	Denver, CO
1991	Duke	Mike Krzyzewski	Kansas	72-65	Christian Laettner, Duke	Indianapolis, IN
1992	Duke	Mike Krzyzewski	Michigan	71-51	Bobby Hurley, Duke	Minneapolis, MN
1993	N. Carolina	Dean Smith	Michigan	77-71	Donald Williams, N. Carolina	New Orleans, LA
1994	Arkansas	Nolan Richardson	Duke	76-72	Corliss Williamson, Arkansas	Charlotte, NC
1995	UCLA	Jim Harrick	Arkansas	89-78	Ed O'Bannon, UCLA	Seattle, WA
1996	Kentucky	Rick Pitino	Syracuse	76-67	Tony Delk, Kentucky	East Rutherford, NJ

All-Time Tournament Records

Individual Performances

Most points in a game
61: Austin Carr, Notre Dame (vs. Ohio, 1970)

58: Bill Bradley, Princeton (vs. Wichita State, 1965)

56: Oscar Robertson, Cincinnati (vs. Arkansas, 1958)

Most points in a championship game
44: Bill Walton, UCLA (vs. Memphis State, 1973)

42: Gail Goodrich, UCLA (vs. Michigan, 1965)

41: Jack Givens, Kentucky (vs. Duke, 1978)

Most points in a tournament
184: Glen Rice, Michigan (1989)

177: Bill Bradley, Princeton (1965)

167: Elvin Hayes, Houston (1968)

Most points in a career
407: Christian Laettner, Duke (1989, 1990, 1991, 1992)

358: Elvin Hayes, Houston (1966, 1967, 1968)

328: Danny Manning, Kansas (1985, 1986, 1987, 1988)

Highest scoring average in a career (minimum 6 games)
41.29: Austin Carr, Notre Dame (1969, 1970, 1971) (289 points in 7 games)

33.67: Bill Bradley, Princeton (1963, 1964, 1965) (303 points in 9 games)

32.40: Oscar Robertson, Cincinnati (1958, 1959, 1960) (324 points in 10 games)

Highest field goal percentage in a tournament (minimum 25 attempts)
.788: Christian Laettner, Duke (1989) (26-33)

.786: Heyward Dotson, Columbia (1968) (22-28)

.781: Kevin Gamble, Iowa (1987) (32-41)

Highest field goal percentage in a career (minimum 50 attempts)
.707: Steve Schall, Arkansas (1977, 1978, 1979) (41-58)

.700: John Shumate, Notre Dame (1974) (35-50)

.686: Bill Walton, UCLA (1972, 1973, 1974) (109-159)

Team Performances

Most points in a game by one team
149: Loyola Marymount (vs. Michigan, 1990)

131: UNLV (vs. Loyola Marymount, 1990)

127: St. Joseph's (vs. Utah, 1961)

Fewest points in a game by one team
20: N. Carolina (vs. Pittsburgh, 1941)

24: Springfield (vs. Indiana, 1940)

26: Pittsburgh (vs. N. Carolina, 1941)

Most points per game in a tournament (minimum 3 games)
105.75: Loyola Marymount (1990) (423 points in 4 games)

105.67: Notre Dame (1970) (317 points in 3 games)

101.00: UNLV (1977) (505 points in 5 games)

Largest average winning margin in a tournament (minimum 3 games)
23.75: UCLA (1967) (95 points in 4 games)

23.00: Loyola-Chicago (1963) (115 points in 5 games)

22.60: Indiana (1981) (113 points in 5 games)

Index